THE ENGLISH HIGHER GRADE SCHOOLS

Woburn Education Series

General Series Editor: Professor Peter Gordon

ISSN: 1462-2076

For over 20 years this series on the history, development and policy of education, under the distinguished editorship of Peter Gordon, has been evolving into a comprehensive and balanced survey of important trends in teaching and educational policy. The series is intended to reflect the changing nature of education in present-day society. The books are divided into four sections – educational policy studies, educational practice, the history of education and social history – and reflect the continuing interest in this area.

For a full series listing, please visit our website: www.woburnpress.com

History of Education

The Victorian School Manager: A Study in the Management of Education 1800–1902
Peter Gordon

Selection for Secondary Education
Peter Gordon

The Study of Education: Inaugural Lectures
Volume I: Early and Modern
Volume II: The Last Decade
Volume III: The Changing Scene
Volume IV: End of an Era?
edited by Peter Gordon

History of Education: The Making of a Discipline
edited by Peter Gordon and Richard Szreter

Educating the Respectable: A Study of Fleet Road Board School, Hampstead,
1879–1903
W.E. Marsden

In History and in Education: Essays Presented to Peter Gordon
edited by Richard Aldrich

An Anglo-Welsh Teaching Dynasty: The Adams Family from the 1840s to the 1930s
W.E. Marsden

Dictionary of British Educationists
Richard Aldrich and Peter Gordon

Biographical Dictionary of North American and European Educationists
Peter Gordon and Richard Aldrich

The Making of the Backward Pupil in Education in England, 1870–1914
Ian Copeland

Social History

The First Teenagers: The Lifestyle of Young Wage-earners in Interwar Britain
David Fowler

James Kay Shuttleworth: Journey of an Outsider
R.J.W. Selleck

Targeting Schools: Drill, Militarism and Imperialism
Alan Penn

THE ENGLISH HIGHER GRADE SCHOOLS

A Lost Opportunity

Meriel Vlaeminke
University of Leicester

WOBURN PRESS
LONDON • PORTLAND, OR

First published in 2000 in Great Britain by
WOBURN PRESS
Newbury House
900 Eastern Avenue
London IG2 7HH

and in the United States of America by
WOBURN PRESS
c/o ISBS
5804 N.E. Hassalo Street
Portland, Oregon 97213-3644

Website: www.woburnpress.com

British Library Cataloguing in Publication Data

Vlaeminke, Meriel
   The English higher grade schools: a lost opportunity. –
(The Woburn education series)
   1. High schools – England – History – 19th century
   2. High schools – England – History – 20th century
   3. Education, Secondary – England – History –
19th century 4. Education, Secondary – England –
History – 20th century
   I. Title
   373.4˙2

ISBN 0 7130 0220 4 (cloth)
ISSN 1462–2076

Library of Congress Cataloging-in-Publication Data

Vlaeminke, Meriel.
   The English higher grade schools: a lost opportunity / Meriel
Vlaeminke.
     p. cm. – (Woburn education series)
   Includes bibliographical references (p.) and index.
   ISBN 0-7130-0220-4 (cloth).
   1. Education, Secondary – England – History. 2. Education,
Secondary – Social aspects – England. I. Title. II. Series.
LA634.V52   1999
373.42–dc21
                                                        99-41037
                                                          CIP

Printed in Great Britain by
The Book Company, Ipswich, Suffolk

CONTENTS

FOREWORD

I find it difficult adequately to express my enthusiasm for this book. It has been waiting to be written for the past 50 years or more, and is certainly one of the most important studies in the history of education recently published. Written with great verve and skill, fully and extensively researched, the author nowhere pulls her punches and presents a clear, highly critical analysis of developments at a crucial turning point in English education, the period 1890–1910 – a period when a series of very positive developments were finally successfully resisted and negated by a powerful Establishment intent on reaffirming the status quo.

The title does not fully reflect the real scope and significance of this book, which charts the growth and significance of the 'alternative system' of education emerging with extraordinary energy under the control of local school boards towards the close of the nineteenth century. As elementary schools established themselves following the 1870 Education Act, many of these thrust upwards in response to local demand, particularly from working- and lower-middle-class populations. With their roots in the elementary schools, these retained their pupils to establish relations with civic universities and colleges. So, a whole, non-selective, organic 'alternative system' was now, apparently spontaneously, coming into being. At the apex were the new-type 'higher grade schools' – the subject of this study.

Under local democratic control, these were a challenge to established institutions – indeed (as some saw it), to the social order as a whole. Opposition multiplied, especially at the newly established Board of Education, but also very much more widely. In 1902 a Conservative government, in face of massive popular opposition, carried an act which abolished the school boards. Concurrent administrative measures cribbed, cabined and confined the higher grade schools, which shortly ceased to exist as an entity. At the same time a highly selective system of 'secondary education', based on the classics and modelled on the exclusive 'public' schools, was carefully nursed into being. So the opportunity for a basic transformation of education was lost. English education now subsided into the bland tripartitism which followed the 1944 Education Act, the resuscitated 'grammar schools' providing an alienating education to a small elite, the mass of the children left in dead-end elementary schools providing no perspectives. Only recently, with the development of comprehensive secondary education, have some of the values of the 1890–1910 transformation been realised.

All this is dealt with in a masterly manner in this fine book. The author brings to life the schools as they really were, with a set of fascinating case studies. She also brilliantly sets the whole period in context, bringing out the wider significance of the often dramatic events and conflicts she records.

The author does not hesitate to draw parallels with contemporary developments in policy-making today. If she records a 'lost opportunity', the efforts made were sometimes heroic and often wholly admirable. There are many lessons here relevant to the present and these are clearly enunciated. We must never lose another such 'opportunity', but this will require clear analytic thinking, collective action and firm leadership.

This book has a contemporary ring and appeal. It cuts through the rhetoric to arrive at the truth. It deserves to be widely read and its lessons taken to heart. The author herself deserves warm congratulations for a fine achievement.

Professor Brian Simon
June 1999

ACKNOWLEDGMENTS

My thanks are due to a number of colleagues at the University of Leicester School of Education, especially Margaret Mathieson, David Reeder and Brian Simon for their stimulating encouragement and support.

LEGISLATION RELATING TO EDUCATION

1869 Endowed Schools Act
1870 Elementary Education Act (Forster's)
1876 Elementary Education Act (Sandon's)
1880 Elementary Education Act (Mundella's)
1888 Local Government Act
1889 Technical Instruction Act
1889 Welsh Intermediate Education Act
1890 Local Taxation (Customs and Excise) Act
1891 Technical Instruction Act
1890 Education Code (1891) Act
1891 Elementary Education Act
1893 Elementary Education (School Attendance) Act
1897 Voluntary Schools Act
1899 Board of Education Act
1900 Cockerton Judgment
1900 Higher Elementary School Minute
1901 Education Act (1st Cockerton)
1902 Education Act (2nd Cockerton)
1902 Education Act (Balfour's)
1903 Education (London) Act
1903 Pupil Teacher Regulations
1904 Elementary School Code
1904 Secondary School Regulations
1906 Education (Feeding of School Children) Act
1907 Education (Administrative Provisions) Act

EDUCATION IN THE 1890s: TENSIONS AND POTENTIAL

THE BROAD DEBATE

It is a common characteristic of historical writing to suggest recurring features, persistent strands, evolutionary tendencies, comparative dimensions, and even sometimes surprising discontinuities or contrasts. The importance of something in the past can only be evaluated in relation to what preceded and followed and what was happening elsewhere. But in considering British education at the end of the twentieth century, the parallels with developments 100 years ago are unusually striking. As the broad educational consensus which had held for much of the twentieth century began to break down from the 1970s onwards, education has been constantly in the spotlight: the focus of high expectations, bitter recriminations and unprecedented legislative attention. Much the same can be said of the 1880s and 1890s.

The British educational experience – then as now – is obstinately unique, despite the increased knowledge and, in some quarters, admiration of other nations' achievements. In the late nineteenth century, Matthew Arnold wrote enthusiastically about Germany and Robert Morant about Switzerland; a century on, the countries of the Pacific Rim have attracted favourable comment. The underlying analysis is much the same: that nations wishing to assert themselves need to develop both a cohesiveness of spirit and a level of economic competence which enable them to establish and safeguard genuine independence. Education is the ideal, perhaps the only, tool for achieving both those goals, and so, typically, governments have taken a strong lead in directing the national education systems for which they are responsible.

The British, it seems, have always done it differently; indeed, if a national system of education is a set of coherently inter-related institutions provided mainly by the state for the education of its people, Britain has never had one. It must be stressed from the outset that the educational experiences of Scotland, Wales and Ireland have been very different from those in England, with the latter periodically asserting its values and priorities over its constituent parts with varying degrees of determination and success. The continuing divergence of Scottish, Welsh and Irish education from key aspects of the central model is a reminder that the tensions between 'English' and 'British' have never been fully resolved. Furthermore, the economic and imperial dominance which Britain achieved in the nineteenth century directly militated against the development of a coherent national system. Not only was a systematic approach to education regarded as unnecessary, but it was seen as likely to inhibit individual endeavour and damage the voluntarist principle which enabled innovatory industrialists and entrepreneurs to thrive. The fact that those economic pioneers were largely placed outside the mainstream of political and cultural life contributed to another enduring handicap which has bedevilled English education: the role of education in the perpetuation of social class differences. England's industrial transformation owed nothing to either the universities or the schools of the governing class, whose members treasured the distance – geographical as well as intellectual and emotional – they were able to maintain from the world of factories, mills, mines, cities, sanitation, poverty and disease. For them, education meant two entirely different things: on the one hand, the elitist, stylised, classical humanism of the public schools and Oxbridge; on the other, the limited, cheap utilitarianism of the publicly provided education system. They were equally important instruments of socialisation.

A further distinctive feature of the British educational experience is the role of religion. Religion and education almost invariably have a close association in their early evolution, and the relation between them has to be confronted at some point. In most countries, where the dominant faith is international – Roman Catholicism or Islam, for example – allegiances outside the country challenge developing notions of nationhood. In England, the Tudor legacy was crucially important in determining that the dominant religious orthodoxy was created by the monarch and, as the established church, closely identified with the ruling elite and with the social and administrative fabric of English life ever since. The Church of England has always, in consequence, been perceived as a safe and supportive locus for the education of the nation's children. The philanthropic/evangelical bent which Anglicanism developed during the nineteenth century ensured that it was actively involved in the provision of differentiated forms of education which matched the preconceptions of the ruling class. In England, then, religion has successfully maintained an important presence in education, which in the secular late twentieth century is enjoying something of a revival.

The role of government in managing these various strands – economic, social, religious – has been an interesting one. Green has argued persuasively that education is one of the key features in the formation of the modern state, possessing as it does unique functions to disseminate national priorities from the top down, and thereby transmit a cohesive national culture along with implicit social and political training. Many countries, he argues, demonstrate a close correlation between periods of intense state formation and spells of dynamic educational change.[1] England, having asserted its dominance over Wales, Scotland and Ireland by the beginning of the eighteenth century, achieved an effective form of national unification earlier than most. Consequently, it was the least interested in education as a tool of nationalism which, as well as promoting an enduring affection for tradition and antiquity, has enabled it to be sanguine in the sharing of power with local and regional bodies. It has also encouraged the evolutionary, piecemeal approach to legislation which, until recently, has characterised governmental endeavour in education as in other fields. With local authorities actively involved in education and often creative in their policy-making, central government has tended to follow rather than direct, to permit or legitimate rather than initiate.

The end of the twentieth century has broken emphatically with that tradition. The systematic diminution of the powers of local education authorities has been accompanied by a claimed devolution of responsibilities to individual institutions' governing bodies (hybrids of unpaid amateurs, professionals and assorted interested parties) which is belied by the multiplication of non-elected centralised bodies such as the Office for Standards in Education, the Funding Agency for Schools and the Qualifications and Curriculum Authority among others. Such a pattern resonates with 'reforms' at the very beginning of the century, when democratic school boards were replaced with local education authorities, which were then forced to adopt individual governing bodies for their secondary schools along with close moulding from a revitalised inspectorate following centrally produced guidance not included in any legislation. The overt intention then – to safeguard any post-elementary education as a scarce and specialised privilege for advantaged groups within society – has become unfashionable now, but the socially segregated 'system' created at the beginning of the century should have alerted us to the dangers of a divided system, now reinforced by other means. The peculiar British circumstance, that state education provision has been largely determined by people who do not participate in it and who adhere to quite different educational priorities for their own class, militates against educational egalitarianism. Institutions do not enjoy parity of esteem, nor do certain styles of education; and the promotion of educational orthodoxy by curriculum and inspection from above does little to change that.

It seems that a complex web of values and priorities underlies the British approach to education, which resists comparisons with other nations. Efforts to understand what is distinctive about the British experience help to generate a remarkably diffuse debate, in which almost every academic discipline has a point of view. Contributions, of necessity, deal primarily in generalisations and broad abstractions, and tend to neglect the actual mechanisms by which values are transmitted. The most important of those mechanisms must be education in its widest sense, and the second half of the nineteenth century has commonly been identified as the period when, it is alleged, Britain should have been modernising its attitudes to cope with the new economic challenges and safeguard its pre-eminence. In a number of respects, education was indeed changing in response to new pressures, the most conspicuous trend being the move towards institutionalisation at all levels. There is thus no substitute for examining closely the late nineteenth-century schools and colleges which transmitted the all-important values, since 'no other set of institutions has been so centrally concerned ... with the transmission of the cultural heritage'.[2]

Some schools and colleges have received due attention. Oxford and Cambridge Universities figure prominently in discussions about philosophical, intellectual and religious change, and the leading English public schools offer unique sociological evidence about the nature of ruling elites and the perpetuation of class distinctions. But, as institutions catering specifically for a small minority of the population, they can tell only part of the story. Despite their deliberate development as institutions neither geographically nor philosophically tied to a particular locality, they can scarcely be viewed as expressing a genuinely national statement about education. The attachment to 'laissez-faire' liberalism, which had restrained state intervention in favour of the voluntary initiative, meant that an overall strategy for education had never been formulated. There was no general view of its purpose, no nationwide 'system' relating to a demographic logic, and no proper articulation of its component parts. Some institutions resembled each other or, finding that they had interests in common, consciously grew more alike, but, provided they could maintain financial independence of the state, they had a virtually free hand in defining their own objectives. Clearly, they had to develop in a way that was roughly in accord with a consensus of opinion, but they were not merely reflective of that consensus; rather, then as now, 'an institution like the public school does not simply transmit values; it selects them and reinforces them'.[3]

Those values came to form a package which has been variously labelled 'the humanistic tradition', 'the liberal-romantic tradition', and 'the cult of the gentleman'. By the late nineteenth century it was characterised[4] by an exclusive devotion to literary studies, especially the classical texts; a consequent disdain for science; a persistent anti-intellectualism and dislike of expertise; a sense of high moral purpose, leading to an emphasis on the importance of character-formation, and to a belief in class superiority and elitism; and, embracing all these, a growing attachment to stability and conformity. Its furtherance involved developing a form of education which was specialised in content and stylised in process, since affective and cultural goals were more important than cognitive ones. Amongst other things, this meant that the educational institutions of the elite could afford – and in fact worked hard – to remain largely aloof from a whole range of pressing educational controversies. Indeed, an increasingly important part of their prestige lay in their assumed capacity to safeguard traditional values and to induce conformity to familiar patterns of behaviour. Class interests cannot therefore be divorced from what members of the elite term the 'national interest', and the survival of certain institutions or styles of education at the expense of others may have little to do with their intrinsic worth for the educational advancement of the whole population.

This book is based on the assumption that institutions which have been less favoured by history can tell us at least as much about the values of Britain's rulers as the schools and universities in which they were themselves educated. It is an assumption supported by what seems to be a persistent inclination in the world of education to glorify antiquity and tradition, as evidenced by the competition among institutions for proof of an early foundation date, the lengthy detailing of old covenants in weighty publications such as the *Victoria County History*, and the taste for old-looking buildings, founders' days, coats of arms and Latin mottoes. This in turn creates a tendency both to undervalue innovatory institutions and to misrepresent moments in history when there was real potential for a change of direction – in other words, when alternative values and priorities were mounting an effective challenge. The end of the nineteenth century was one such moment, witnessing a critical test for the established elite and its familiar values. Other sections of the population were utilising the haphazard collection of educational resources at their disposal to construct a dynamic and self-contained 'system' of education which, disconcertingly, had no apparent desire to emulate the priorities of the elite. By the end of the century, this new system was approaching completion, and it is possible to identify four distinct ways in which it seemed to be challenging the established order. In the areas of technical, secondary and elementary education and in educational administration, tensions were building to a climax and significant measures of reform seemed to be needed urgently. To understand each of them it is necessary to look at institutions other than those which have been customarily regarded as the repositories of Britain's educational tradition.

TENSIONS IN TECHNICAL EDUCATION

Probably the most important 'new' controversy thrusting into the world of education was the whole area of technical, scientific and vocational education. In the nineteenth century these three, while not exactly synonymous, were so closely related at a practical and institutional level that fine distinctions will not be laboured over in this discussion. It was an area of education which had not been a pressing issue while industrialisation was in progress or during the subsequent half-century or so of world dominance. Britain's industrial revolution had succeeded in the absence of any formal encouragement or controls, and it had become a key part of the Victorian gospel not to intervene. One of the unsurprising outcomes of this was that industrialists had come to expect little help from the nation's elite, and tended to accept that the point of education was to safeguard the cultural heritage and develop general qualities of leadership, not to increase technical competence and feed skilled personnel into industry. Relations settled into a barren pattern, in which industrialists failed to appreciate the value of scientific research or technical training, university-based scientists resisted what they regarded as the taint of applied research, and most members of the elite had little respect for either group of 'experts'.

In the latter part of the nineteenth century there were signs that attitudes were changing. A number of more perceptive Victorians, aware that Britain's economic supremacy was coming under challenge, made intelligent guesses at the reasons. Prominent amongst them was the inadequacy of educational provision to respond to the more technically demanding 'second' industrial revolution of the latter part of the nineteenth century. By the 1890s, they had succeeded in forcing the issues on to the political and cultural agenda. The first input of state money into the endowed schools was to encourage practical science and manual instruction, and in the publicly provided sector those subjects were positively booming, from elementary schools up to new technical colleges and university courses. To the pro-science lobby, these developments did nothing more than accord science something approaching its rightful place after years of neglect, and there was great enthusiasm for what was happening. From the Birmingham witness telling the Cross Commission that 'the little blackguards in the poor districts ... have an extremely sharp intelligence, and they can be specially awakened by science',[5] to the rejoicing of Samuelson that 'the impetus given to technical education [140 technical schools and colleges started between 1891 and 1893] was beyond the most sanguine expectations of its warmest advocates',[6] real change seemed to be in the air.

But the success of the movement was too dramatic for those who believed that education should be based on other priorities, and who themselves had little knowledge or experience of the alternatives. Convinced that 'good' grammar schools were being ruined, and that the whole literary tradition of education was under threat, they managed to ·create a climate of opinion that saw technical and secondary education as two distinct things, the former being inimical to the latter. The Bryce Commission heard much of that kind of anxiety, and although it paid tribute to the 'equal' claims of literary, scientific and technical elements in education, it nevertheless concluded:

> there is little danger at the present day that we should fail to recognize the necessity of improving and extending science and technical instruction. It is less certain that we may not run some risk of a lop-sided development in education, in which the teaching of science, theoretical and applied, may so predominate as to entail comparative neglect of studies which are of less obvious and immediate utility, though not of less moment for the formation of mind and character.[7]

That comment rang the alarm bells for many of those involved in the higher levels of the educational world, and the considerable weight of opinion in favour of a literary-based education was mobilised. Despite the rapid progress in technical and scientific education, it had far fewer resources on which to draw, and when the tensions over curriculum came to be resolved, the two sides proved to be very unevenly matched.

TENSIONS IN SECONDARY EDUCATION

The institutions which felt most directly threatened by the technical education movement were the lesser endowed schools. By the close of the nineteenth century, the restructuring of England's ancient educational endowments was coming to a natural end, after 70 or so years of erratic progress. At first, a handful of schools which were highly favoured – either in terms of financial security or the fortuitous arrival of a dynamic headmaster – had reformed themselves in a way that seemed to accord with the needs of a certain part of the population. Blessed by the Clarendon Commission, they were attracting considerable prestige, not least through their strengthening connections with the nation's intellectual, religious and political elite. This helped them to assume a role as models of educational excellence, which proved to be an irresistibly powerful influence on the Schools Inquiry Commissioners, who set about restructuring England's endowed schools around the pinnacle of the classical 'first-grade' school. Significantly, that model had been delineated before there was any concern about the nation's economic performance, although its more elaborate rituals were mostly added after the schools began taking larger numbers from the rising bourgeoisie. Some schools profited handsomely from the reorganisation, and so another tier of schools joined the original nine. The attachment was formalised in the creation of the Headmasters' Conference, which came into being specifically to resist state interference and which played a key part in giving a common image to a widely differing collection of schools.

But what of the rest of the endowed schools – the majority – which still could not manage to become viable, despite reformed 'schemes' and reorganised endowments? Few of them were content with the essentially negative designation of 'second-grade' or 'third-grade' status, but there was no obvious way out of the financial, intellectual and social constraints within which they were accustomed to operating. The Bryce Assistant-Commissioners reporting in 1894–95 found a lot of endowed schools were so impoverished, unpopular or badly run that they were virtually moribund, offering only elementary education or even 'in abeyance'. By about 1900, then, the endowed schools were far from being a homogeneous group of institutions sharing a particular identity. Rather, the nineteenth-century reorganisation of secondary education had resulted in a 'polarisation of endowed grammar schools into two groups', with 'the gap between successful and unsuccessful schools becoming wider'.[8]

At that point in their history, many endowed schools were in a perilous condition and could have been coaxed in a variety of directions. A growing number were developing links with the publicly funded sector of education through scholarships and capitation grants, and, despite some grumbling, were moving fairly smoothly towards closer cooperation with the various local educational authorities. Others had seen a different way out of their difficulties. The shared educational background (in the absence of any other) of the teachers in many endowed and most public schools encouraged the former to emphasise their identity of interest with the latter, even when their schools had almost nothing in common. The endowed schools needed allies and quite consciously sought them among their more prestigious fellows in the educational world, and through that alliance were able to elicit sympathy from the central decision-makers. They thereby ensured that when the long-awaited reorganisation of secondary education arrived, all endowed schools were treated as part of the independent sector which, as has been suggested, was essentially class-based and poorly attuned to the needs of industrial communities.

TENSIONS IN ELEMENTARY EDUCATION

One of the firmest convictions of the struggling endowed schools was that their problems were not of their own making or soluble by their own efforts. They saw themselves as the victims of unfair competition from the publicly provided sector of education, which by the 1890s had grown much grander than had originally been expected. State support for elementary schools had been conceived of as a completely different activity from the sort of education outlined in the previous section. It seemed to be the best way to tackle the serious social problems associated with urban poverty, for a strong strand of Victorian opinion clung to the idea that the poor quality of life of the urban working classes was the fault of the people concerned, not the circumstances in which they lived. And yet there was always a reluctance to spend too much money on the correcting process, and improvements in elementary education were never free of stringent financial constraints.

The deep tensions implicit in deciding what elementary education was for, and how much of the nation's resources should be invested in it, were approaching a climax by the end of the nineteenth century. The creation

of the elementary school 'system', including the 1870 Elementary
Education Act, was based on assumptions about the age, social class and
educational needs of the recipients which had never been made explicit
and which fairly rapidly became disquietingly blurred and complicated.
By the end of the century, the public elementary education system was
attracting increasing numbers of older pupils as well as children from a
widening range of social classes, and to cater for both, curricular
constraints had been progressively loosened and standards allowed to rise.
In the process, the Science and Art Department, a body founded for quite
different educational purposes, assumed an important presence in
'elementary' education although the relationship between the two was yet
to be properly defined.

During that quarter-century, the central authority had bent with the
winds of change as elementary education broke its boundaries in all
directions, and even started to forge links with colleges of higher
education. Depending on whom was in office, the Education Department
vacillated between feeling vaguely uneasy about what was happening but
lacking a rationale to stop it, and positively welcoming the progress
towards better opportunities for the mass of the population. Adherents to
the latter view held sway in the first half of the 1890s, and helped to
engender 'an era of new educational hope ... the whole emphasis was
indeed delightfully positive'.[9] Public elementary education was given
such a boost that it was beginning to pose a serious challenge to both its
two chief competitors, the voluntary elementary schools and the poorer
endowed secondary schools. The accession to power of a strong
Conservative government (after an election in which education played
little part) was extremely fortuitous for both. Powerful lobbies from the
Anglicans and the endowed school heads played upon the government's
instinctive sympathies and greatly enhanced their chances of having the
tensions within elementary education resolved in their favour.

TENSIONS IN EDUCATIONAL ADMINISTRATION

Underlying all three of the areas of tension described above was a conflict
in outlook between the centre and the periphery; this conflict had major
repercussions for the exercise of power at local level. Continuing
affection for the voluntary principle in education meant that the centre had
refrained from laying down a universal model, whether of technical,
secondary or elementary education. But that did not mean that it was
uninterested in how things took shape and nor, as became clear towards

the end of the 1890s, was it neutral. As institutions which it favoured – Church of England schools and endowed grammar schools – seemed to be threatened with extinction, it abandoned its permissive stance of 25 years and looked for ways of restoring the old balance, primarily by curbing the elementary education system. Local wishes became relatively unimportant and the industrial areas which had gained most from the expansion of public education – and which were often those worst served by voluntary effort – were brought into sharp conflict with the central authority.

By the end of the nineteenth century, those towns and cities were in a position to put up a more determined resistance than would have been the case a few years earlier. Urban government had become more sophisticated and more self-assured, accompanied by (cause and effect are difficult to disentangle) a growing involvement in the life of their towns among the prosperous business communities. Status could be acquired by serving one's local community, and so while wealthy men moved their residences out to the suburbs, sent their sons to distant public schools, and invested their money far from their home town – or even their home land – they nevertheless retained an emotional commitment to their locality. In Birmingham, for example, it was said at the beginning of this century that prominent citizens 'do not hold themselves aloof from local affairs' and a later writer has identified that city's early recognition of 'a new vision of the function and nature of the corporation' as the main reason for its social and economic elite resisting the pull to the metropolis.[10]

The metropolitan elite was far removed from this world of gas supplies, sanitation and poor relief funds. Sharing the public school and Oxbridge background of the aristocracy and the governing elite, these privileged groups together made up 'Society' and followed 'the Season' around London, country houses, Oxbridge, Eton, Henley and Ascot.[11] Its members never visited industrial cities and were deeply uneasy about what they understood to be dirty, smoky, disease-ridden places, full of drunken and immoral inhabitants. It seemed inconceivable that the needs of the urban masses were of a similar order to those of the aspiring middle class, and local leaders who thought otherwise clearly needed to be guided in the 'right' direction. The Education Department, through its retention of recruitment by patronage, remained even more exclusively the preserve of the metropolitan elite than most government departments. Visiting inspectors had little in common with local inspectors or with most of the nation's teachers; the urban school boards became the object of violent attacks; locally based attempts to exert control over endowed schools were resisted;[12] and the old universities were quite deliberately employed to 'hold the pass against the onslaught of the surge of democracy in the towns' through supervision of the civic universities.[13] Local administrators, who in some circumstances imitated the metropolitan upper middle class, found their loyalties sorely tested, as their home cities seemed to be best served by the very things least favoured at Whitehall: the pursuit of scientific and vocational goals in education, and the continuing upward growth of the publicly provided elementary school system.

HIGHER GRADE SCHOOLS: A FOCUS OF TENSIONS

One group of institutions was intimately involved in all four of the tensions outlined above. The higher grade schools were the highest achievement of the school board elementary system, by virtue of which they were perceived as rivals to the older secondary schools, and they placed a much stronger emphasis on scientific, technical and vocational education. The first of the higher grade schools came into being in 1876 (in Bradford);[14] 25 years later they were declared illegal by the Cockerton judgment; and within another five years they had ceased to exist. It is therefore possible to isolate them as a phenomenon, one which closely coincided in time with the major tensions which were gathering in the world of education. It is particularly important to penetrate the unfavourable 'official' view, to try to catch the spirit of the schools and understand how they were perceived by their pupils, teachers, parents and other local people. Did they feel that the schools were merely a stop-gap waiting to be replaced, or did they have a recognisable identity which was known and approved? If Robert Morant was correct when he said that the term 'higher grade' 'is used by an infinity of Schools up and down the country and has no definite connotation whatever',[15] it would be impossible to study the 'higher grade school' as a distinctive type of educational institution. There are indeed a number of practical constraints.

Since the higher grade schools were not the product of any central planning and had uncertain legal status, there was no centralised recording of their activities. Nobody in the central administration was responsible for them and they straddled all three of the statutory controlling bodies – the Education Department, the Science and Art Department and, to a lesser extent, the Charity Commissioners – at a time when those three were so autonomous that they scarcely spoke to each other. The Science and Art Department had the most to do with them, but, as for most of its existence it was primarily a grant-awarding, examining body, that is precisely the extent of the information it recorded. It is difficult, although not impossible, to disentangle the information relating to higher grade schools from the listings for the hundreds of assorted institutes, schools, colleges and classes which utilised the Science and Art Department's examinations. And the dubious legality of higher grade developments encouraged cautious school boards to stress those features which were characteristic of good quality elementary schools and therefore an indisputable part of their responsibilities. 'Higher grade' information is consequently often as jumbled up with elementary school archives as it is with the Science and Art Department's records.

At the local and institutional levels, it seems that changes of status and moves to better locations over the years have taken a heavier toll of higher grade school records than of more settled institutions. Where they do exist, the mundane business of daily administration – attendance figures, equipment needs, examination entries and earnings – tends to dominate. Overworked higher grade school headteachers, often lacking clerical assistance, were rather more prone to lamentations about their state of nervous exhaustion than to a wealth of factual detail, personal comment and philosophical interpretation. Even the most successful former pupils were generally too busy earning their living, as teachers or clerks or engineers, to produce the 'Alma Mater' type of histories which proliferate in the annals of public and endowed schools.

The difficulty in locating reliable information is, no doubt, one of the reasons for the poor representation which the higher grade schools have received from educational historians. Few omit reference to the schools, with assessments varying from the dismissive to the enthusiastic, but interpretations are coloured by attitudes to a range of other issues, such as the role of the school boards, the nature of the secondary school curriculum, and the significance of the 1902 Education Act. Detail is often lacking, and there seems to be a recurring desire to seek out recognisable patterns from the past, as if to prove that innovations or sudden changes of direction were in fact stages along a carefully managed evolutionary path. Institutions and trends which fell by the wayside tend to be the chief victims of such an approach. The survey which follows summarises the strengths and weaknesses of recorded opinion about the higher grade schools and their place in the history of education, as well as indicating the themes which this book will illuminate.

HIGHER GRADE SCHOOLS: THE VERDICT SO FAR

There is little dispute within the historical literature that what are generally known as the 'higher grade schools' were those founded by the school boards as a means of providing a higher level of education for some of their pupils. As such they were innovatory, adding a new component to the nation's educational provision: 'the first enterprising ... attempt to provide education for all'.[16] It is commonly suggested that there were 65 of them, mostly located in the industrial cities of the North and Midlands; the inaccuracy of both statements will be explained later. Writers have puzzled whether to include them with the public elementary school system or with the endowed secondary schools, and so phrases like 'secondary-type schooling', 'secondary in all but name' and 'pseudo-secondary features' are commonly used. The use of the term 'grade' was in keeping with the educational jargon of the time, reinforced by the Schools Inquiry Commission's plan to match secondary schooling with social class as determined by school-leaving age. By the 1890s higher grade schools were being seen as equivalent to 'third-grade' schools, although at least one headmaster resisted this categorisation, proclaiming that 'his own school is of no grade, but will be developed according to the requirements of the district'.[17]

Higher grade schools are nearly always assumed to have provided a distinctively scientific and technical curriculum; indeed much of the contemporary criticism of the schools cited this as an undesirable attribute. The Bryce Commission, while acknowledging the importance of scientific and technical studies, nevertheless fuelled anxieties about the 'lop-sided' nature of the curriculum by suggesting that literary subjects might be pushed into an irrevocable decline. Many subsequent commentators have followed this interpretation; true secondary education consists of literary or humanitarian subjects, with science occupying, at best, a subordinate role and technological or vocational training lying firmly outside or beyond the secondary school. Hence, Archer felt that such public money as went to secondary schools before 1902 amounted to the virtual subsidising of scientific secondary education, which was 'unfair discrimination against the more literary type of education';[18] Adamson repeated the charges that the higher grade curriculum was 'wanting in breadth' and 'unduly biased if not warped'; and Cruickshank has criticised 'the imbalance of the curriculum, the neglect of the humanities and particularly of the English language' of these 'hybrid institutions'.

However, the opposing view has had its proponents, encouraged by two of the more important twentieth-century reports. The Hadow Report in 1927 noted that the organised science schools functioning within higher grade schools were popular with parents and represented 'a natural development' of the science teaching long associated with the best elementary schools.[19] And Young's much-quoted introduction to the Spens Report of 1939 included these sentences:

> The most salient defect in the new Regulations for Secondary Schools issued in 1904 is that they failed to take note of the comparatively rich experience of secondary curricula of a practical and quasi-vocational nature which had been evolved in the Higher Grade Schools, the Organised Science Schools and the Technical Day Schools. The new Regulations were based wholly on the tradition of the Grammar Schools and Public Schools.[20]

Writing soon after, Graves believed that the organised science school met a real need 'for some quasi-vocational alternative to the traditional grammar school curriculum', and that 'the rich secondary curriculum of the higher grade, science and technical schools' was ignored by the 1902 settlement.[21] Lowe has recently added a new dimension, in arguing that the Board of Education was under pressure from the Treasury to minimise costs 'by establishing a "model" of secondary education to which only a minority of schools could conform'.[22] Clearly, opinions about curriculum change over time and one has to question pronouncements about what constituted 'general education', a 'balanced curriculum' or 'excessive specialisation' to people almost exclusively educated in the nineteenth-century literary tradition with all its vast resources and prestige.

There are differing interpretations of whether the higher grade schools should have existed at all. Among the approving were Selby-Bigge ('distinguished by their active and progressive spirit, they contributed greatly to the advance of education') and Lowndes ('so cruelly cut back – one of the "might have beens" of English educational history').[23] More critical were those who implied that school boards were being deliberately provocative in assuming powers to which they were not entitled, and since the overt challenge to the existence of the higher grade schools came about by legal process, rather than political or administrative decision, an unusual amount of attention has been focused on their precise status in law. Most commentators have shrunk from the unequivocal verdicts of, for example, Halevy (the higher grade schools were 'illegally maintained') and Mann (they 'rested on no legal basis whatever'),[24] and have favoured terms like 'doubtful legality', 'equivocal position', 'irregular position' or 'haphazard growth'. It has been pointed out that the actual words of the Education Act of 1870 – what Hyndman termed the 'semantic ambiguities'[25] – did not seem to impose such a restriction, provided 'elementary education is the principal part of the education given'.

Perhaps more important, although rarely stated, is the fact that the school boards had taken on many responsibilities which existing laws and rules did not explicitly permit them to do, but from which subsequent legislation took its lead. In the education of pupil teachers, infants and handicapped children, and the organisation of school meals, medicals and physical exercise, the school boards had perceived a need and responded positively, thereby contributing much towards defining the wider role of the nation's education service. The 'dubious legality' question is therefore not a particularly fruitful matter for discussion, and the notion that Morant 'discovered what nobody else knew',[26] and 'was astonished to discover' that the higher grade schools were 'carried on in open defiance of the law of the land'[27] seems always to have been more than a little naive. Whether or not the school boards were technically entitled to be doing what they were, their actions were hardly a secret, either from their electorates or from the Education Department, and there is no doubt that the effects of the Cockerton verdict could easily have been reversed or modified by the nation's policy-makers had they been so inclined.

SCHOOL BOARDS: HEROIC INNOVATORS OR REPOSITORIES OF INEPTITUDE?

Discussion of the 'dubious legality' of the higher grade schools is often placed in the wider context of observations about the generally poor state of educational administration at the end of the nineteenth century. It is cited as one of many examples of inadequate legislation, poor planning and coordination, muddled ideology and a lackadaisical inclination to improvise. Adamson, for example, devoted a whole chapter to the 'administrative muddle', writing of the 'chaos', the 'national disinclination to think things out', 'the overlapping and waste'; Mann found the educational scene of the 1890s to be 'almost indescribable'; and Leese saw it as 'utter confusion'.[28] Ten members of the Cabinet had some say in educational institutions, and it was said to be 'scandalous' that no single body controlled education.[29] Of the three main administrative bodies, it has been suggested that the Charity Commission was being allowed to wither away, the atmosphere at the Education Department was 'troubled and potentially inflammable', and the Science and Art Department's 'multifarious activities were now causing great confusion in the organization of education'.[30] This lack of central direction has been variously held responsible for the 'jungle' and 'chaotic muddle' of secondary education, the 'lop-sided' and 'warped' state of the secondary curriculum, and – the most favoured target – 'that overgrown Moby Dick', the school board system.[31]

More than any other set of institutions, the higher grade schools were dependent on the continued existence and support of the school boards. The schools' own headmasters were in no doubt that the two belonged together, arguing that to replace the boards with council committees would be 'disastrous to the expansion of our educational system', since school board management was the only way of 'retaining the present close connection between Elementary and Secondary Education'.[32] Many of the larger and medium-sized school boards have earned unqualified praise from subsequent commentators: 'men of vision and vigour and courage' in both Barnsley and Sheffield, 'magnificent service' in Birmingham, or 'self-taught, versatile, industrious, devoted to public service, free-thinking, independent' in Bradford.[33] Overall, Armytage thought the school boards 'engaged some of the liveliest minds of the times. Each school board produced its great men', while to Sutherland such people were 'the likeliest candidates for the role of heroic innovators' in the world of education.[34] As the abolition of the school boards became imminent, a well-informed contemporary, Kekewich, confessed himself 'not quite able to understand why ... having done their work admirably, [they] were not to be rewarded and honoured, but led out to execution'.[35]

In sharp contrast, some contemporaries loathed the school boards with a passion. They were portrayed as 'positively evil' because of their dangerously pagan and radical outlook, or as 'repositories of bucolic prejudice and ineptitude'; there was emotive talk from anti-school board churchmen of anti-Christ and 'the day of judgment', of promoting vice and increasing crime.[36] Members of the influential Cecil family were implacable and scathing opponents,[37] and there cannot be many crusades originating from such aristocratic, High Church sources which have been so widely applauded in later years. Sneyd-Kinnersley said, 'I rocked the cradle of many Boards in 1871, and mine were two of the dry eyes that noted the interment ... sometimes it was a farce, sometimes a tragedy.'[38] Curtis cited Morant's comment that they 'had long outlived their period of usefulness', and himself believed that 'few mourned the decease of the School Boards save the School Boards themselves'.[39] So what is to be made of this marked divergence of opinion about the school boards, 'the idol of one party and the bugbear of another'?[40]

The answer is a political one. At the heart of the school boards' success lay their importance as organs of local democracy, described in 1903 as 'that gem, the principle of popular control, [which] had been burglariously stolen from them and replaced by mere paste'[41] and some years later as 'the most democratically constituted of all elected bodies of local government'.[42] The fact that a lot of small rural school boards were apathetic or incompetent is irrelevant; the real target was the strong, successful urban boards, which represented a serious challenge to central power and to 'traditional' values, especially as the strong Liberal, nonconformist presence on many of them was unlikely to be sympathetic to what the government saw as the most pressing problems in education: the rescue of the denominational and endowed schools. That the Church Party played an active political role at that time is indisputable. Morant's remark about 'getting up steam' against the school boards by appealing to the voluntary school lobby is well known, and it has since been proved that a very well organised and vociferous section of the Church of England played a key role in promoting 'bitter and unreasonable hostility to the School Board system'.[43] There has been speculation that the twentieth century would certainly have seen greater Labour and trade union representation on the school boards, which 'must have been at least one reason why the Church Party was anxious to replace a system of voting for school boards with one of appointing education committees'.[44]

A leading higher grade school headmaster predicted in 1895 that 'an indirectly elected and nominated body cannot possibly be so well in touch with the ratepayers as one elected by them. Its action will tend to be weak, its policy vacillating. Where it should be strong it will hesitate, where it should be yielding it will be obstinate ... [education] will glide into a backwater'.[45] His pessimism was confirmed in 1913, when half the country's directors of education, and no fewer than 72 per cent of those in boroughs and urban districts, indicated that they preferred the *ad hoc* system, because they were anxious about the 'decay in local interest' in education.[46] In the 1950s Eaglesham overcame his initial prejudice against the school boards to end up convinced 'that the systematic and extensive development of the *ad hoc* principle might in the long run have provided a sounder system of local educational administration than that established by the 1902 Act'.[47]

THE 1902 ACT: SUPREME ACHIEVEMENT OR DISASTROUS PACKAGE?

However, enthusiasm for the 1902 Education Act has been widely expressed and sometimes lyrical: a 'major advance', a 'landmark', a 'transformation', a 'supreme achievement', 'nothing short of revolution', 'a social revolution of the first magnitude', and 'incomparably more cohesive and effective'. Part of the approval is for the new administrative arrangements, with the county council structure replacing the school boards as the basis of local educational administration. To Halevy, 'it was plainly out of the question to unify the local administration of the Education Acts on the basis of the school boards ... it was inevitable that the County Councils should be preferred'. Cruickshank felt that the LEAs were a logical development from the county councils, which already had 'substantial expertise' through the technical instruction committees,[48] although in fact those committees were barely ten years old and had no experience of dealing with the educational needs of all children or the education service as a whole. The manner in which some of them initially familiarised themselves with their task – appealing for information in the local press, or in one case, consulting the sanitation sub-committee – was indicative of what an alien introduction they were to the education scene. Their most noted achievement had been the creation of technical colleges, and a significant proportion of their energy and money was devoted to sponsoring scattered evening classes in bee-keeping or wood-carving. But they had played a 'crucial part' in restoring the fortunes of the struggling endowed schools and, it has been suggested, 'this mutual support between the county authorities and the grammar schools helps to explain the direction of policy for secondary education after 1902'.[49]

Much has been made of the importance of the new relationship between central and local authorities, which has been somewhat effusively characterised as a 'unique partnership ... in all parts it is sustained by this spirit of partnership'.[50] The 1902 Act is said to have inaugurated 'a coherent system of administration' and meant that 'the community nationally and locally assumed responsibility for all forms in a sense never before realized'.[51] Many of the new education committees, it has been suggested, 'had strong (and often strange) ideas about the kinds of secondary schools they wanted', and since they were all preoccupied with keeping down the rates, there is all the more reason to be thankful for Morant's 'clear vision and dynamic energy' goading 'progressive and laggard local education authorities alike into incessant action'.[52] In fact the local education authorities had considerably less power than the 1902 Act seemed to imply. Graves, for example, stressed that the local authorities were obliged by the Board's Regulations to follow central policy assiduously, and Hyndman confirmed that the 1904 Regulations were a 'classic illustration of how central authority could exert pressure upon one particular sector of education when it really desired to'.[53] Eaglesham reckoned that for the Board to say that the local education authority would 'be absolute master of secular education was nonsense. But the statement was repeated time and again; and somehow the bluff worked'.[54]

In general, it is hard to see any automatic way in which the quality of educational administration was improved by the new system. A number of built-in anomalies, such as the Part II/Part III authorities and the continued existence of voluntary school managers, detract significantly from the oft-acclaimed systemisation, and to Clarke writing in 1940, the English education system was still 'extraordinarily complex ... as illogical as it is ill-defined'.[55] And it was certainly less answerable to popular wishes. It had taken an amendment from Yoxall, the NUT General Secretary, to ensure that at least a majority of each education committee should comprise elected councillors. A significant loss was for the rights of women, who could (and did) stand for election to the school boards on equal terms, but now figured as a small required element in the co-optive membership of education committees. Midwinter has suggested that in the change to the county council system, education became just one of numerous services in the queue for the attention of an 'obscure and distant' local authority, bogged down in a 'bewildering series of committees' and regarded with 'suspicion and envy' because of its costliness.[56] To Simon, the breaking of the direct relationship between the people and the local school system was one of the key factors which made the 1902 Education Act 'a disastrous package'.[57] In moving the administration of education a decisive step away from its popular roots, the 1902 Act made it more susceptible to centralised control and, quite simply, less democratic.

If, then, the educational administration created by the 1902 Act is susceptible to such criticism, what of the work which it did? Tributes like 'at last ... England possessed a State system of education', or 'a co-ordinated national system of education was at last introduced',[58] have been questioned on the grounds that the settlement was neither national nor a system.[59] Enthusiasm for the bringing together of elementary and secondary education as part of a single whole – 'the two forms of education starting at the two ends had at length met in the middle'[60] – has to be discarded because the 1902 Act 'did not, alas, create a completely articulated system of public education ... the 1902 structure was made up of two imperfectly co-ordinated parts, elementary and "other than elementary"'.[61] As Sir George Kekewich explained at the time:

co-ordination has been talked of as if it meant simply that higher and lower education were under the same school authority. That was not co-ordination, because co-ordination meant that the curriculum should be so arranged as to be properly stepped from one school to another.[62]

There has also to be a big question mark over the Board of Education's approach to existing secondary schools, which did not merely fail to draw the majority into the 'system', but actually enhanced their separate and privileged status. Archer doubted whether a state system of education can 'be regarded as satisfactory as long as schools which can afford to do so insist on boycotting it'.[63] No government since has successfully tackled this entrenched division, so that we reach the end of the twentieth century with renewed attempts to pretend that the state and independent systems have the same goals and can work together.

And what of the widely expressed assumption that the new secondary schools made a significant contribution to improving educational opportunity for all children of ability? What of claims that the 1902 Act 'placed advanced instruction within the reach of the major part of the people', or that 'in future there was no county or town in which the lower middle class was unprovided with secondary schools where for a low fee, or even without payment, their children could receive an education as good as that given to the children of the gentry or the upper middle class'?[64] Surprisingly little has been made of the insistence, often against local wishes, on a minimum school fee, which disqualified from secondary education far more children than scholarships or free places could support, or of the remarkable fact that large numbers of children declined to compete for secondary school places even when maintenance support was available. Perhaps the distinctive identity given to the grammar school became so familiar during the course of the twentieth century that it is forgotten how strange – and unwelcoming – it was to many children facing it for the first time. Graves concluded that 'practically speaking, no alternative now existed for the ambitious poor boy of 12',[65] echoing contemporary criticisms made by Michael Sadler in his reports to various LEAs that for children aged 12 to 15, 'remarkably little had been done'. Although Sadler's comments on the higher grade schools were 'to say the least of them, chilly', yet he 'never contemplated their abolition without their being replaced by something better', and firmly believed in 'retaining every instrument of tested value'.[66]

If it should prove to be the case that the new system of secondary education badly failed large numbers of children who wished to continue their schooling and had previously been able to do so, then its merits would have to be seriously questioned. Few writers have explored this fundamental issue. Marsden suggested that in attaching high status to the 'social quarantining' of the grammar schools, to the detriment of the 'educational sophistication' of the higher grade schools,[67] the Board of Education faced opponents with an impossible dilemma, which served to muzzle their protests. The NUT and the Labour Party could only press for more grammar schools and scholarships because technical and higher grade schools would be seen as 'poor substitutes for grammar schools';[68] in the words of the NUT's own historians, the teachers were presented with a choice between 'half a loaf or no bread'.[69] And if the changed nature of the education on offer deserves further attention, so too does the scale on which it was available. The belief that after 1902 secondary schooling expanded dramatically, with its implicit assumption that more and different children were being educated in new schools, is almost unanimously expressed. In fact, the main achievement of the 1902 settlement was to rescue hundreds of ailing endowed schools, which essentially carried on educating the same children in much the same way as before. In the absence of full statistics, nobody knew how many secondary school pupils there were, and it will be suggested later that the new arrangements represented a diminution rather than an enhancement of opportunities.

CENTRAL AUTHORITY: BURSTING WITH BRAINS OR TORTUOUS AND IGNOBLE?

Consideration by educational historians of the central authority, the other half of the 'unique administrative partnership' created at the turn of the century, has been completely dominated by Robert Morant. Some of them have become unusually extravagant in their judgments. Words like 'unique', 'remarkable', 'extraordinary' and 'genius' abound in discussions about Robert Morant. To Beatrice Webb he was 'a man of genius ... [who] has done more to improve English administration than any other man', while three-quarters of a century later English education was said to be fortunate to have been 'directed by a man of clear vision and dynamic energy'.[70] He has been characterised as a 'remarkably able and single-minded educational administrator', a 'unique reformer' and the greatest Permanent Secretary ever to serve the Board of Education.[71]

There are, however, always deep reservations about the manner in which Morant achieved what he did. It seems to be almost impossible to review his personality in a favourable light. Described variously as 'a strange mortal, not quite sane', 'brilliant but erratic and indiscreet' and 'the "eminence grise" of the Board of Education', he had 'great failings as a human being', and was 'as autocratic, ruthless and ambitious as any self-made industrial magnate'.[72] One of his most severe critics has written of Morant's 'unsubtle blend of fawning charm towards his superiors and malevolent spite towards subordinates'.[73] His most commonly agreed personal qualities were his industriousness – 'a man of demoniac energy, with a consuming passion for work'[74] – and his intolerance towards opposition of any kind. Nearly all writers note that his handling of opponents was ruthless and unscrupulous, combining elements of flattery, bluff, deceit, and, if needs be, a violent temper. Eaglesham detailed some of Morant's dealings with colleagues who had fallen out of favour, using words like 'unreasonable', 'violent', 'vehement', 'sledgehammer', 'blistering', 'devastating', 'storm', 'fume' and 'explosive' to describe the rows with individuals and other government departments.[75] Two men who knew Morant at work were struck by his single-minded ambition and his enjoyment of intrigue. One said of him that he was 'occasionally hysterical in mood and manner …. and by nature and by habit a maker of intrigue, advancing on his goal by several devious personal channels';[76] and the other that he had 'a profound conviction that all opposition derived from the devil … That he was over-weeningly ambitious, tortuous and indifferent to common standards of honour, is not in doubt.'[77]

Taylor portrayed Morant's spectacular rise in the central educational administration as a quite consciously engineered exercise, during which he repeatedly sought out powerful allies, switched allegiances, and then vilified any possible rivals, including former friends.[78] Arriving in the Department in 1895, with experience of virtually ruling Siam (Thailand) rather than the usual tedious civil service apprenticeship, he must immediately have seen the opportunities for a conscientious and well-informed leader to cut through the confusion, especially as there was a consensus in favour of change. It has to be said that in taking full advantage of those possibilities Morant's preparation was impeccable. His first job after his remarkable promotion in 1899 was to set about creating 'the department of his dreams', which has been adjudged his second most important achievement, bettered only by the planning and implementation of the 1902 Act.[79] Among his senior colleagues, he easily outmanoeuvred Kekewich, forcing him into early and undignified retirement, and, in driving out Michael Sadler, he rid the Board of the one man of comparable ability to himself. Sadler himself later wrote of a 'restlessly ambitious side' to Morant's nature, and suggested that 'at critical moments in his career ... he was not scrupulous [but] impatient, masterful, prejudiced and a little reckless. I think he would have seen his way, if he had been a young German in 1933, to serve Hitler strenuously.'[80]

By 1902, when he became Permanent Secretary, Morant was moving in the highest social and political circles and was a close and trusted ally of the Prime Minister; politicians certainly held no fears for him. Occupying a vacuum at the Board of Education, he quickly emerged unmistakably as the experienced expert: the ideal man to be in command of both practical details and visionary plans. This made it possible for him to clear the ground of any remaining vested interests which might have given him problems, notably the school boards and their higher grade schools, abolishing both before their successors were announced so that opposition was minimised and the eventual solutions more readily welcomed. He then cultivated aloofness from all the spokesmen and experts who might have disagreed with him, notably the new local authorities and the main part of the teaching profession. The National Union of Teachers, to whose leaders Morant showed 'scarcely concealed contempt', experienced an 'extraordinary breakdown of confidence' while he was at the Board; the Union's historians concluded that relations were never so bitter as when Morant was in charge.[81] Only intense and long-felt dislike can explain the determination with which the major teachers' organisation and its allies pursued Morant out of the Board of Education in 1911. The thrust of the onslaught was highly personal, directing itself against a 'bureaucratic despotism' and an 'autocratic and reactionary officer', and *The Schoolmaster* demanded that civil servants be 'more open minded, less haughtily prejudiced, more patient, more accessible to argument, less class conscious, and less cocksure than some of them have been'.[82]

One of his successors as Permanent Secretary believed Morant to be 'incapable of thinking in terms of partnership',[83] and later writers have drawn attention to his basically anti-democratic urge to 'submit the impulses of the many ignorant to the guidance and control of the few wise' and to keep control of the Board's relations with the public 'strictly in his own hands',[84] an interpretation which is confirmed by the ubiquity of his handwriting on documents within the Board of Education, and the care with which he briefed colleagues in what to say.[85] He also failed to utilise any of the advisory mechanisms provided for the Board of Education, thereby contributing to the insulation of its officials from a wide spectrum of educational opinion. The 'Board' established in 1899 was never actually constituted, merely creating the 'redundant paraphernalia of a non-existent Board', and providing a set of 'imaginary colleagues'. The proposed Educational Council of advisory experts never existed, Morant arranged for the Office of Special Enquiries and Reports to lose all its originality (as well as its most talented researcher, Sadler), and the Consultative Committee never gained sufficient independence to become genuinely innovative.

Furthermore, Gorst had closed off the possibility of any elementary teacher becoming an HMI, and the Board of Education, uniquely among government departments, retained recruitment by patronage; it was 'almost the last surviving self-perpetuating oligarchy in the British Isles'.[86] The 1912 Civil Service Commission was far from impressed by the Board of Education's recruitment methods, pointing to cases of favouritism and showing that its appointees were no better qualified than those who entered other government departments after examination. The Board, it thought, furnished 'a striking condemnation of the system of political nomination. It became notorious that its senior officials were prone to allow personal views to influence their official actions.'[87] Spencer, with an insider's view, depicted the Board's permanent officials as 'entirely without first-hand acquaintance with the "proletarian" class of education they control ... They lack imagination and they lack positive enthusiasm, though many of them burst with brains.'[88] In similar vein, Bishop believed that Morant succeeded in surrounding himself with people 'whose ignorance of, indeed contempt for, elementary education was matched only by their lack of interest in it'.[89]

Much the same could be said of their dismissive attitude towards their 'colleagues' from the Science and Art Department. The physical and ideological isolation of that Department, and the ensuing competition for supremacy between the secondary and technical branches of the office, were to be particularly damaging for scientific education and the higher grade schools. Sneyd-Kinnersley characterised the antagonism between the two thus: 'the Montague and Capulet retainers never met; only they bit their thumbs when the other house was mentioned'.[90] Opinions about the Science and Art Department are extremely divided. Some historians follow Acland's condemnation of its examinations-based 'payment by results' mode of operation – 'the very worst way in which a secondary school can receive public aid'[91] – while others have acknowledged the contribution of the Science and Art Department to making the education of thousands of children (and adults) more interesting and fruitful. It 'had done a vast amount of good, and had more than justified its existence' thought the higher grade school heads, and Selby-Bigge believed that 'at small cost' it did 'valuable pioneering work' in promoting a sound educational blend of general and specialist instruction.[92]

More recent analysis has shown that the Science and Art Department's insistence on meticulous rules and marking under the supervision of highly qualified examiners blended remarkably well with 'the vagaries of local initiative' and constituted 'a unique organisational form in our educational history'.[93] But the adoption of Science and Art Department work in schools had been an expedient, its relationship with the normal education system never defined, and, with the convenient retirement of its determined head just one month before the passing of the Board of Education Act, the Department fell prey to all the personal and political wranglings within the new organisation.[94] The uncertainty after 1899 about how everyone would fit into the restructured Board of Education, and the lobbying from outside pressure groups, disrupted the normally settled routines of central administration. Bishop was critical of the 'exceptionally permissive character' of the 1899 legislation, and overall was led to the conclusion that the rise of the central authority for education was mostly due to bad luck and poor judgment: 'a slow, tortuous, makeshift, muddled, unplanned, disjointed and ignoble process'.[95]

Morant, meanwhile, was able to create the team of his choice. HM Inspectorate – the 'eyes and ears of the Department' – was just moving into its most important period to date, and Morant was fully aware of its potential power. His judgment then is confirmed today by our knowledge of the impact on schools of a rigorous and interventionist inspection system, reconstituted to replace what had evolved into a virtually autonomous and widely respected HM Inspectorate. But, at the beginning of the century, the Board of Education's retention of patronage gave its head almost total control of the personnel selected, and Morant must have known exactly what he was doing when he selected men like Headlam and Mackail, both distinguished classical scholars. Barnett has said of this triumvirate:

> it is hard to imagine that the shaping of British state education at a crucial point in its development could have fallen into the hands of men more sublimely oblivious, or dismissive, of Britain's urgent educational needs as an industrial society already outmatched by its rivals.

To him, Morant set out 'not to provide England with education for capability (either general or technical) that could match that of her rivals, but to demolish what little had been gradually built up by this time'.[96] Barnett's comments help to pinpoint the key issue concerning Morant: if much that was good was discarded in the process of systemisation, and the nation's overall educational potential stunted in order to safeguard part of it, then Morant's ideals and achievements are as open to criticism as his manner and methods.

The vacuum that Morant filled within the administration of education was paralleled by a comparable void in the political sphere. There is striking agreement among historians over the dismal state of the political leadership of education at that highly significant point in its history. Lord Salisbury, it has been said, was essentially an anachronism, whose 'antiquated notions of what an educational system should be became increasingly irrelevant and increasingly embarrassing'.[97] All the Cecils, their family biographer concluded, shared their father's affection for creeds which were 'already unfashionable, and sometimes obsolete'.[98] It has now been proved that 'Hotel Cecil' was not just a catchy nickname for an unusual family presence in high political circles, but rather an active, clandestine and highly effective group. Several Cecils were involved in the events which led up to the Cockerton judgment, for them the successful outcome of their 'campaign of guerrilla warfare' against the London School Board, during which they 'nobbled' Sir John Gorst and identified Morant as an ideal spy for Balfour.[99]

Balfour, the Cecil cousin who assumed the parliamentary leadership of education as well as the premiership, has generally been commended for his intelligence and shrewdness, but he was hardly the man to create an education system designed to serve the whole population. It has been written of him that 'he was willing to engage in battle only when the traditional institutions he cherished or his own privileged status or life style seemed threatened', and, like his uncle, his interest in the 1902 legislation derived from a determination to rescue the voluntary schools, for 'whether the nation's children went to school or not was a matter of deep indifference to a man noted for his intellectual elitism and his lack of concern for "democratic" issues'. His sister commented that he regarded education as 'a tricky political topic, fraught with pitfalls and full of intricate discussions of detail. Not only that but it was boring.'[100] Balfour's shameless clinging to office until the end of 1905 and his well-known pledge to thwart the new government through the House of Lords – in which task he received the active assistance of three Cecil brothers[101] – are proof of how out of touch they all were with modern democratic conditions.

Supporting the two prime ministers before and after 1902 were Cabinets which were 'impatient and tired with the whole question of education', and became so chaotic that Morant found it impossible to discover what had actually been decided at meetings.[102] Not surprisingly, many Members of Parliament 'seem to have been genuinely confused' by the debates on the Bill.[103] As for the Education Department itself, it had in 1902 a largely undistinguished political past, the typical President often knowing 'more about cattle plague than he did about the education code', while the typical Vice-President 'came in like a lion ... and went out like a lamb'.[104] Morant revealed to Beatrice Webb his contempt for most of the politicians he worked with, and he seems to have been right. The Duke of Devonshire, appointed President in 1895, failed 'through inertia and stupidity to grasp any complicated detail half an hour after he had listened to the clearest exposition of it'. His senior civil servant, Sir George Kekewich, said of him: 'He gave me the impression of being so wrapped up in his own dignity and family pride, that he regarded commoners such as myself as people to be kept at a distance. He was a living wet blanket.'[105] Vice-President Sir John Gorst, an able but difficult man, became 'cynical and careless, having given up even the semblance of any interest in the office'. Both chose to resign in the summer of 1902 in the middle of the protracted Commons struggle over the 1902 Bill. The new president, the Marquis of Londonderry, was portrayed as 'a bull in a china shop' whose appointment was greeted with incredulity by the press, while his deputy, Sir William Anson, 'knew so little ... that it was barely worth talking to him' and struck Michael Sadler as a 'misadventurous opportunist Whig'.[106]

The twentieth-century system of education was thus created by a clever but unscrupulous civil servant and by politicians whose low standard of competence was repeatedly lamented by Beatrice Webb, not least because of their confusion about education in general and the schooling of the ordinary people in particular. Even the individuals who created the new system were surprised at the ways it worked out in practice; Balfour's plaintive 'I did not realise that the Act would mean more expense and more bureaucracy' is well known in this context. Was the transformation that was accomplished by the Board of Education in the first decade of this century as it resolved the various tensions in public education outlined earlier, the best, or the only, possible solution? It is one of the aims of this book to demonstrate that in the higher grade school movement English education had a source of great strength, and that the rejection of both its educational ideology and its organisational principles was a wasteful, ill-informed and retrogressive step. The higher grade schools were a vital constituent of a developing range of educational institutions which included organised schools of science, pupil teacher centres, technical colleges, evening classes and university colleges, which were all blossoming at the close of the nineteenth century in response to an upsurge of educational demand.[107] If – as will be argued in this book – they were making a unique contribution to English education, their removal from the scene constitutes a lost opportunity the scale and significance of which have not yet been appreciated.

From the existing limited and sometimes inaccurate representations of the higher grade schools surveyed in this chapter, the focus sharpens in Chapter 2 to give a detailed analysis of the distinctive features of the schools. Drawing on the schools' own records, this chapter identifies these features as curriculum, staffing and organisation, premises, fees and class of pupils, length and nature of school career, girls in higher grade schools, and the organic connection with elementary and further education. Chapter 3 narrows the focus to explore fully the optimistic and expansionist beginnings of just three higher grade schools – St George, Fairfield Road and Merrywood in the city of Bristol – before 1902. The Bristol case study continues in Chapter 4, which recounts the three schools' frustrating experiences after 1902 as they struggled to find a role within the newly constituted secondary education system. Chapter 5 steps back to the national perspective, picking up the themes of Chapter 2 to describe the fate of all higher grade schools after 1902, and thereby discovering much about the priorities which shaped the new system. Chapter 6 returns to the larger picture outlined in Chapter 1, looking at what happened to the tensions evident in education in the 1890s and demonstrating that the formation of the twentieth-century education system represented a huge waste of potential. In the concluding chapter, the higher grade school phenomenon is considered in the context of the broad sweep of British educational history.

NOTES

1. A. Green, *Education and State Formation* (London: Macmillan, 1990).
2. F.K. Ringer, *Education and Society in Modern Europe* (Bloomington and London: Indiana University Press, 1979), p. 9.
3. R. Wilkinson, *The Prefects: British Leadership and the Public School Tradition* (London: Oxford University Press, 1964), p. x.
4. By S. Rothblatt, *Tradition and Change in English Liberal Education: An Essay in History and Culture* (London: Faber, 1976).
5. Quoted by C. Heward, 'Education, Examinations and the Artisans: The Department of Science and Art in Birmingham, 1853–1902', in R. Macleod (ed.), *Days of Judgment: Science, Examinations and the Organization of Knowledge in Late Victorian England* (Driffield: Nafferton Books, 1982), p. 54.
6. Reported in the *Record of Technical and Secondary Education*, III, 13 (1894).
7. *Royal Commission on Secondary Education (Bryce Commission)*, I (1895), p. 48.
8. H. Steedman, 'Defining Institutions: The Endowed Grammar Schools and the Systemisation of English Secondary Education', in D.K. Muller, F. Ringer and B. Simon, *The Rise of the Modern*

Educational System: Structural Change and Social Reproduction 1870–1920 (Cambridge: Cambridge University Press, 1987), p. 128.

9. E.J.R. Eaglesham, *From School Board to Local Authority* (London: Routledge & Kegan Paul, 1956), pp. 59, 103.

10. J.H. Muirhead (ed.), *Birmingham Institutions* (Birmingham: Cornish Bros, 1911), p. 139; E.P. Hennock, *Fit and Proper Persons: Ideal and Reality in Nineteenth-Century Urban Government* (London: Edward Arnold, 1973), pp. 172–3. The radical nonconformist George Dixon was a good example; he interrupted a promising parliamentary career to devote himself to his ailing wife and to Birmingham's affairs, serving 26 years on the most active school board in the country. 'Radical Joe' Chamberlain remained a local hero for his work in turning Birmingham into the best governed city in Britain, alongside his career in national politics. The city was fortunate to have congenial Edgbaston just a mile from the city centre.

11. As described by L. Davidoff, *The Best Circles: Social Etiquette and the Season* (London: Croom Helm, 1973).

12. The battle over King Edward School, Birmingham in the 1860s and 1880s was an example of this kind of conflict, as described by R.C. Gilson, 'The Schools of King Edward VI', in Muirhead, *Birmingham Institutions*, pp. 523–60, and D. Smith, *Conflict and Compromise – Class Formation in English Society 1830–1914: A Comparative Study of Birmingham and Sheffield* (London: Routledge & Kegan Paul, 1982) pp. 176–83.

13. D.I. Allsobrook, 'An Investigation of Precedents for the Recommendations of the Schools Inquiry Commission 1864–67' (University of Leicester PhD thesis, 1979), p. 662. P. Gordon and J. White in *Philosophers as Educational Reformers: The Influence of Idealism on British Educational Thought and Practice* (London: Routledge & Kegan Paul, 1979), pp. 121–2, described how personal links between, for example, Jowett at Balliol and Percival of Clifton College and later the bishopric of Hereford, led to an open invitation to the Oxford colleges to get closely involved with provincial university colleges, 'in order to avoid local influences, which would tend towards the practical wants of the neighbourhood but which would produce little or nothing in the way of liberal culture'. Bristol University College, over which Balliol and New College had considerable influence, was their greatest success.

14. The designation was probably first used by a school in Cambridge, but it was of a rather different type.

15. In the proposed *Higher Elementary Schools Minute*, 6 April 1900.

16. A.S. Bishop, *The Rise of a Central Authority for English Education* (Cambridge: Cambridge University Press, 1971), p. 178.

17. Leeds' Dr Forsyth quoted in *The Schoolmaster*, 7 December 1895.

18. R.L. Archer, *Secondary Education in the Nineteenth Century* (Cambridge: Cambridge University Press, 1921), p. 308; J.W. Adamson, *English Education 1789–1902* (Cambridge: Cambridge University Press, 1930), pp. 371, 455; M. Cruickshank, 'A Defence of the 1902 Act', *History of Education Society Bulletin*, 19 (1977), p. 6.

19. Board of Education, *Report of the Consultative Committee on The Education of the Adolescent (Hadow Report)* (1927) p. 18.

20. Board of Education, *Report of the Consultative Committee on Secondary Education (Spens Report)* (1939), pp. 66–7.

21. J. Graves, *Policy and Progress in Secondary Education 1902–1942* (London: Thomas Nelson, 1943), pp. 63, 78.

22. R. Lowe, 'Robert Morant and the Secondary School Regulations of 1904', *Journal of Educational Administration and History*, 16, 1 (1984), pp. 1, 12.

23. L.A. Selby-Bigge, *The Board of Education* (London: G.P. Putnam's Sons, 1927), p. 180 – Selby Bigge was Permanent Secretary to the Board of Education 1911–25; G.A.N. Lowndes, *The Silent Social Revolution: An Account of the Expansion of Public Education in England and Wales 1895–1935* (London: Oxford University Press, 1937), p. 53.

24. E. Halevy, *Imperialism and the Rise of Labour* (London: Benn, 1951), p. 198; Graves, *Policy and Progress*, p. 30.

25. M. Hyndman, *Schools and Schooling in England and Wales* (London: Harper & Row, 1978), p. 60.

26. R.C.K. Ensor, *England 1870–1914* (Oxford: Clarendon Press, 1936), p. 355.

27. J.F. Mann, *Education* (London: Pitman, 1979), p. 19.

28. Adamson, *English Education*, Ch. 16; Mann, *Education*, p. 18; J. Leese, *Personalities and Power in English Education* (Leeds: E.J. Arnold, 1950), p. 226. It is worth considering that late-ninenteenth-century 'overlapping' may be the same as twentieth-century extension of opportunities.

29. Halevy, *Imperialism*, p. 148.

30. Bishop, *Rise of a Central Authority*, pp. 129, 192, 255.

31. E.J.R. Eaglesham, *The Foundations of Twentieth-Century Education in England* (London: Routledge & Kegan Paul, 1967), p. 28; J.N. Hewitson, *The Grammar School Tradition in a Comprehensive World* (London: Routledge & Kegan Paul, 1969), p. 18; Adamson, *English Education*, p. 455; E. Midwinter, *Schools in Society: The Evolution of English Education* (London: Batsford Academic, 1980), p. 75.

32. Quoted in *The Schoolmaster*, 7 December 1895 and 26 April 1896, from conference speeches of the Association of Headmasters of Higher Grade and Organised Schools of Science.

33. A.M. Davies, *The Barnsley School Board 1871–1903* (Barnsley: Cheesman, 1965), p. 189; J.H. Bingham, *The Sheffield School Board 1870–1903* (Sheffield: Northend, 1949), p. 279; *School Government Chronicle*, 16 May 1903; Bradford Corporation, *Education in Bradford since 1870* (Bradford: Bradford Corporation, 1970), p. 33.

34. W.H.G. Armytage, *Four Hundred Years of English Education* (Cambridge: Cambridge University Press, 1964), p. 145; G. Sutherland, *Policy-Making in Elementary Education 1870–1895* (London: Oxford University Press, 1973), p. 104.

35. Reported in the *School Government Chronicle*, 9 May 1903.

36. A. Rogers, 'Churches and Children: A Study in the Controversy over the 1902 Education Act', *British Journal of Educational Studies*, 8, 1 (1959), p. 33; Hyndman, *Schools and Schooling*, p. 209; B. Simon, *Education and the Labour Movement 1870–1920* (London: Lawrence & Wishart, 1965), p. 227.

37. For the Cecil 'conspiracy', see T. Taylor, 'The Cecils and the Cockerton Case: High Politics and Low Intentions', *History of Education Society Bulletin*, 37 (1986).

38. E.M. Sneyd-Kinnersley, *H.M.I. Some Passages in the Life of One of H.M. Inspectors of Schools* (London: Macmillan, 1908), p. 171. His first-hand assessment (p. 8) of the Anglesey board could scarcely have been more damning: 'five men whose opinion on a pig might be accepted ... but on school matters the pig's opinion would be equally valuable'.

39. S.J. Curtis, *Education in Britain since 1900* (London: Dakers, 1952), pp. 32, 36.

40. Sneyd-Kinnersley, *H.M.I.*, p. 170.

41. *School Government Chronicle*, 16 May 1903: the words of Rev. McCarthy, the radical Anglican headmaster of one of Birmingham's King Edward grammar schools. A long-serving member of the city's school board, and passionately devoted to the cause of public education, he refused to serve on the education committee as a matter of principle.

42. J.S. Hurt, *Elementary Schooling and the Working Classes 1860–1918* (London: Routledge & Kegan Paul, 1979), p. 75.

43. Rogers, 'Churches', p. 35; and T. Taylor, 'Lord Cranborne, the Church Party and Anglican Education 1893–1902: From Politics to Pressure', *History of Education*, 22, 2 (1993).

44. C. Griggs, *The Trades Union Congress and the Struggle for Education 1868–1925* (Lewes: Falmer Press, 1983), p. 163. It may well also have been one reason why the Liberal government of 1906 had little desire to revert to the former system of direct election.

45. John Bidgood of Gateshead, quoted in *The Schoolmaster*, 7 December 1895.

46. J. Lawson and H. Silver, *A Social History of Education in England* (London: Methuen, 1973), p. 379. They also point out that the *ad hoc*, directly elected principle survived in Scotland until the 1930s, moves to copy the 1902 English model being defeated.

47. Eaglesham, *From School Board*, p. vii.

48. Halevy, *Imperialism*, pp. 196, 206; Cruickshank, 'Defence', p. 5.

49. R. Bourne and B. MacArthur, *The Struggle for Education 1870–1970: A Pictorial History of Popular Education and the National Union of Teachers* (London: Schoolmaster Publishing, 1970), p. 46.

50. H.C. Dent, *Education in England and Wales* (London: Hodder & Stoughton, 1982), p. 179.

51. Adamson, *English Education*, p. 469.

52. H.C. Dent, *1870–1970: Century of Growth in English Education* (Harlow: Longmans, 1970), pp. 60–1.

53. Graves, *Policy and Progress*, p. 52; Hyndman, *Schools and Schooling*, p. 215.
54. Eaglesham, *Foundations*, p. 47.
55. F. Clarke, *Education and Social Change: An English Interpretation* (London: Shaldon Press, 1940), p. 34. Various writers have noted the complications associated with the smaller Part III authorities; for example, Curtis, *Education in Britain*, p. 43, said they were 'restricted and handicapped' and 'the source of much contention' over the years.
56. Midwinter, *Schools in Society*, p. 95.
57. Simon, 'The 1902 Education Act: A Wrong Turning', *History of Education Society Bulletin*, 19 (1977), p. 12.
58. Adamson, *English Education*, p. 471; H.C. Barnard, *A History of English Education from 1760* (London: University of London Press, 1947), p. 211.
59. C. Birchenough, *History of Elementary Education in England and Wales from 1800 to the Present Day* (London: University Tutorial Press, 1938), p. 179, noted the comment of the President of the Board of Education in 1913 that 'the existing system suffered from the double defect of being neither national nor a system'.
60. Archer, *Secondary Education*, p. 318.
61. Dent, *Education in England and Wales*, p. 11.
62. Reported in the *School Government Chronicle*, 9 May 1903.
63. Archer, *Secondary Education*, p. 315.
64. Halevy, *Imperialism*, p. 205.
65. Graves, *Policy and Progress*, p. 80.
66. L. Grier, *Achievement in Education: The Work of Michael Ernest Sadler* (London: Constable, 1952), p. 139.
67. W.E. Marsden, 'Schools for the Urban Lower Middle Class: Third Grade or Higher Grade', in P. Searby (ed.), *Educating the Victorian Middle Class* (Leicester: History of Education Society, 1982), p. 54.
68. A. Tropp, *The School Teachers: The Growth of the Teaching Profession in England and Wales from 1800 to the Present Day* (London: Heinemann, 1957), p. 192.
69. Bourne and MacArthur, *Struggle*, p. 47
70. Quoted in A.V. Judges, 'The Educational Influence of the Webbs', *British Journal of Educational Studies*, 10, 1 (1961), p. 44; Dent, *Century of Growth*, p. 60.
71. N. Mackenzie (ed.), *The Letters of Sidney and Beatrice Webb* (Cambridge: Cambridge University Press, 1978), p. 138; C. Martin, *A Short History of English Schools 1750–1965* (Hove: Wayland, 1979), p. 81; Eaglesham, *From School Board*, p. 2.
72. Judges, 'Educational Influence', p. 44; Dent, *Century of Growth*, p. 57; K.M. Hughes, 'A Political Party and Education. Reflections on the Liberal Party's Educational Policy, 1867–1902', *British Journal of Educational Studies*, 8, 2 (1960), p. 125; Tropp, *School Teachers*, p. 184; W.O. Lester Smith, *Education in Great Britain* (London: Oxford University Press, 1958), p. 117.
73. T. Taylor, '"An Early Arrival of the Fascist Mentality": Robert Morant's Rise to Power', *Journal of Educational Administration and History*, 17, 2 (1985), p. 48.
74. Eaglesham, *Foundations*, p. 39.
75. E.J.R. Eaglesham, 'The Centenary of Sir Robert Morant', *British Journal of Educational Studies*, 12, 1 (1963), pp. 8–12.
76. Sir Arthur Salter, quoted in Grier, *Achievement*, p. 81.
77. J. Craig, *A History of Red Tape: An Account of the Origin and Development of the Civil Service* (London: Macdonald & Evans, 1955), p. 155.
78. Taylor, '"Early Arrival"'.
79. Eaglesham, 'Centenary', p. 8.
80. Quoted in Grier, *Achievement*, p. 80. Michael Sadler, a distinguished Oxford scholar, made his name through the university extension movement, served on the Bryce Commission and then (1895) joined the Education Department as Director of the newly created Office for Special Reports and Inquiries. Morant entered the Department as his assistant.
81. Bourne and MacArthur, *Struggle*, p. 57.
82. B.M. Allen, *Sir Robert Morant: A Great Public Servant* (London: Macmillan, 1934), pp. 261–2; Bourne and MacArthur, *Struggle*, p. 57.
83. Sir Maurice Holmes, quoted in Curtis, *Education in Britain*, p. 46.
84. Armytage, *Four Hundred Years*, p. 183; Graves, *Policy and Progress*, p. 89.

85. This disputes the views of O.L. Banks, *Parity and Prestige in English Secondary Education* (London: Routledge & Kegan Paul, 1955), p. 11, that the 'influence of Robert Morant ... has often been not only exaggerated but misunderstood'; and of Dent, *Century of Growth*, p. 66, who criticised the approach which found it 'so easy (and emotionally satisfying) to portray Morant as the machiavellian aristocrat'.

86. J. Duckworth, 'The Board of Education and the Establishment of the Curriculum in the New Secondary Schools of the Twentieth Century', *History of Education Society Bulletin*, 16 (1975), p. 38.

87. P.G. Richards, *Patronage in British Government* (London: Allen & Unwin, 1963), pp. 58–9.

88. F.H. Spencer, *An Inspector's Testament* (Edinburgh: Edinburgh University Press, 1938), p. 313.

89. Bishop, *Rise of a Central Authority*, p. 272.

90. Sneyd-Kinnersley, *H.M.I.*, p. 143.

91. A.H.D. Acland and H. Llewellyn-Smith (eds), *Studies in Secondary Education* (London: Percival and Co., 1892), pp. 303–4.

92. James Scotson of Manchester, reported in *The Schoolmaster*, 14 January 1893 (before the Department's most significant reforms); Selby-Bigge, *Board of Education*, pp. 13, 142. Grants from the Department totalled just £314,000 in 1901–2.

93. Heward, 'Education, Examinations and the Artisans', and H. Butterworth, 'The Science and Art Department Examinations: Origins and Achievements', both in Macleod, *Days of Judgment*, pp. 36–7, 46.. This model of an examination system has striking resemblances to current practice.

94. Major-General Sir John Donnelly mounted a 'last-ditch defence of his cherished system' before he went, as described by H. Butterworth, 'The Department of Science and Art (1853–1900) and the Development of Secondary Education', *History of Education Society Bulletin*, 6 (1970), p. 40; and he died in 1902 just before 'the machinery he had so patiently constructed [was] systematically dismantled by Robert Morant'. Bishop, *Rise of a Central Authority*, p. 197.

95. Bishop, *Rise of a Central Authority*, p. 276.

96. C. Barnett, *The Audit of War: The Illusion and Reality of Britain as a Great Nation* (London: Macmillan, 1986), pp. 223, 225.

97   T. Taylor, 'Lord Salisbury and the Politics of Education', *Journal of Educational Administration and History*, 16, 2 (1984), pp. 1, 8.

98. K. Rose, *The Later Cecils* (London: Weidenfeld & Nicolson, 1975), p. 321.

99. Taylor, 'The Cecils', pp. 36–42. He says, 'Was there a Tory plot? The answer has to be, yes there was, and quite a well-advanced one at that.'

100. S.H. Zebel, *Balfour: A Political Biography* (London: Cambridge University Press, 1973), p. 89; Taylor, '"Early Arrival"', pp. 49–50.

101. According to Rose, *Later Cecils*, pp. 78, 249–50, James, the new Lord Salisbury, tried petulance, threats and approaches to the King and the Archbishop of Canterbury, while the venomous Hugh adopted 'reckless' and 'irresponsible' tactics in the Commons, including shabby tricks to obstruct debates and a screaming attack on the 'traitor' Asquith.

102. N. and J. Mackenzie (eds), *The Diary of Beatrice Webb, 2, 1892–1905* (London: Virago, 1983), p. 247.

103. Eaglesham, *Foundations*, p. 44.

104. Sneyd-Kinnersley, *H.M.I.*, pp. 145–6. An inspector for 35 years (until 1906), he never saw a President.

105. N. and J. Mackenzie, *Diary*, p. 257; G. Kekewich, *The Education Department and After* (London: Constable, 1920), p. 96.

106. N. and J. Mackenzie, *Diary*, p. 265; N. Daglish, *Education Policy-Making in England and Wales: The Crucible Years, 1895–1911* (London: Woburn Press, 1996), p. 178.

107. Only the university colleges continued their development in the twentieth century; no doubt their susceptibility to 'metropolitan' influence helped protect them.

2

THE HIGHER GRADE SCHOOL PHENOMENON: AN ANALYSIS

The analysis of higher grade schools contained in this chapter aims to remedy the gaps in our knowledge of what the schools were actually like. In the process, their distinctive characteristics will be evaluated, with particular attention to those which have been neglected or misunderstood in the writing of educational history. What emerges – and it is a perhaps surprising continuity – is that they were not just a brave attempt to conjure up some form of higher elementary schooling out of a set of basically unfavourable circumstances, and even less were they an imitation of 'traditional' secondary schooling. Rather, they saw themselves as embodying a particular approach to education; not, of course, free from practical constraints but wholly positive and constructive nonetheless. Their style of schooling was clearly of special importance to certain classes of society, but was not exclusive of others; it had a validity in its own right, with enormous potential for the future.

This conclusion is reached by concentrating on certain cities in order to gauge the total effect of the higher grade school phenomenon on an area, rather than selecting individual schools disjointed from each other and from their environments. Bristol, a city which was unusually well endowed with secondary schools and yet found that higher grade schools filled a major gap in its educational provision, is the subject of a detailed investigation. It was not one of the pioneers, but within a very few years in the 1890s became heavily committed to higher grade school development, finding that its cautious entry into the field aroused an enthusiastic response among its citizens. Birmingham and Nottingham are also studied in some detail, both of them areas in which higher grade schools made an early appearance. The former is of particular interest as a city which was noted in the second half of the nineteenth century for its radical and positive approach to popular education, and the latter as one of the few cities which tried the unhappy experiment of converting to higher elementary schools.

The main focus in time is the 20-year period of which the 1902 Education Act is the midpoint. The first half of that period was what might be termed the 'maturity' of the higher grade school movement, when early problems had been largely solved, and when a spell of sympathetic handling from the central controlling bodies gave the movement considerable impetus. After 1902, when technically the schools ceased to exist, it is important to examine what happened to them; they did not change overnight and retained their distinctive identity until at least 1907 when the moulding process to which they were subjected began to have a decisive effect.

THE HIGHER GRADE SCHOOL: A DISTINCT IDENTITY

F.H. Spencer, who had a wider experience of education than most, observed that the High Pavement Higher Grade School in Nottingham, where he started his teaching career in 1894, was 'famous, at least in the local sense some "Board Schools" were. Grown men to-day will talk of Ithaca Road, or Stenhouse Street School with an insolent pride'.[1] Occasional glimpses like this of the loyalty and pride in their higher grade schools expressed by former pupils and teachers was just one facet of the understanding which contemporaries had of the schools. It may have suited Morant and the Board of Education to represent them as an undefinable hotchpotch of institutions, but there is no doubt that by the 1890s a lot of people knew what the higher grade schools were – what they did and why they were different from other public elementary schools. In other words, they had an identity. School boards discussed motions about higher grade schools without labouring over definitions, and local press coverage did not feel the need to include explanatory notes, even when the idea was being discussed for the first time in an area. Contact between school boards and higher grade schools in different parts of the country became regular and cordial through correspondence, visits and meetings, especially of the headmasters' own association. There was every sign that the higher grade school movement was becoming increasingly coherent and assured on a national scale.

Within a particular community the formal opening of a new higher grade school was usually a notable public event, graced by local and sometimes national dignitaries and eloquent speeches, and drawing crowds of people and detailed newspaper reports. Open days, concerts and prize-givings were well attended (Manchester Central School's first 'at home' attracted 1,000 visitors, and St George School's 1896 concert at the Albert Hall in Bristol was 'crammed to the doors, hundreds had to be turned away'),[2] and the schools usually turned out in force at activities like the opening of a tramway or the neighbourhood procession on Coronation Day in 1902. Most heads allocated weekly times – one or two afternoons every week – when parents could visit, and one in a solidly working-class area was delighted to receive over 100 responses to the reports on pupils sent to parents. He inferred from this that a 'vast amount of interest and anxiety for the welfare of the children exists, often where not expected', and that parents were 'fully alive to the great privileges and benefits which our Schools offer'.[3] The impact which the higher grade schools had can be gauged by the fact that the label often persisted locally, long after the official designation ceased to exist; at the close of the nineteenth century they most certainly had a distinct and widely understood identity.

This is not to say that they were all the same. A major advantage of the absence of central direction was that it permitted a greater flexibility to higher grade schools than was available to public elementary schools or, after 1904, to state secondary schools. The majority were very new and still evolving, or, as one headmaster put it in 1895, 'all of us are young, some of us are mere infants in arms ... we are a new species'.[4] In addition, they were genuinely local in conception, with supply following a clearly articulated demand. In Bristol, for example, one headmaster notified the school board in 1896 that he would soon have a number of children who had passed Standard VII for whom something would have to be provided,[5] while in Bradford most of the six higher grade schools came about as the result of pressure from local residents.[6] The Barnsley School Board was told by one of its members that 'a Higher Grade School is sorely needed as, after Standard IV, the children make little progress. My own child passed this Standard before she was 10 years old', and by another:

> my child will pass Standard V in October. I do not know what I am going to do with her afterwards. I shall not send her to a private school because I am not satisfied with their class of education, and to send her to Sheffield High School will cost about £80 a year. Most middle-class men are in this position. We ought to keep pace with the times.[7]

In these circumstances, uniformity was neither possible nor desirable, a view which was emphasised by a leading higher grade school head in 1895: 'Higher grade schools are of different types in different parts of the country, and to contend that they should be established upon one universal system would be to make a great mistake.'[8]

Both the Barnsley speakers obviously had an awareness of a recognisable trend around the country, and it remains true that the common characteristics of the higher grade schools were more striking than their differences. The key factor was a simple one: they offered a higher standard of education than ordinary public elementary schools. Even Morant acknowledged that education 'at a higher level' was their main function, and local administrators, teachers, parents, pupils and some employers knew that. They were living proof that the Education Department's attempts to provide for older elementary pupils by creating 'class' and 'specific' subjects and a Standard VII were inadequate, and the higher standard of education was therefore offered by means of a different curriculum. It is not an overstatement to say that without the Science and Art Department the higher grade schools could not have existed, although it should be noted that 'higher grade' was not synonymous with 'school of science' as defined by the Science and Art Department. Many higher grade schools incorporated schools of science for their more advanced pupils, but no higher grade school was solely a school of science, nor were schools of science automatically higher grade schools: they could be part of technical colleges, or endowed or voluntary schools. Some endowed schools, like Bablake in Coventry or the Perse School in Cambridge, had turned themselves into schools of science, but in other respects – notably the cheap and automatic access to elementary school children – they fulfilled a different role.

The school board higher grade schools were unlike any other institutions in England and arguably had a stronger identity than the endowed schools, which at that time were extraordinarily varied in almost every respect. And higher grade schools were growing fast. The Bryce Commission wrote of 65 such schools, the National Union of Teachers of 80 four years later, and it is known that several school boards had plans for others at various stages of progress.[9] The Science and Art Department's records for 1898–1900 show that there were 87 organised schools of science in publicly provided institutions in 24 counties and London. There were also sizeable daytime examination entries from many other schools. Some were the large and well-known higher grade schools, such as Leeds Central Higher Grade School (730 candidates, with another 169 at the Southern branch); Gateshead Higher Grade School (323); Bolton Central Higher Grade Board School (359); and Hull Central

Higher Grade School, one of three in that town, (306). Bradford's five higher grade schools and classes were entering over 1,000 candidates annually; Manchester had nearly 2,000 candidates in ten schools, with over 1,000 more in the Municipal Technical School and two schools of science and art, while in Liverpool no fewer than 20 institutions (including one school of science, four pupil teachers' colleges, three higher grade schools and 11 board schools) were involved in the Department's examinations.

These figures are solid evidence of the enthusiasm for learning and qualifications in some of the larger cities of the North, with which higher grade schools have been typically associated. When to these are added sizeable institutions in towns like Cambridge, Plymouth, Bristol, Portsmouth, Grimsby, Norwich, Nottingham, Oxford, Bath, Ipswich and Brighton, and hundreds of smaller examination entries from every county in England except Buckinghamshire and Rutland, the scale of the higher grade school movement can be appreciated. The momentum it was developing and the enthusiasm it engendered were to be found all over the country. One can only wonder what might have been achieved if this forerunner of the comprehensive school had been allowed to flourish 70 years earlier than the time when all children were in fact admitted to secondary schools on equal terms.

CURRICULUM

Higher grade schools normally required their entrants to have reached a designated Standard in the Education Department Code, although which one varied with the nature of the school. Those like Birmingham and Sheffield, which functioned as central schools drawing pupils from all elementary schools, expected a higher Standard to have been achieved, VI or VII. The majority, as in Bristol and Nottingham, which were 'all-through' schools with an additional intake from other elementary schools at the higher level, were happier to admit to the higher grade department from Standard IV or V. Both types usually favoured an introductory first year of exclusively Education Code work at Standard VI or VII, before embarking on the Science and Art Department's prescribed school of science course. That could be spread over four years, two fairly general years followed by up to two more specialist years. Each year of the syllabus also geared itself to other examinations, such as the school boards' tests of pupil teachers, the College of Preceptors' examinations, Oxford and Cambridge Junior and Senior Locals, music examinations, civil service examinations and London University matriculation.

Of the schools closely analysed in this study, not one was exclusively scientific and technical, and all showed a careful regard for constructing as wide an education as teaching resources and examination requirements permitted. Indeed, the most striking feature of most schools' prospectuses was the long list of subjects they hoped to fit onto the timetable. At the High Pavement Higher Grade School, for example, all the senior classes studied Shakespeare and other literature, history, writing, arithmetic, recitation, geography, several sciences, French, music, domestic economy, needlework and shorthand, and the local newspaper paid tribute to the 'ample evidence of the comprehensive curriculum adopted'.[10] The timetables reproduced in the Bryce Report[11] show that at the Leeds Central School, all boys and girls studied English, history, geography, Latin, French, mathematics, at least two sciences, drawing, manual instruction and physical education, with religious instruction, German, shorthand, bookkeeping, geometry and dressmaking also included at various points during the four-year course. Sciences claimed the largest share of the time – between 11.5 and 14.5 hours (according to age) of a 27-hour week – but clearly other subjects were not ignored, and this was before the Science and Art Department's biggest step towards liberalising its curriculum. By 1899, one of that Department's senior inspectors was delighted with the great variety of curricula that had developed as a result, which could only happen when 'outside control is reduced to a minimum, and examinations in only a few subjects have to be faced'. With the reservations that French needed more time in a lot of schools and that some endowed schools of science were 'hopelessly inefficient', he concluded that 'in only a minority of schools can the amount of Science instruction be described as excessive. This is a matter of commendation.'[12]

Yet schools like these came in for relentless criticism from influential people whose own education would seem to have been conspicuously narrow in terms of curriculum. It is likely that many of them did not know the full range of what was taught in higher grade schools, and inferred from the 'school of science' label and the importance of science examinations that no other subjects were taught. There were more fundamental objections too. Most of the leading educationists of the 1890s attended English public schools and Oxbridge in the 1850s and 1860s when no science was taught. They knew little about it and believed that it was an inferior intellectual discipline, of utility to the lower classes pursuing industrial occupations, but lacking the humanising qualities which were the true hallmark of education as they understood it. Even a 'reformer' like T.H. Green could say that although he felt 'the diffidence proper to one who has no thorough acquaintance' with the physical sciences, he was nevertheless confident that they were an 'inferior educational organ ... doubtless more acceptable to the majority of boys than Latin or Greek, but for the simple reason that they are easier'.[13]

By the 1890s much of the anxiety about the way the secondary school curriculum was developing was focused on the Science and Art Department. Enjoying virtual autonomy from the Education Department, even after their nominal amalgamation in 1899, the Science and Art Department was becoming threateningly powerful. To traditionalists its way of operating was just about acceptable for part-time adults, particularly of the lower classes, but was considered totally inappropriate for the schooling of children. There was heavy criticism of its emphasis on the examinations and specialisation associated with 'payment by results', and organised schools of science were particularly unpopular. The higher grade schools had a much more positive view of the Science and Art Department. James Scotson's faith in the Department has already been mentioned and his colleague in Gateshead, John Bidgood, was convinced that its courses were a response to an expressed need rather than an arbitrary imposition from above, for 'the Organised Science School scheme was never elaborated until schools nearly corresponding to them were already in existence'.[14] And, with certain modifications, which the Department seemed to be willing to implement, the higher grade schools were able increasingly to accommodate a wide diversity of needs. Bradford, which had six higher grade schools and therefore probably the most complete system of higher grade education of all cities, was leading the way in this respect by varying the curriculum to produce certain specialities within the system. Two schools, one boys' and one girls', were designated as centres for art and commercial subjects, while the others concentrated on science.[15]

Most higher grade schools, being large and well equipped, were able to offer choices between subjects or even between courses, especially as their funding arrangements improved. Perhaps most significantly, they did so without glorifying certain areas of study and demeaning others, and by rejecting the notion that children (of both sexes) destined for a particular occupation must be trained in a certain way. In achieving this formidable goal, it is hard to deny that the typical higher grade school curriculum looks commendably balanced and 'modern'. The interpretation of terms like 'general', 'over-specialised' and 'liberal' as used by traditionalists around the turn of the century must therefore be treated with caution. The idea that education should and could comprise a wide range of subjects, which is now taken for granted, is very much a rediscovery of the higher grade school tradition, and the movement increasingly saw itself as pioneering a new style of curriculum, which was useful but not utilitarian and combined practical, intellectual, cultural and physical pursuits. In much the same way that late twentieth-century teachers objected to the assisted-places scheme, the higher grade school headteachers were resentful of the Bryce Commission's suggestion that promising pupils should be transferred to grammar schools: 'Does the Commission think that the parents of our children do not know what they want?'[16]

STAFFING AND ORGANISATION

A related characteristic of higher grade schools was their higher level of staffing in terms of academic qualifications and professional competence. It was a major problem in most newly established schools, as it is for any innovative organisation, but the latter part of the nineteenth century saw great progress in the status and aspirations of the elementary teaching profession. By the turn of the century one-third of all elementary teachers were trained and certificated, and access to degree courses was much improved by the development of university colleges. Elementary teachers were in a state of transition, ready to embrace further advances in their academic and social opportunities, and with their leading union in an 'extremely strong position'.[17] The higher grade movement played an important role in bringing them to this position, but in so doing, attracted growing animosity from the untrained graduate teachers of endowed secondary schools. The resulting confrontation and its unsatisfactory resolution emphasised divisions within the profession which have still not been fully eradicated.

In the early higher grade school days a heavy burden devolved upon the headteachers, who were chosen with care and generally given a lot of responsibility for developing the new style of education. They sometimes seem to have been running their schools virtually single-handed. During St George School's first year, the head noted whole days sitting in with a weak teacher's class, or teaching 130 girls in the central hall because of staff absence, while his colleague at Queen's Walk School in Nottingham was, in March 1897, 'still waiting for help. Since Christmas, the Head Teacher has had to take one, two or sometimes three Classes at a time.'[18] Some of them seem to have been veritable polymaths. David Forsyth of Leeds Central School held a DSc in geology, mainly taught Latin, wrote textbooks on chemistry, perspective, Shakespeare and copperplate penmanship, and was also described as a mathematician. He was said to be a great believer in the 'lack of finality in education'![19]

Within a relatively short time, recruitment problems eased as a new breed of teacher developed. Increasingly, the typical higher grade school teacher had been educated in a higher grade school, pupil teacher centre and training or university college, in all of which significant advances were being made. Indeed, the higher grade schools have been seen as 'equally important for the prestige of the profession' as the pupil teacher centres themselves.[20] The recent judgment that their achievement amounted to 'servicing elementary schools with cheap teaching fodder'[21] seems more than a little harsh. The school boards worked hard to staff their higher grade schools as well as possible, by organising recruiting visits to training colleges, arranging transfers between schools, and by offering higher salaries, rewards for newly acquired qualifications and favourable promotion prospects. Not surprisingly, higher grade school teachers rapidly became something of an elite within the elementary teaching profession[22] and working in those institutions was recognised as a specialism. Teachers commonly moved between higher grade schools, schools of science, pupil teacher centres, technical colleges and sometimes teacher training departments; there was very little interchange of staff with the endowed school sector.[23]

Higher grade school teachers generally continued their education on the job. They were likely to be encouraged to pursue further studies and enhance their qualifications, either by attending holiday courses in individual subjects or through enrolling for external degrees. Leave of absence was freely given and successes noted with pleasure, and a number of teachers obviously maintained some form of part-time study for the greater part of their working lives. F.H. Spencer vividly described the protracted and solitary labours associated with gaining an external London degree, particularly when there was no centre near enough to attend, scholars and tutors were far away and correspondence courses too costly.[24] Studying for further qualifications was additional to school-based professional development. Headteachers accustomed to the training role associated with the pupil teacher system,[25] paid considerable attention to passing on their own expertise and getting the best out of their assistants. Points which one headteacher thought worthy of note were: 'enthusiasm', 'displaying much kindness and sympathy to their charges', 'influence of the best kind', 'a cultured gentleman and a splendid worker and disciplinarian', and 'excellent assiduity and skill in teaching'. Heads were highly critical of poor teachers, but equally generous in their praise when those same staff managed to raise their standards, or when they had thoroughly good teachers working in their schools. At St George School in Bristol, a rather dismal entry in the log book to the effect that 'the weakness of staff is reacting on the whole work of the Higher Grade School ... We seem to be very unfortunate in regard to the staffing of the School', was transformed eight years later to:

> I have here to recognise the splendid zeal and enthusiasm displayed by members of the staff individually and collectively. The great secret of the success of this school year after year in the face of many discouraging conditions and hindrances to work of a higher kind – lies in the fact that nothing can daunt the 'esprit de corps' of the teachers. No trouble, no extra work, no sacrifice of time is counted an obstacle in carrying out their school duties. It is with real pleasure that I put this testimony to the loyalty and zeal of the present staff of the school on record.[26]

One of the heads' foremost concerns was to establish good relations between staff and pupils and their attitude to discipline and punishments seems to have been thoroughly enlightened. The use of the cane was an early issue at the Bridge Street School in Birmingham, when the head was accused by a junior colleague of 'resorting too much to the milder method of personal persuasion', and he explained that 'in gross cases I have found it more beneficial to make a lad apologize to this teacher, instead of resorting to corporal punishment'. Soon after St George School's opening, Mr Pickles had reason to speak to certain of the staff who were 'in the habit of resorting to corporal punishment on unnecessary occasions', and he had repeated problems with Mr Watson in the workshop, who 'makes no discrimination between the strong sturdy boys and the physically weak', and whose physical methods were in 'serious breach of the School Board's Regulations'. Mr Hugh at the High Pavement School in Nottingham found that 'in all the upper standards the assistants say they get, through using the "mark card", such an amount of co-operation from parents, as reduces to a minimum the need of punishment of any kind whatever'.[27] Wherever A.P. Laurie, the Bryce Assistant-Commissioner, went in the West Riding, he found that 'the most perfect discipline reigns throughout' in the higher grade schools,[28] and it is possible to read many HMI reports before finding an adverse comment on the general atmosphere and conduct in a higher grade school.

The concern of all higher grade school heads for the 'moral tone' of their schools and the personal development of their pupils is a persistent and striking feature of the records. In at least two instances, the organisation of extra-curricular activities – the 'School Journey' at Barnsley Central School,[29] and the daily class cricket matches in the park adjoining St George School, Bristol – were held to have contributed significantly to good relations within school. The latter were said to have been 'most helpful in encouraging the growth of that "esprit de corps" which is so necessary to a school of this character', and two unpopular teachers who were helping to supervise 'have strengthened their position in the regard of the boys'.[30] The head of Bridge Street School even introduced a short 'Moral Lesson' for all classes on Friday afternoons, and was so pleased with the results that it was soon extended to two 30-minute lessons a week.[31] Two Bristolians recalled their former headmasters from higher grade school days as men of the 'highest moral calibre',[32] and higher grade school heads often assumed considerable status and influence, becoming almost legendary figures to successive generations of a particular locality.

As to what went on in the classroom, there were surprisingly progressive attitudes to learning, bearing in mind the constant pressure from external examinations. One head worried that 'the work done in certain classes is far too superficial for a school of this character. Too much insistence is laid on mere facts or pieces of information while the thinking process is ignored.' Another recorded his opposition to the dictating of notes in chemistry, which he saw as a 'positive waste of time and as depriving the boys of the benefit of teaching and explanations' and was anxious that the pupils should learn to consider themselves 'as students rather than as schoolboys', with more private study and a more thoughtful approach. A third was quite sure of the connection between interesting teaching and the 'remarkably good' attendance in the upper part of his school: 'it is now exceptional for a boy to absent himself from any other cause than that of illness'.[33]

Several of the higher grade school heads experimented with what became the normal practice in twentieth-century grammar schools but was not common then: the deployment of staff to teach specialist subjects to all children. This must have seemed an obvious move in an environment which rewarded examination successes, especially once the training of teachers had begun to emphasise expertise in particular areas of the curriculum. But the heads were never completely happy with this scheme of organisation, worrying in particular that the academic gain to the pupils was outweighed by the loss of personal and moral guidance from the form teacher system. As the head of Mundella School, Nottingham, explained when noting three cases of truancy in the upper part of the school:

Such a thing has not occurred in this School for years and I am reluctantly coming to the conclusion that the specializing which I am trying in all the Classes of the School of Science, is not for the good of the Scholars morally. The teacher feels he is responsible only for the Subject he teaches, and the tone of the classes suffers much in consequence.

A fellow headmaster registered similar reservations: 'there is too little "esprit de corps" among the older boys. A good form master is wanted for each class. The specialist system is a failure in cultivating a proper school spirit.'[34]

Overall, the day-to-day writings of those early headteachers are a remarkable tribute to the enlightened and thoughtful attitudes they brought to the job, and it is hard to dispel the impression that there were some very fine teachers indeed in the higher grade sector of the education system. A.P. Laurie repeatedly drew unfavourable comparisons between the average Oxbridge graduate amateurs of the grammar schools and the enthusiastic, professional higher grade teachers. While the former were 'sleepy' and 'wanting in vigour', producing 'the usual want of attention on the part of the boys in the class-room which is so common when the teacher is untrained', the latter represented 'a new type of teacher, young, brilliant, and enthusiastic, students of the best methods of teaching … everywhere one sees examples of the perfection of method in teaching'. He was particularly impressed by a science lesson given by the headmaster of Belle Vue School in Bradford, Richard Lishman, of whose teaching the HMI wrote on successive visits, 'left nothing to be desired. The Board ought not to be content with any science teaching which is not of this character'; 'a feature of striking and exceptional merit'; and 'one of the best taught classes I have visited … [he] teaches to perfection'.[35]

A higher grade school headship was the most prestigious occupation to which poorer children had access, and the higher grade/pupil teacher system was the route by which the most able and ambitious among them could fulfil their aspirations. Teaching thus became the only profession which was readily accessible to the working classes, and also the only one which admitted women on any significant scale. There must have been many families in which the elevation to such academic and social heights of a son or daughter was a source of enormous pride. The various school registers contain many examples of carpenters, gardeners, railway workers and bootmakers whose children, particularly the daughters, became teachers and/or gained university degrees. F.H. Spencer, himself a former pupil and teacher in higher grade schools, had a clear and affectionate idea of his social class origins: 'I wish statesmen had been thrown up among that class of teacher, the class of the sober, skilful, essentially respectable artisan class. But it is hardly to be expected, for "we" are not "raised" to be leaders.'[36] The gulf between the leaders and the led was to be fully exposed in the early years of the twentieth century. This aspiring class of teachers, who owed much to the school boards' investment in higher grade education and to their sponsorship of improved opportunities for their teaching forces, were poorly rewarded by those who shaped England's new system of secondary education. It was no wonder that they resented the Board of Education's determination to banish them from the secondary school system after 1902.

PREMISES

By the time the urban school boards became interested in developing higher grade provision, most of them were accustomed to the responsibility of building new schools and had become familiar with the necessary procedures and some of the problems. In the early days, extra classes were usually fitted into existing school premises, or occasionally accommodated temporarily in other buildings, such as a disused Cadbury's factory in Birmingham.[37] But a high proportion of higher grade schools were purpose-built, or at least extensively converted, almost invariably as show-piece schools. They were large even by today's standards: for example, Fairfield Road in Bristol was built for over 1,000 pupils, Sheffield Higher Grade School had 1,200 and Leeds Central School 2,600, of whom about 1,000 were in Standard VII or above. They were better equipped and more spaciously laid out than ordinary elementary schools and, it has been suggested, more ornate in order to 'emphasize the achievements of the school boards' and to connote the special associations of higher learning. These show-piece board schools were often, along with the churches, the most impressive buildings in crowded urban landscapes, not least because pressure on land necessitated a minimum of two storeys, usually more. They readily became the focus of admiration and aspiration for local citizens and of approving interest to the steady stream of outside visitors which all successful higher grade schools entertained. The construction of the three-storey St George School in Bristol was said to have fascinated local residents,[38] and a young Walter Southgate found Mowlem Street School in east London an 'awesome building'.[39]

Higher grade schools were nearly always the major capital undertaking of their respective school boards, which took out big long-term loans to pay for them. For example, St George School cost £14,000 to erect and boasted heating, lighting and ventilation 'on the most modern principles', large playgrounds, proximity to a public park of 40 acres and 'a thoroughly well-appointed Chemistry Laboratory, a large Science Lecture Room, a Workshop, a Dining Room, and accommodation of every kind conducive to the well-being of the scholars'.[40] Its bigger sister school under the Bristol School Board, Fairfield Road, cost £24,000 just a few years later and was similarly well planned. In Nottingham the High Pavement School moved to a location where 'everything possible had been done to make the building as perfect as possible'. As well as the usual laboratories and lecture rooms, it had a swimming bath, a gymnasium, a laundry and a garden, and Sir George Kekewich personally inscribed in the log book: 'I had the pleasure of visiting this beautiful School.'[41] In all higher grade schools the provision of good laboratories and workshops was the biggest difference from ordinary elementary schools – and from public and grammar schools – and criticisms or threats of possible loss of grant from visiting inspectors prompted speedy rectification of inadequacies or defects.

In view of the careful planning and heavy financial outlay which the school boards lavished on their higher grade schools, it is clear they were not thinking of short-term expedients. Pupil teacher centres, which were smaller and less demanding of facilities, were much more likely to be housed in makeshift accommodation, although by the turn of the century they too were being promised specialist premises in a number of areas. The school boards, having received the necessary Education Department approval to take on big loans, certainly saw their new higher grade schools as major investments for the future educational resources of the district: a number of the buildings are still in use. It was therefore all the more shattering, both to their pride and their practical capabilities, when the Board of Education started raising fundamental objections to the quality of the facilities after 1900.[42] It rapidly became clear that the Board's perception of the physical needs of secondary schooling was so much at variance with that of the urban local authorities that it preferred to see a thriving school die than accept an alternative approach to the provision of buildings and facilities.

FEES AND CLASS OF PUPIL

The question of fees in higher grade schools was another area of conflict between the school boards and the central authority. On both sides there were many who believed that it was appropriate to make some charge for non-elementary education, but there the consensus ended. From the school boards' point of view, it was important to make sure that the difference between an ordinary elementary school and a new-style higher grade school was understood by parents who very likely had no experience of either; the income derived from the fees was fairly inconsequential to the schools. Some boards, like Birmingham, Sheffield and Bradford, relied on getting their message across in other ways and provided higher grade education free to the pupils, but most favoured the charging of fees, anything from 1d to 9d per week. Totalling, at most, £1 13s 0d per year, this was much cheaper than any endowed or private school. Almost as important was the way in which the fees were administered: they were payable weekly; they never seem to have gone up; there was usually an elastic number of free places; and heads sometimes used their own and other resources in cases of need. It has been impossible to find an example of a willing higher grade school pupil being turned away for financial reasons.

The Education Department tortured itself over whether it was alright for higher grade schools to charge fees. It had no agreed policy on the matter and more memoranda were pushed up and down the various levels of officialdom on this than on any other question. The granting of free elementary education in 1891 only complicated the matter, and the Act was minutely examined for clues, and precedents desperately sought and quoted. The key paragraph in the Elementary Education Act of 1891 allowed, exceptionally, schools to receive the new per capita grant and charge fees (not exceeding 6d per week), provided that one of three conditions was met. There had to be sufficient free elementary school places in the district for those who wanted them, or there had to have been 'a change of population in the district', or fees must be shown to be 'for the educational benefit of the district'. School boards therefore made much in their applications to the Department of the respectable tradesmen, clerks and superior artisans who were likely to patronise their new school, their desire to pay a small contribution, and the obvious advantage to the district of a superior level of teaching, a more varied curriculum and access to further courses of study.

Bristol's three higher grade schools, conceived in 1891, 1894 and 1896, well illustrate the muddle surrounding this whole question. The Education Department, having initially been advised by its local HMI that the St George School Board was unlikely to be able to carry out its grandiose plan, was taken aback to be informed in the summer of 1894 that the new school was about to open and a decision on fees was urgently required. Half a dozen precedents were examined before it was decided to 'treat the case exceptionally' and allow a 5d per week fee, with 25 per cent free places, for three years.[43] Merrywood was just as problematic to the Department and, after initially refusing to sanction fees, the Department was eventually trapped into a similar agreement because of its ineptitude over earlier correspondence and decisions. By the time Fairfield Road was under discussion, the Department had accumulated a number of precedents and, taking into consideration the adequate provision of free places in the district, the 'superior social grade of the parents', and the higher standard of education, it was more ready to accept that alone of the school boards' schools, higher grade schools could charge fees and still receive full government grants.

From the copious correspondence on the various questions of fees, it seems that the school boards understood and interpreted the legislation rather more successfully than did the Education Department, presenting well-argued cases and quoting previous communications of which the Department had often lost track. It is interesting, in the light of twentieth-century developments, that deep reservations were expressed about the 25 per cent free places, awarded on the results of a competitive examination. Bristol's local HMI objected, as Acland had done, that 'these so-called scholarships are usually gained not by the poorest children who would be unable to pay the fee, but by the well-to-do children who could easily do so', although as 'it would scarcely be possible to ask for a declaration of poverty on the part of the parents it is difficult to suggest an alternative system'. His only suggestion was that 'free places should in all cases mean unconditionally free to the first applicants' and have nothing to do with ability as demonstrated in a test.[44]

Parents were sometimes confused and there were occasional complaints that higher grade schools combed too wide an area for their pupils and excluded those who lived nearby. No doubt the higher grade schools were keen to have as many children as possible who were likely to take full advantage of the education offered, by staying longer and taking examinations, and the school boards saw them as serving whole areas rather than particular neighbourhoods. But there is no evidence that they operated anything like the rigorous selection mechanisms of the twentieth-century grammar schools: neither the fees nor the entrance test were used for that purpose. At one point the Bristol School Board put on record its undertaking that 'care will be taken that no promising boy or girl shall be excluded from the advantages of the school by reason of the parents' inability to pay the suggested fee'.[45] Nationwide, the guiding principles seem to have been to fill – and often overfill – the higher grade schools; never to exclude a child able and willing to attend; and to safeguard the schools' place within the public elementary school provision of their respective neighbourhoods. Indeed, after 1902, the head of St George School was prepared to forgo secondary school status rather than lose his elementary 'feeder' classes.[46]

Even 3d or 5d per week was beyond the reach of some families, and it is true that the poorest sections of the working class were under-represented in the higher grade schools. The Chairman of the Manchester School Board told the Cross Commission that a 9d fee was 'prohibitory' for the labouring classes, and regretted that in consequence 'the higher grade schools are not open to the labouring classes as they ought to be'.[47] There is no ready-made statistical measure to identify a point in the income scale at which people could afford to educate their children for longer than the statutory minimum, as so many other factors – such as the number of dependants in the family or whether the wife had a regular income – affected individual circumstances. But, generalising from the results of various surveys conducted around the turn of the century,[48] families with an income of up to 30 shillings per week (the national average for manual workers was 27 shillings in 1906) spent every spare penny on food. The poorest, under about 20 shillings per week, could afford only a severely deficient diet; those who earned a little more did not have any money to spare, but were merely able to afford a slightly more varied and nutritious diet. It is therefore not surprising that relatively few families in that situation extended their children's schooling at all, for their earnings made a real difference to the family's standard of living, especially at a time (1896–1912) when the purchasing power of the pound was dropping by about 20 per cent. At the beginning of that period, skilled workers earned about 40 shillings per week, and that seems to have been about the lowest income on which extended schooling was normally a possibility; lower-middle-class white-collar workers, such as small shop-keepers, clerks, postal workers and schoolteachers, who all earned around £100 a year, were thus included.

In many of the discussions over the provision of higher grade education and its cost to parents, school boards made reference to the class of person who would willingly pay a small weekly charge but who could not contemplate the fees normally associated with endowed or private secondary schools. There is no reason to disbelieve the accuracy of their assessment, which is confirmed by the schools' own records. A detailed analysis of 316 parents of pupils at the Birmingham Seventh Standard School in 1892–93 showed that only 5 per cent were professional people, employers or managers; 9 per cent unskilled working class; 19 per cent were semi-professional, merchants and traders; and 67 per cent were skilled or semi-skilled workers, clerks and in other white-collar occupations.[49] At national level, data collected to inform a series of meetings in 1897 between headmasters of secondary and higher grade schools showed that the parents at 43 higher grade schools were 12.4 per cent middle class, 47.6 per cent lower middle class and 40 per cent working class, compared with figures for 43 secondary schools of 42 per cent, 48.8 per cent and 9.1 per cent.[50]

It is also important to remember that poorer members of the working class were excluded from higher grade education by the force of their economic circumstances and not by any overt or covert policy of the schools. If the higher grade schools had wished to be socially selective, they could certainly have managed it more effectively by adopting barriers like termly fees, school uniform or 'extra' charges for some school subjects. In fact it is striking what efforts were made by families and teachers to keep an exceptional pupil at school, sometimes with scholarships and maintenance awards being rustled up from school board or private sources. One headmaster, referring to the science examinations in 1904, recorded that he 'offered to pay fees of £4-5-6 [£4 5s 6d] out of my own pocket rather than enforce it from the boys and girls',[51] and others seemed to manage to 'find' jobs with a minimal wage, such as helping in the school office or the laboratories. F.H. Spencer recounted how, having not left and gone to 'The Factory' at the age of 13 along with many of his classmates, he did odd jobs for the headmaster, including taking the school pence to the pawn shop to exchange for gold, and then, for a wage of 2 shillings per week, became a 'monitor' to a dozen mentally deficient children in the cloakroom.[52] So if in the short period of the higher grade schools' existence, not many of the poorest children climbed all the way from the bottom of the ladder to the top, some did and, theoretically, all could. Certainly the higher grade school heads were unshakeable in their conviction that they offered opportunities to children who would not have been able to get them anywhere else.

However, neither that nor the financial struggle which some families obviously had in the pursuit of education, made much impression on the widely held view that the patrons of higher grade schools could and should pay more. In particular, the grammar school headmasters were absolutely convinced that higher grade schools constituted unfair competition and were stealing their pupils purely on the grounds of cost. A.P. Laurie on behalf of the Bryce Commission carried out a special investigation into that very complaint in the West Riding and concluded that few higher grade school pupils would ever go to grammar schools, some because they could not afford to and more because they would not choose to, because of the poor teaching and the outdated curriculum. However, more weight was attached to the view expressed by a succession of witnesses that secondary education should cost more, and the only point at issue was how much secondary schools needed to charge in order to be self-supporting. Bryce himself had earlier written that £4 to £6 per annum was sufficient only if the teachers starved, and the two men from the headmasters' association favoured £12.[53] Such sums placed secondary education firmly and exclusively in the grip of the comfortable middle classes, who managed to resist for another 40 years the demands of a less favoured – and much larger – section of the population.

LENGTH AND NATURE OF SCHOOL CAREER

Almost as important as fees as a differential between social classes was the confidence with which families could predict their future circumstances, which clearly had a bearing on the expectations associated with their children's educational potential. The elementary education system as a whole paid less attention to the age of its customers than to their attainment as defined by the Code Standards, and the 1870 Elementary Education Act, planned merely to plug the gaps for the most disadvantaged, had made no provision for older children staying at school. It did not anticipate the national trend for children to stay longer at elementary school, so that during the 1890s the numbers between ages 12 and 15 rose every year and those over 15 reached a peak of 8,822 in 1896–97 before dropping a little during the years when higher grade education was most under threat.[54] In response, legislation during the decade pushed the general leaving age from 10 to 12, and from 1900 a leaving age of 14 was permitted if local authorities wished, an option which most of the bigger urban school boards took up. Beyond that, the politicians and the Education Department had left the local authorities to sort out their own problems about what to do with such children: how to place them in schools and what to teach them. In the absence of any other ideas, the development of higher grade schools had seemed an acceptable solution.

In the importance attached to attainment rather than age within the system lay two of the biggest disadvantages under which the higher grade schools laboured. Understandably, they were keener to admit a bright 11 year old who had passed Standard IV or V than a dogged 14 year old who had just reached the same Standard, but the elementary schools were often reluctant to lose their most capable and willing pupils before they had completed the Standards and any class or specific subjects which they could provide. Consequently there are examples of uncooperative, even obstructionist, tactics on the part of ordinary elementary school heads and teachers. The St George School log book noted that elementary teachers 'use every endeavour to dissuade parents from sending their children to the Higher Grade Schools', and there were parental reports of elementary school heads 'making it rough' for one boy, and excluding another because his brother was transferring to St George.[55] One can only imagine the depth of resentment and jealousy which underlay such occurrences; to many ordinary elementary teachers, their higher grade school colleagues were better paid, doing more stimulating work with brighter children, and gaining more prestige and better promotion prospects.

The second disadvantage was that the varying ages and levels of ability of pupils on admission, together with the nature of the courses available, made it very difficult to plan an identifiable 'higher grade curriculum' and therefore to have a 'typical school career'. This did not stop the schools from planning precise and progressive courses lasting four or five years, but with pupils starting and, even more, dropping out at different stages, only a minority actually worked through the whole course. The Science and Art Department syllabuses were broken down into several stages, so that pupils could be examined each year at a different level, and a range of other tests and examinations could also be attempted. With each complete year self-contained and potentially fruitful to the pupil, it was possible for children to attend for almost any length of time and still have something to show for their stay in terms of progress and qualifications. Looking back from a time when all children basically follow the same route through school and aim for the same examinations, it is hard to conceive how the teachers managed to cater for the differing goals and aspirations of their 40 or so children. Since their pupils did indeed pass a variety of examinations, one can only assume that they succeeded. Their achievement is all the more remarkable when they only knew with certainty what pupils they would have when they turned up at the beginning of the new school year; teachers and school boards had to be eminently flexible when timetables, staffing, rooms, equipment and syllabuses could be settled only after the start of term. Perhaps the absence of both a lower and an upper age limit in the higher grade schools contributed to an atmosphere of excitement and untapped potential, for while there may have been no such thing as a typical higher grade course, obversely, the course could be almost limitless in scope and duration.

All this is not to say that the teachers were happy when their pupils left after just one or two years,[56] and when numbers dwindled in the upper classes. The log books and school board minutes show an almost obsessive preoccupation with keeping children at school longer, especially when course requirements rewarded the third and fourth years with bigger grants. Increasingly, higher grade school entrants and their parents were asked to sign agreements or undertakings to remain for a specified length of course, on penalty of paying £2 or £3 to help compensate for the loss of grant incurred by premature departure. The single fact that many children left after less than two years in a higher grade school and went into employment offers incontrovertible proof of their socio-economic background; middle-class parents getting secondary education on the cheap were hardly likely to put their children to work at the age of 13 or 14. The registers of the Birmingham Municipal Technical College Day School support this view, showing that of the entrants in the autumn of 1897, when the school opened, 70 per cent stayed two years or less, a figure which had fallen to 50 per cent of the autumn 1902 entrants, an encouraging trend for the school. Nearly all of the school's leavers went into employment.[57]

However long they stayed, higher grade school pupils worked very hard to make the most of their opportunity. At examination time in 1900, some St George School boys and girls were 'close to breakdown according to their parents' because they were working so hard, and a Birmingham parent came to see the head of Bridge Street School to say that 'he regrets ... that his sons have been overworked', although they would remain at school for another year nonetheless. A.P. Laurie in the West Riding was everywhere impressed by the attentiveness and interest shown by the higher grade school children, and observed that boys from homes where there was little education often came for one year and by 'their own eagerness' persuaded their parents to let them stay for two or three. There is strong evidence, too, that they liked school very much indeed. Mention has already been made of the generally excellent attendance and of the need for only the lightest of discipline. The schools were nearly always full and bursting at the seams: Sheffield's higher grade school 'has to turn away many children who would be glad to come'; Bridge Street School had temporarily to introduce its own entrance examination to weed out weaker candidates; and St George School recorded a November attendance of 91 per cent 'without using the attendance officer'. The People's College, reopening in 1901 as a much reduced higher elementary school, faced the absurd situation of having 242 more children than the Board of Education said it had room for. While strongly arguing their right to stay, the head reduced the numbers as best he could, but refused to eject those who wanted to stay and was obliged to form what he called 'the "shell" or Extra class' which had 'to move every lesson to an unoccupied room'.[58]

Overall, in those higher grade schools where such information can be traced, the trend was for the age of entry to move downwards towards 12 (generally regarded as the optimum), and the length of school career to creep upwards gradually, with an increasing proportion of pupils staying to the age of 17 or 18. All the signs are that the schools were doing as much as could be done to increase the school life of their various pupils from their differing backgrounds. To fix a four-year minimum course, as Morant did, was not actually to solve the problem but merely to exclude those children who wanted – or could only afford – to do less. Such children were very important to the higher grade schools, whose heads accepted that, for many, just one year of more advanced schooling was a precious acquisition and a considerable burden to their families. The Bristol School Board acknowledged this when, at the very same meeting that it approved the parental undertaking not to withdraw children prematurely, it deputed its two most experienced higher grade headmasters to draw up a scheme of instruction for those who could not remain more than one year after the completion of the Standards.[59] The schools' capacity usefully to extend the education of such children alongside more able and ambitious pupils was a major achievement and a great loss in the reorganised system. In fact, it is impossible to think of any other type of school which has successfully catered for such disparate requirements among its pupils; Morant's secondary schools, with their four-year course and minimum £3 per annum fee, must rank among the least successful.

GIRLS IN HIGHER GRADE SCHOOLS: EQUAL EDUCATION

A highly significant aspect of the inclusive nature of higher grade education lay in its attitude to girls. Like many educationists at the time (and since), school boards and their headteachers were genuinely unsure about what was the ideal curriculum for girls, but they showed a willingness to innovate and to offer opportunities which was very much at odds with class-based ideas about the role of women in society and the economy. That view decreed that upper- and middle-class women did not normally work, either for money or in the home, and that the rest of the female population had just two functions: to service their social betters, and to devote themselves to running their homes and raising their families. The educational needs of the latter were, therefore, limited: a basic command of the three Rs, religious instruction and as much training as possible in domestic skills. However, for most working-class women the reality of the situation was very different from this vision of dutiful domesticity, and statistical evidence relating to three key determinants – marriage, family size and employment – proves the inaccuracy of a number of popular myths.

Only about half the nation's women (over 15 years of age) were married at any given time. The average age of marriage was 25 and rising, there was a 1 in 10 chance of being widowed, and 'the proportion of women never marrying rose to levels probably unprecedented in much of north-western Europe by the end of the nineteenth century'.[60] With the average number of live births for each woman standing at 3.5, with perceptible rather than dramatic differences between social classes, it is certain that Victorian and Edwardian parents limited the size of their families.[61] Contemporary surveys and reports confirm that working-class women took it for granted that, around the demands of their families, they did paid work: either piece-work for a former employer, or work in a whole range of domestic or service occupations.[62] A team of Birmingham investigators, for example, found the incessant labours of the local women 'little short of miraculous', while more recent researchers interviewed elderly ladies who never stopped working but officially 'never worked'. Even the official figures reveal that over one-third of women of all ages were employed, with growing numbers taking up the new opportunities opening up in the civil service, clerical work and as shop assistants, as well as teaching and nursing.[63]

All of this adds up to a perhaps unexpected picture of women being very actively involved in the economic process. It is clear that it was the normal practice for most girls to enter employment when they finished at school, and to expect to remain there for at least ten years before they married, with a strong likelihood of working again at some point in their lives. The possibility of enhanced educational opportunities was therefore of real significance because, even more than for boys, the skills and qualifications gained at school could mean entrance to a completely different type of job. With the older professions still closed to women, no occupation which was open to them was selective on the basis of social class, or required extended training in a specialised institution or milieu. The qualifications acquired at school could be the working-class girl's main aid to occupational mobility, and suitable preparation and training were increasingly demanded of the public education system.

The higher grade schools and allied institutions found themselves playing a key role in this transformation, which often conflicted with the Board of Education's growing enthusiasm for domestic subjects. The latter was given a formidable boost around the turn of the century by the apparently sudden realisation that Britain was not a healthy nation: the birth rate was declining, infant mortality was still too high, epidemic diseases would not go away, and thousands of recruits for the Boer War had to be discarded because of their poor physical condition. An assortment of remedial activists, ranging from the social Darwinist– eugenist movement to the promoters of milk depots, were almost unanimous about the cause of the problems: the irresponsibility and ineptitude of urban lower-class women. The Chief Medical Officer to the Board of Education even stated that 'expressed bluntly, it is the ignorance and carelessness of mothers that directly causes a large proportion of the infant mortality'.[64] The solution lay in the dissemination through education of habits of thrifty housekeeping and responsible motherhood. By the 1890s, needlework could occupy as much as a third of the week for elementary school girls, domestic economy was a compulsory subject (with options in cookery, laundry work and hygiene), and the Technical Instruction Committees' main contribution for girls was the provision of more domestic centres and courses.

There were strong objections. To aspiring lower-middle and working-class families, education had much more important things to offer their daughters than the basic domestic training believed to be essential for them by their social superiors. One contemporary feminist complained bitterly about the encroachment that four to five hours per week of sewing made into girls' education, especially when 'they have seldom shown much liking' for it, and it was in any case 'largely rendered useless' by ready-made clothes and sewing machines.[65] The London School Board's first superintendent of cookery recorded that the 'prejudice against it was almost insuperable, and parents put every obstacle in the way of their children attending the classes',[66] while Mrs Pillow, in a special report for the Education Department, exclaimed that 'extraordinary as it may seem in the face of the general ignorance on culinary matters, mothers frequently complained that their daughters "wasted their time" in going to cookery lessons'.[67] Some school boards definitely dragged their feet over domestic subjects. Birmingham constructed just one kitchen for 230 girls at its otherwise superbly equipped Waverley Road Higher Grade School, while Bristol refused to build a new cookery room at St George School, and ordered that girls should study less needlework and more geography to enhance their chances in the pupil teacher examinations.

Most higher grade schools tried to accommodate the growing demand for 'commercial' education, although it should be noted that what they called 'commercial courses' were not narrowly skills-based or vocational. The Bryce Assistant-Commissioner in Birmingham discussed at some length the English, geography, mathematics and French taught to the higher grade schools' commercial pupils, and HMIs at Mundella Higher Grade School noted that 'efforts to give the literary work a more commercial turn, without diminishing its educational value, is very interesting, and appears successful'. Manchester's Central Higher Grade School was able to run a separate commercial department financed by the school's success on the science side, which greatly impressed Mr and Mrs Kitchener on behalf of the Bryce Commission; it had its own woman head and about 150 girls studying religious knowledge, arithmetic, English language and literature, French, geography, art drawing, music and singing, manual instruction, domestic economy, drill and bookkeeping and shorthand.[68] The absence of science was the main difference from the normal higher grade school curriculum, which had implications for pupil teachers when HMIs tried to guide them on to the commercial side in the belief that teachers did not need to know much science. But it is difficult to see quite why commercial education fell so badly out of favour at the Board of Education, or why, as Eaglesham has suggested, vocational education of the commercial variety was 'for long anathema' to Morant, who behaved 'almost as if no education was preferable' to it.[69]

However, although 'commercial' education was a key attraction to girls staying on at school, it was not the only one. Some higher grade schools tried out subjects like hygiene and physiology, but middle-class visitors were repeatedly impressed by the enthusiasm shown by girls for mathematics and science, and went away racking their brains as to why the girls should be so keen to participate in something assumed to be of no earthly use to them. Mrs Kitchener, who was convinced that Science and Art Department courses were inappropriately scientific and 'masculine' for girls, was particularly intrigued by this phenomenon. She noted that at the Bolton Higher Grade School, where 65 girls were in the organised science school, 'the girls looked so bright and interested that it was clear that they were using their minds'; while in an algebra lesson at the Ducie Avenue Higher Grade School in Manchester 'the girls were so intent on the subject that hardly a head was turned when I passed through the classroom'; and at Waterloo Higher Grade School in Oldham 20 girls looked 'uncommonly bright and happy' working alongside 48 boys in the school's splendid chemistry laboratory. She learned from Miss Moss at the Manchester Central Higher Grade School that a surprisingly large number of girls (about half) chose to go into the organised science school rather than her own commercial section, including those who were planning to become pupil teachers. In Miss Moss's experience, the girls emerged 'more intelligent, more alive in mind' at the end of a year in the science school, and Mrs Kitchener herself acknowledged the evident value to girls of studying subjects like chemistry and mathematics as a form of 'intellectual gymnastics'.[70]

Mrs Kitchener also recounted the remarkable lesson learned by the Liverpool School Board when it planned a central science school for boys only, on the assumption that girls would prefer to stay with their elementary school teachers and not have to walk about the streets. The girls of six board schools organised a petition 'asking that they might have the same advantages as the boys' and when the school board agreed, 120 girls put their names down for the science school. There they made up half the numbers and were said by the headmaster to do very well. Mrs Kitchener regarded this as a striking example of girls demanding knowledge for its own sake and, pondering this 'curious fact', concluded that the girls she had come across opted for the best teaching and the highest standards of work and qualifications that were available to them.[71] What emerges strongly from this kind of evidence is that the girls themselves were determined that they would not be fobbed off with a second-rate education; their subjects and courses must carry the same status and lead to the same qualification as the boys.

Higher grade school girls responded well to being treated as equals. Headteachers expected their female pupils and staff to attend as regularly, and to perform as well as their male counterparts, and were neither over-solicitous about their welfare nor surprised by their achievements. The head of Brae Street in Liverpool was 'very proud of his girls' (the ones who had petitioned to be allowed in), Halifax headmaster Dyche believed that 'the girl would work much harder than the boy', and at Ducie Avenue in Manchester, the head acknowledged that the 'presence of the girls was a distinct help to him in maintaining discipline'.[72] At one time the head of St George School was very much concerned that some 'intelligent girls are languishing', so he allocated himself and three school of science teachers to teach them intensively for a week, thereby bringing about 'splendid progress'. The Science Inspector's Report for 1896 included the comment that 'the Girls' section is a distinct success and is even superior to the Boys' section', and a few years later St George School girls won five out of the six Elton scholarships on offer in Bristol, and also had the top-placed candidate in the city in the Oxford Senior Local Examinations.[73] There is no reason to think that the girls at this higher grade school were untypical of others like them, and indeed the most striking aspects of their catalogue of successes was that only the visiting inspectors thought it so unusual as to merit special mention and appreciation.

Since a fair proportion of successful higher grade school girls became teachers, not infrequently in their own or other higher grade schools, it is no surprise to find equally high standards among women teachers. In fact, given the overall pattern of occupational recruitment at the turn of the century, female higher grade school teachers were probably the cream of their generation in terms of intellect, personality and career commitment. Although no co-educational higher grade school had a woman head, all had some female teachers and not necessarily with the more junior forms or teaching 'feminine' subjects. Most had at least a notional girls' school or section under a senior assistant mistress with acknowledged status, some of whom were obviously formidable characters. Miss Beard, in charge of the girls' part of the People's College in Nottingham, generally 'acted for herself' and in 1901 she sharply (and probably unwisely) informed the visiting HMIs that 'she always did Higher Grade work, was still doing it, and intended to continue to do it'.[74] F.H. Spencer recalled a colleague at High Pavement School who was 'very able' and 'so efficient' that she was indispensable to the school,[75] and various heads recorded warm tributes to their female colleagues. At St George, for instance, one who left to become a university lecturer was described as 'a severe loss to the school … Not only has she always exercised a wonderful influence for good over the girls' department, but her abilities are of an unusually high order, and her skill in teaching unsurpassed'. At the same school, the head noted that in the organisation of extra-curricular events like the school concert, 'the lady teachers and children worked like Trojans. Strange antipathy in the work, on the part of several men on the staff', and he was very appreciative of the women teachers' plan to help prepare warm meals for the children at lunch time.[76]

A number of higher grade schools experimented with co-educational classes, sometimes forced on them by having awkwardly unequal numbers to staff and accommodate. The heads were generally pleased with the results. At St George, it was recorded that the mixed second-year class was working 'for the mutual advantage of each. With care the mixed system will work better than the separate one', one noted advantage being that 'the boys are restrained from boisterous conduct by the presence of girls'. Mr Pickles developed a few reservations over the years, thinking at one time that 'the girls become too "laddish" in their general behaviour', and worrying on another occasion that the sexes were mixing too freely out of school hours: 'some boys lose their heads and "sweet-hearting" results'.[77] However, there was never any question of the girls not studying basically the same curriculum as the boys or not aiming at the same standards. Indeed, it is likely that in relative terms more girls studied science and mathematics on an equal footing with boys – and not infrequently outshone them in competitive examinations and awards – than at any time before or since.

It remains to consider whether higher grade school girls mostly did go into paid employment, and whether the investment they had made in a longer and more advanced education paid off in terms of the jobs they got. The admissions registers of St George School in Bristol, which did not significantly change its character until 1907, show that of 140 girls who were admitted to the upper (secondary) part of the school between 1902 and 1906, a remarkably high proportion (over two-thirds) held or were awarded scholarships of some sort, indicating that, despite the unusually low fee at St George, extraordinary methods had to be found to enable them to continue their schooling. No fewer than 54 of them went into teaching, 13 of whom were known to have progressed to a training college or university;[78] 25 became typists; 21 became clerks or took 'business posts'; and 19 took up a variety of jobs, such as shop assistants, Telephone Office employees and librarians.[79] No fewer than 110 of these 140 girls therefore went into jobs where their better education could have proved useful. Since it is unlikely that fee-paying girls' secondary schools could have catered for more than the occasional exceptional pupil from a poorer home and a public elementary school, it has to be concluded that the higher grade school was offering a unique opportunity to such girls. St George School was in an unusually poor area where the incentives to do well at school were great, but its achievements in the field of girls' education were not unusual. Of 63 girls admitted to Fairfield Road School in Bristol up to 1906, 27 went into teaching; ten became clerks or trained for the Post Office; a further ten moved on to a typing or commercial school; four went to other schools or the university; three were described as 'invalids'; and only four were recorded as being 'at home'.[80]

The early twentieth century was an important time for the advancement of women into professional and semi-professional careers. The higher grade/science schools/pupil teacher network of institutions, in liaison with university and technical colleges, played a crucial role in meeting the needs of girls with ability and ambition but little money, who would not have been able to consider those careers but for their achievements in the public education system. A circular put out by the NUT identified the 'pioneer work in the education of girls' as one of the higher grade schools' main achievements, explaining that girls 'receive a

first class preparation for earning a living by instruction in commercial
subjects, but they are also fitted for household duties'.[81] The very
important role which the higher grade schools played in the education of
girls accords with the picture already presented of how seriously the girls
took their school work, and of how well they responded to the near-equal
treatment they received. It is very probable that had the higher grade
schools been allowed to continue, the content and purpose of girls'
education would have been one of the major areas of experimentation.
Looking back from a time when there is much concern that girls are out-
performing boys, after nearly a century when the under-achievement of
girls was an expectation, the higher grade schools stand out as being a
long way ahead of their time in that respect.

THE ORGANIC CONNECTION WITH ELEMENTARY AND FURTHER EDUCATION

The single generation of children who attended higher grade schools was
unique in that most of their parents had not had the opportunity of any
post-elementary schooling, and most of their children would have to pay
rather more dearly for a similar privilege. There was therefore no
traditional expectation of what a higher education was like or of what
opportunities could open up, and there was a gradual discovery of
aptitudes and aspirations during the course of the school career. In other
words, most parents of 4 or 5 year olds starting at a public elementary
school had no idea, beyond the statutory minimum requirements (and they
could change), of what lay ahead and it was only the successful
completion of each stage which guided them to attempt the next one. As
has been shown, the schools responded to this reality by designing courses
which required only a one-year commitment as well as being part of a
more extended whole, and the inclinations of the children themselves
were an important determinant. They were treading new ground, and
familiarity with the system, the school, the teachers, the type of work and
the cost must have been a highly significant factor in encouraging their
continuance in education.

The organic connection with public elementary schools, offering both
continuity and familiarity, was thus crucially important for the higher
grade schools. Those schools which housed all ages, from 4 to 19, were
emphatically part of the school board elementary system: Jack Church at
Surrey Lane Higher Grade School was separated from his brother Richard
in the infants school only by a set of stairs.[82] Such schools obviously had

the opportunity to get to know their pupils over an extended period and to guide their education in a coordinated fashion. And even those which relied on taking a proportion of their pupils from a large number of elementary schools – and some of them travelled considerable distances – knew, with considerable certainty, what and how their pupils had previously been taught. To the newcomers, who often transferred in blocks or whole classes, the school board higher grade schools presented a fairly familiar face in a number of aspects: the structure of the curriculum, the methods of examination and inspection, the general style of teaching, the sort of extra-curricular activities, the amount and weekly payment of any fees, even the appearance of the building. The alternative was spelled out in a response from the National Union of Teachers to a critical speech by Sir John Gorst at the Incorporated Association of Headmasters' banquet:

> Put your higher grade school at the other end of the town, under separate management, and with the inevitable 'classy' atmosphere, the institution is straightway reserved exclusively for middle-class people and the bright child of the artisan home fails to find out its existence. He cuts short his school-life on passing the sixth and seventh standard, to enter the labour market.[83]

This was the practical side of a more philosophical interpretation of the role of the higher grade schools, which was widely voiced at the time by their supporters. Acland and Llewellyn Smith correctly identified the vacant space they filled when they argued in 1892 that existing secondary schools were in no way continuation schools for the children of artisans and that the 'most urgent need' was to devise some form of secondary education which catered for 'workmen's children'.[84] Several witnesses to the Bryce Commission picked up this theme: Dr Forsyth of Leeds Higher Grade School said that 'the grammar school would not serve the purpose, because of the difference in its aims and methods'; the Clerk of the Sheffield School Board felt that 'ex-7th Standard Scholars could not go to the grammar school, as the curriculum is unsuited to them'; and Birmingham's Reverend McCarthy was emphatic that 'endowed secondary schools [of one of which he was headmaster] are not continuation schools for pupils who have passed through public elementary schools'.[85] It is worth noting that at the same time that higher grade schools of 1,000 to 2,000 children were full to overflowing, many endowed schools were struggling to find more than a few dozen pupils. For example, Bristol Grammar School was 'nearer to disaster' than at any time in the nineteenth century, with the numbers and quality of entrants dropping;[86] Sheffield Grammar School was undersubscribed, with a sixth form sometimes of only three pupils, owing to the 'very great difficulty' in getting boys to stay beyond the age of 15 or 16; and Leeds Grammar School, where the boys were 'inattentive' and the masters 'sleepy', had lost about 100 pupils.[87]

Statements about the unsuitability of endowed secondary schools for public elementary school pupils in no way masked a feeling that they were not sufficiently clever or well-educated to transfer. In fact, the low academic attainment of candidates wishing to transfer into some higher grade schools from private or voluntary schools was a worry to the headteachers, and they rarely won awards in open competition with board school children. The head of St George School in Bristol, having examined several girls from private schools for admission to Standard V, found that 'the majority of them came out very poorly', and he wrote to their parents 'advising a further course of study in an elementary school'.[88] Possibly such children were those who were not doing very well at their private schools, but it is significant that the school inspector at Bradford noted that 'board school boys are among the most industrious, the most capable, and the most teachable of those who have been admitted into the Bradford Grammar School'.[89] After 1907 the reservations of many grammar school heads were overcome when they found their 'Free Place' entrants from public elementary schools becoming their academic pace-setters. The impossibility of competing with contemporaries educated at board schools has been cited as one of the main deterrents to middle-class girls entering the elementary teaching profession; they required extra private tuition to get into a training college, and the work was physically and mentally harder than they were used to.[90]

The higher grade headmasters constantly reiterated the crucial importance of the organic connection between their schools and the public elementary system, all under the umbrella of the school board system. They were convinced that any break in the connection or radical change in the controlling authority would not only ruin their schools, but would leave the type of child for whom they catered adrift in an alien environment. The dangers inherent in an enforced segregation of elementary and secondary education were precisely forecast by Llewellyn Smith, in a passage that deserves quoting at some length. Arguing that the mere opening up of a scholarship link between elementary and secondary was not enough, he wrote:

> What it does is to take a few boys from one class, and place them
> among a number of boys of another class, coming from a different

kind of home and aiming at a different kind of career. The newcomers must assimilate themselves to their new surroundings under the penalty of miserable isolation during their school career. They are, as a rule, clever boys, and masters say they 'mix in well' – that is, they readily imitate the manner and catch the idea of those around them. In other words, such sons of artisans as secure scholarships tend to receive in the higher school the stamp of middle-class ideas, and an almost irresistible bias towards a middle-class trade or profession. If this be, as it is, a perversion of the aim of continuation schools, some powerful corrective must be applied.[91]

Morant could not have more totally ignored this advice in his determined separation of secondary from elementary education. The imposition of rigid stipulations about course length, age limits, cost, curriculum and teaching qualifications was entirely alien to the higher grade system. It created artificial constraints on what had been a well-integrated system, which permitted efficient but flexible use of buildings, resources and staff, and offered every encouragement to hesitant pupils and families with disparate educational needs and goals.

THE VISION OF THE HIGHER GRADE SCHOOL HEADTEACHERS

To conclude this analysis of higher grade schools, it is appropriate to give the last word to the schools' most informed and committed spokesmen, their headteachers.[92] While they were obviously partisan in their opinions, they were, of course, more intimately knowledgable about the schools' characteristics and place in the community than anyone else. They seem too to have had a wise view of the educational needs of the total community and a capacity to see the educational process as a whole. From the first, when the idea of a professional association was mooted in late 1892, they were completely confident of the special nature of the job they were doing, and extremely enthusiastic about it. They unashamedly declared themselves to be involved in 'education more advanced than is often recognised as "elementary"', but saw it as an unbroken extension of the public elementary education system. Their work was declared to comprise a continuation of ordinary and specific elementary subjects, including manual instruction for boys and domestic subjects for girls; an introduction 'for all pupils' to scientific study, particularly mathematics and chemistry; provision of commercial subjects; and due attention to

English literature, geography, history, languages (including Latin and Greek if desired) and religious training. The natural development out of the elementary system – 'the apex of the broad-based pyramid' – was so obvious to the higher grade heads as scarcely to need stating, at least until the schools and the school boards came under attack.

The headmasters acknowledged that their schools were still evolving and had their faults, but were emphatic that they were involved with an 'important type of school ... which, in the opinion of many, is one representative of the secondary school of the future'. Yet in no way did they see it as a poor imitation of the secondary school as it was traditionally known in England. Not surprisingly they were somewhat unsure of the exact scope of their work, preferring to label it as 'intermediate', somewhere between the rapidly progressing elementary schools and the dramatically improved civic universities. This was a position which no other schools were able or willing to occupy. While they did not rule out passing their cleverest children on to the universities, they resisted the idea that universities should dominate secondary education. They saw servicing (with the aid of scholarships) the other variants of higher and continuation education as their special province – the technical colleges, art colleges, evening schools and the like – while also providing sufficient diversity to prepare pupils for the full range of future occupations and training. Civil, mechanical and electrical engineering, surveying, dyeworks, factories, chemical works, architects' offices, art rooms and designers' studios were specifically mentioned as likely areas of employment. The heads were happy to accept the paramount duty of educating children for 'the practical needs of after life', but passionately argued their right to access to literary culture and to 'knowledge of their own glorious inheritance'.

Early on there is no sign that the higher grade heads saw the endowed schools as particular rivals or threats to them, although the nature of their work inevitably made them unsympathetic to the class-based view of secondary education and aware of how much better the nation would be served by an alternative or more varied system. Dr Forsyth opened his address to the first conference of the Association of Headmasters of Higher Grade and Organised Schools of Science with the assertion that 'higher education must not in any sense be considered the privilege of any particular class, it must be the common prerogative of all'. Over the years he elaborated the argument, with reference to the widely discussed 'national interest' debate; if a secondary education system was to be 'truly national', it must be 'within the reach of all, even the poorest classes'. The endowed schools were unfitted to serve the national interest because their exclusive fees and the classical nature of their training debarred far too many of the nation's children and did not generate the necessary kinds of expertise and skills. Perhaps, it was suggested, the nation's endowments should be rearranged to benefit the nation's children as a whole. In achieving this goal, specially elected local boards of management along school board lines had a 'very strong' claim to be in charge. They could build on the higher grade and organised science school experience to construct 'genuine secondary or intermediate education' such as would serve 'the needs of their districts' and also 'suit the social circumstances of the great bulk of the population'.

The awareness of local needs and social class issues were held to be the two determinants which made the higher grade schools unique and gave them their 'charter of existence'. Their supporters believed that in a way which no other institution of secondary education could claim, higher grade schools were entitled to 'recognition and consideration as national secondary schools'. The headmasters expected to be important people in any reshaping of education, providing a fund of experience for the new secondary school authorities to draw upon, and thereby exercising a formative influence on any scheme of secondary education. In the light of the energy they put into their own schools and their broad understanding of the nation's educational needs, it is hard to dispute their right so to do, or to remain unimpressed by their optimistic commitment and dedication.

NOTES

1. Spencer, *Inspector's Testament*, p. 157. Spencer, born into a nonconformist artisan family in 1872, attended a board school in Swindon where he became a pupil teacher and then trained at Borough Road College. While teaching in London, he got involved in university extension lectures, took a part-time degree and did some work for Graham Wallas and the Webbs, and was asked to head the new day department of the City of London Polytechnic. He was then invited to become an HMI (Technical Branch) and finished his career (in 1933) as Chief Inspector under the London Education Committee.
2. J. Roach, *Secondary Education in England 1870–1902* (London: Routledge, 1991), p. 103; St George School, Bristol, Log Book, 2 October 1896.
3. St George School, Log Book, 25 January 1897, 3 February 1897.
4. Gateshead's John Bidgood in *The Schoolmaster*, 9 February 1895.
5. Bristol School Board, School Management Committee, Minutes, 17 September 1896.
6. Bradford Corporation, *Education in Bradford*, p. 19.
7. Davies, *Barnsley School Board*, p. 164.
8. John Thornton of Bolton in *The Schoolmaster*, 9 December 1895.
9. As evidenced in reports in *The Schoolmaster*, in various local archives, such as School Board Minutes; in central records, notably the individual School Files held in the Public Records Office, and in the annual published *Reports of the Department of Science and Art*. That department's reports for 1898, 1899 and 1900 supply the statistics which follow in this paragraph.
10. High Pavement School, Nottingham, Log Book; and D. Wardle, *Education and Society in Nineteenth-Century Nottingham* (London: Cambridge University Press, 1971), pp. 131–2, which gives other similar examples.
11. *Bryce Commission*, IX, pp. 414–15, 422–3. The timetable of Sheffield Central School was similar

to that of Leeds.

12. Department of Science and Art, *46th Report* (1899), p. 11.
13. *Schools Inquiry Commission (Taunton Commission)* VIII, (1868), p. 150.
14. Quoted in *The Schoolmaster*, 7 December 1895.
15. Bradford Corporation, *Education in Bradford*, pp. 21, 160. All pupils did English, French, history, geography, art, chemistry, mathematics and physics, and all girls did domestic economy and all boys manual instruction, but then different schools offered algebra, bookkeeping, Euclid, shorthand, German, animal physiology or hygiene.
16. Quoted in *The Schoolmaster*, 7 December 1895.
17. Tropp, *School Teachers*, pp. 147, 151.
18. St George School, Log Book, 15 March 1895, 19 September 1895, 14 February 1896, 11 March 1896; Queen's Walk School, Nottingham, Log Book, 22 March 1897.
19. E.W. Jenkins, *'A Magnificent Pile': A Centenary History of the Leeds Central High School* (Leeds: City of Leeds School, 1985), pp. 55, 57.
20. F. Widdowson, *Going Up Into the Next Class: Women and Elementary Teacher Training, 1840–1914* (London: WRRC, 1980), p. 41.
21. W. Robinson, 'Pupil Teachers: The Achilles Heel of Higher Grade Girls' Schools 1882–1904?', *History of Education*, 22, 3 (1993), p. 241.
22. Robinson, 'Pupil Teachers', p. 250, disputes this when she says they were 'hardly the elite of the teaching profession', but it is difficult to know where else the London School Board was likely to find the 'highly qualified and dedicated teachers' which she felt the higher grade schools lacked.
23. A typical (successful) career progression was that of Frederick Pickles. Having been educated at Bradford Technical College and Edinburgh University, he taught at Belle Vue Higher Grade School, Bradford, the Pupil Teacher Centre in Bradford and the Pupil Teacher Centre in Birmingham before moving to Bristol in 1895 to become head of St George Higher Grade School.
24. Spencer, *Inspector's Testament* (1938), pp. 171–2. Teachers quite often gained their first degree in their mid-20s or 30s (by which time they had been teaching for several years), possibly with a masters degree some years later.
25. And after the move to pupil teacher centres, higher grade schools were favoured for observation visits and teaching practice, and their teachers were often involved in part-time lecturing.
26. St George School, Log Book, 17 April 1896, 17 December 1904.
27. Bridge Street School, Birmingham, Log Book, 14 October 1885; St George School, Log Book, 6 December 1895, 14 September 1897, 29 January 1900, 18 December 1900; High Pavement School, Log Book, 25 September 1893.
28. *Bryce Commission*, VII, p. 161.
29. Davies, *Barnsley School Board*, pp. 176–9. He describes how, despite the Education Department's opposition – 'If it [the Barnsley School Board] does not show more common-sense in future ... it ought to go to the wall and let something else take its place' – the first 'School Journey' was organised, and approvingly written up by Michael Sadler in one of his Special Reports.
30. St George School, Log Book, 14 May 1897, 19 May 1897.
31. Bridge Street School, Log Book, 15 March 1892, 15 March 1893.
32. Interviews with George Creech (St George School) and Ellen Hallett (Fairfield Road School).
33. St George School, Log Book, 28 February 1896; Bridge Street School, Log Book, 13 March 1885, 9 March 1892; Queen's Walk School, Log Book, 10 July 1884, 1 June 1885.
34. Mundella School, Nottingham, Log Book, 9 February 1900; St George School, Log Book, 29 June 1904.
35. *Bryce Commission*, VII, pp. 140, 161, 166, 194.
36. Spencer, *Inspector's Testament*, p. 228. Tropp, *School Teachers*, pp. 149–52, explores the growing radicalisation of the elementary teaching profession, including the NUT leadership; Richard Lishman, the 'premier' higher grade school head in Bradford, was a vigorous campaigner for Socialism and an active supporter of the ILP, J. Jackson, *Belle Vue Boys' School* (Bradford: typescript, 1976), p. 27.
37. This was not a successful arrangement. Classroom temperatures of between 35 and 45 degrees were recorded and, during the course of one winter, one teacher was away with a kidney

complaint after catching cold in his schoolroom, another resigned because 'he finds the school too unhealthy to work in', a new appointee declined to come because 'the school premises are not conducive to good health', the headmaster was unwell with neuralgia and nervous exhaustion, and another teacher was 'extremely ill and overtaxed' and later died. Bridge Street School, Log Book, 6 February 1888, 30 October 1888, 14 February 1889, 12 April 1889, 7 February 1895.

38. T.J.A. Rogers, 'First in the West', in *The Georgian Jubilee Number: St George Secondary School, Bristol 1894–1944* (school magazine) (1944), p. 9.

39. W. Southgate, *That's the Way it Was. A Working Class Autobiography 1890–1950* (Oxted: New Clarion Press, 1982), p. 21. Conan Doyle's description (through Sherlock Holmes) of the board schools as 'lighthouses' is well-known, and to Charles Booth, 'each school stands up from its playground like a church in God's acre ringing its bell', quoted in D. Rubinstein, 'Socialization and the London School Board 1870–1904', in P. McCann, (ed.), *Popular Education And Socialization in the Nineteenth Century* (London: Methuen, 1977), p. 237.

40. St George School Board, Higher Grade and Technical School Prospectus 1894–5.

41. High Pavement School, Log Book, 20 July 1894, 9 April 1895, 23 November 1900. According to evidence given to the *Bryce Commission,* VIII, p. 80, Sheffield's school cost a staggering £52,000 (site and buildings) plus £29,000 (laboratories, workshops, and so on).

42. The head of the People's College in Nottingham, with strong local support, resisted the Board's new stringent requirements for five years until the school, in a 'depleted and moribund' state, closed in 1907. The People's College, Log Book, 19 September 1901, 2 July 1906, 26 July 1907. Barnsley's Central School experienced a similar 'severe shock', according to Davies, *Barnsley School Board*, pp. 185–7, and after a bitter dispute, the Education Committee, declining to spend a large sum of money on the relatively small school the Board wanted, turned its thriving higher grade school into an ordinary elementary school. Public Record Office (PRO) Ed.20/47.

43. PRO Ed.21/6162.

44. PRO Ed.21/6142.

45. PRO Ed.21/6128.

46. St George School, Log Book, 23 October 1903, 13 November 1903, 6 May 1904, 21 June 1904.

47. Lawson and Silver, *Social History of Education*, p. 338.

48. See especially J. Burnett, *Plenty and Want: A Social History of Diet in England From 1815 to the Present Day* (London: Nelson, 1966), Chapters 6 and 8.

49. C.N.J. Scudamore, 'The Social Background of Pupils at the Bridge Street Higher Grade School, Birmingham' (University of Birmingham MEd thesis, 1976), pp. 118–20. Using an imaginative variety of indices (rateable values of houses, returns of infectious diseases and distribution of pawnbrokers as well as occupations), he proved that the school board was not deluding itself in thinking that Bridge Street School primarily served the working class, albeit its more skilled members.

50. Cited in various places, including F. Campbell, *Eleven-Plus and All That: The Grammar School in a Changing Society* (London: Watts, 1956), p. 140. 'Middle class' was defined as independent means, professional, teachers, heads of firms; 'lower middle class' as managers, retail traders, commercial travellers, shop assistants, clerks, public officials, foremen; 'working class' as skilled tradesmen, unskilled workmen, labourers, etc. The series of meetings resulted in a Joint Memorandum agreeing the different functions of the two kinds of schools, as described by Daglish, *Education Policy-Making*, pp. 75–9.

51. St George School, Log Book, 8 July 1904. In similar vein, the head of Wyggeston Boys' School (which in the absence of a higher grade board school in Leicester, took more scholarship pupils than most endowed schools) promised, 'I will find the money myself if needs be' to enable a bright boy, the son of 'a working man', to continue at St John's College, Cambridge. Wyggeston Schools, Governors' Minute Book, 2 May 1900.

52. Spencer, *Inspector's Testament*, pp. 69–73.

53. J. Bryce, 'Introduction' to Acland and Llewellyn Smith, *Studies in Secondary Education*, p. xix; *Bryce Commission*, VII, p. 71.

54. Board of Education, *Statistics*.

55. St George School, Log Book, 14 September 1900, 27 September 1900, 18 June 1902, 29 June 1903, 3 July 1903, 8 July 1903.

56. And they were infuriated by pupils who left part-way through a year and failed to take any examinations, especially as this usually meant loss of grant.

57. Birmingham Municipal Technical School, Register of Day Scholars.
58. *Bryce Commission*, VII, p. 174; St George School, Log Book, 8 November 1901; People's College, Log Book, 26 September 1901.
59. Bristol School Board, School Management Committee, Minutes, 21 January 1898.
60. H.J. Habakkuk, 'The Economic History of Modern Britain', p. 154, and J. Hajnal, 'European Marriage Patterns in Perspective', pp. 103, 130, both in D.V. Glass and D.E.C. Eversley (eds), *Population in History: Essays in Historical Demography* (London: Edward Arnold, 1965).
61. C. Rollett and J. Parker, 'Population and Family', in A.H. Halsey (ed.), *Trends in British Society since 1900* (London: Macmillan, 1972), Tables 2.16 and 2.18.
62. E. Cadbury, M.C. Matheson and G. Shann, *Women's Work and Wages: A Phase of Life in an Industrial City* (London: T. Fisher Unwin, 1906); D. Gittins, *Fair Sex: Family Size and Structure, 1900–1939* (London: Hutchinson, 1982). Walter Southgate, in *That's the Way it Was*, wrote of his mother's expertise at managing the pawnbroker as well as working in the laundry and helping with births and laying out.
63. G.S. Bain, R. Bacon and J. Pimlott, 'The Labour Force', in Halsey, *Trends*, Tables 4.3, 4.4 and 4.5; B.L. Hutchins, *Women in Modern Industry* (Wakefield: EP Publishing 1980; reprint of 1915 edition), p. 80.
64. Quoted in C. Dyhouse, *Girls Growing Up in Late Victorian and Edwardian England* (London: Routledge & Kegan Paul, 1981), p. 96. *The Report of the Inter-Departmental Committee on Physical Deterioration* (1904) was particularly influential.
65. C.S. Bremner, *Education of Girls and Women in Great Britain* (London: Swan Sonnenschein, 1897), p. 47.
66. J. Kamm, *Hope Deferred: Girls' Education in English History* (London: Methuen, 1965), p. 164; Dyhouse, *Girls Growing Up*, p. 90.
67. Education Department, *Special Reports on Education Subjects* (1896).
68. *Bryce Commission*, VI, p. 265 and VII, pp. 57–8; Mundella School, Log Book, 16 July 1900.
69. Eaglesham, 'Centenary', p. 14.
70. *Bryce Commission*, VI, pp. 275, 278, 354, 362, 374–6.
71. *Bryce Commission*, VI, pp. 253–5.
72. *Bryce Commission*, VI, pp. 374, 384; *School Government Chronicle*, 3 January 1903.
73. St George School, Log Book, 26 November 1894, 17 April 1896, 2 October 1896, 28 July 1897, 25 June 1900, 13 January 1905, 1 September 1905.
74. People's College, Log Book, 26 September 1901, 13 November 1901, 18 October 1903; Nottingham School Board, Minutes, 12 November 1897. Miss Beard was perhaps fortified by her 'school' having received a remarkable accolade four years earlier from Morant, then employed in the Education Department Library, 'congratulating her upon its excellent curriculum, and stating that the school appears to be superior to any similar one in the South of England'. Trained at Homerton College, Miss Beard had previously been headmistress of a large mixed elementary school in Coventry, where she was described as 'an assiduous and painstaking governess'. She resigned in 1904, apparently in disgust at the Board of Education's treatment of her school. PRO Ed.20/116.
75. Spencer, *Inspector's Testament*, p. 158.
76. St George School, Log Book, 26 August 1895, 18 December 1895, 26 January 1904.
77. St George School, Log Book, 28 September 1896, 16 February 1903, 20 May 1904.
78. Former pupil and student-teacher Mary Creech recalled that according to local custom in Bristol, the Grammar School produced lawyers, the Cathedral School clergymen, Colston's School doctors, and St George School teachers and technicians.
79. St George School, Admission Registers. A standard admission register was introduced into all maintained schools in 1908–9, so they were drawn up retrospectively for entrants before then. Hence, 'successful' pupils and scholarship holders are proportionately over-represented, although, presumably, pupils who had left earlier were even more likely to have gone into employment.
80. Fairfield Road School, Admission Registers.
81. Draft of *NUT Circular* (?1897) in collection of miscellaneous minutes, etc., in the archives of the NUT.
82. R. Church, *Over the Bridge: An Essay in Autobiography* (London: Reprint Society/Heinemann, 1956), p. 46.

83. *The Schoolmaster*, 19 January 1901.
84. Acland and Llewellyn Smith, *Studies*, pp. 306–7
85. *Bryce Commission*, VII, pp. 74, 80, 98.
86. C.P. Hill, *The History of Bristol Grammar School* (London: Pitman, 1951), pp. 117, 128. This was nevertheless an improvement on 1829, when there was not a single pupil! (p. 65).
87. *Bryce Commission*, VII, pp. 163–6.
88. St George School, Log Book, 31 August 1896.
89. E. Wilson, 'The Development of Secondary Education in Bradford from 1895 to 1928' (University of Leeds MEd thesis, 1968), p. 125.
90. F. Widdowson, *Going Up*, pp. 15–16.
91. Acland and Llewellyn Smith, *Studies*, p. 187.
92. This section is based on reports in *The Schoolmaster*.

3

BRISTOL: SCHOOL BOARD AND HIGHER GRADE SCHOOLS, 1894–1903

For reasons going far back into its history, Bristol had more endowed schools per head of the population than any other major city. Furthermore, it had managed to keep them relatively accessible to the city's children, including a significant number from less well-off families, despite periodic pressure to develop them in other directions. It had been largely out of frustration at not being able to turn the grammar school into a full-blown, non-local public school that a group of local clerics and professional people founded Clifton College in 1862. And the efforts of the Endowed Schools Commissioners to pool the city's considerable charitable resources to produce an orderly system of fee-paying first, second and third grade schools had failed in the face of local devotion to at least the spirit of the original foundations. Assistant Commissioner Joshua Fitch's five-year battle with the various Bristol trustees was one of the longest and most bitter of any that resulted from the Endowed Schools Act, and it has since been observed that the Bristol public just 'stopped short of burning Fitch in effigy'.[2] The battle has been cited as one of the main reasons for the demise of the Endowed Schools Commission, and it left Bristol's endowed schools fundamentally unchanged.

By the beginning of the 1890s, then, Bristol's secondary education provision was as follows. Quite separate was Clifton College, already a first grade proprietary boarding school, but always one of the few public schools to emphasise science in the curriculum and to admit day-boys on equal terms. Bristol Grammar School had hung on to its first-grade status, a classical school with a modern side, thanks to nearly £10,000 diverted from other charities and a share of the 'whisky money'³ distributed by the Technical Instruction Committee from 1891. This helped to fund a completely new school building and some scholarships, but the school was struggling to find a role between the prestigious public schools, which it envied, and the developing higher grade schools, which it feared, until the arrival in 1906 of its greatest headmaster, Cyril Norwood. The Cathedral School, after several fruitless reorganisations, took 120 boys between 8 and 17, including 18 free choristers and five other scholarship boys. The nucleus of the group of men and women which founded Clifton College was also instrumental in the establishment of Clifton High School for Girls (1877) and Redland High School for Girls (1882), in the mould of the Girls' Public Day School Trust's high schools. Both were flourishing, fee-paying institutions, although the latter took a number of scholarship girls from elementary schools in return for grants from the Technical Instruction Committee. Bristol also boasted an array of private schools, a few of them quite long-established and reputable (notably Badminton School) and some no doubt offering a form of secondary schooling, especially to girls.

Hospital foundations proved to be the biggest stumbling-block to the Endowed Schools Commission and Bristol had three of them, all lucrative and all fondly regarded by its citizens. Among their other charitable works, they traditionally provided residential education for needy children, giving them two or three years' post-elementary instruction in useful subjects designed to prepare them for domestic service or apprenticeships. Their respective trustees sturdily resisted Fitch's attempts to upgrade them socially and academically by the charging of substantial fees, and they emerged little changed in 1875. The Queen Elizabeth's Hospital, or City School, remained predominantly a school for poor boys, with 160 free boarders, comprising 60 poor orphans and 100 chosen by examination from the Bristol elementary schools. A few could proceed to the Grammar School, where they were said to have noticeably raised the standards of achievement in mathematics. The Red Maids' School remained a small charitable boarding school with a quaint uniform, and although it was gradually moving away from the thorough preparation of girls for domestic service towards a 'sound, practical and liberal education', it was far from being the top-level girls' high school that Fitch envisaged.

The most important foundation, Colston's Hospital Fund, was in the hands of the Society of Merchant Venturers⁴ and supported several charitable institutions in the city, including a boys' school. This had earlier made a controversial move out of the city centre to Stapleton on the outskirts, where it provided a fairly limited boarding education to fee-payers, and free to 100 elementary schoolboys with exhibitions, to enable the best to proceed to 'higher and first-grade schools'. Wise investment of the Colston money by the Merchant Venturers enabled them to carry out their commitment to open a girls' school – Colston's Day School – in 1891, 'to provide a sound practical education of girls of 7 years and upwards', and some free places were available. Both schools were explicitly Anglican. The Merchant Venturers also ran a unique institution, the former Diocesan Trade School, which they completely refurbished and reopened in 1885 as the Merchant Venturers' Technical College and School. With a moderate fee (from £5 per annum) and a scholarship system, this flourishing institution catered for boys from the age of 9 and girls from 15 right through to university entrance. It had various day and evening departments, and a large and well-qualified staff offering a wide range of subjects, especially on the science and technical side. By the 1890s, it was feeling the effects of the competition provided by the cheaper evening classes of the University College, which also included a Day Training College for women teachers. The Technical College principal, Julius Wertheimer, consequently had some anxieties about the future role of the College and was sensitive to any possible rivalry from other institutions.

The relative accessibility of Bristol's endowed schools prevented the secondary education void experienced in other cities, which at least a couple of dozen urban school boards were attempting to fill by the 1880s. At most of Bristol's endowed schools, fees were comparatively low and scholarships were available, and the introduction of the Technical Instruction Committee's scholarship system added to the impression that poor children of ability were not neglected. Furthermore, the people involved in running Bristol's educational institutions were an unusually cohesive group.[5] They were more or less united in their dedication to extending opportunities regardless of class, income or sex, and any sectarian squabbles which might have disturbed their work had long since been resolved in the city.[6] There is no doubt that the potential prestige of some of the schools was stunted by the rejection of Fitch's scheme, but there is something not wholly unattractive about the determination of the trustees to put other criteria ahead of that one. Bristolians had relied for nearly 300 years on a basic provision of social services – for the old, the sick, the uneducated, the orphaned, the pregnant, the insane – from charitable sources. Their reluctance to advance with changing opinion towards an entirely class-based system of secondary education probably harmed very few and benefited a good many.

THE SCHOOL BOARD AND HIGHER GRADE SCHOOLS, 1890–1900

So Bristol could congratulate itself, with some justification, on the fact that it was not impossible for the more fortunate and capable of its children, whatever their parents' income, to take their education further than the statutory elementary stage. The School Board had therefore concentrated on improving the provision of elementary schools, while playing a part in keeping open the routes through to the existing post-elementary schools. Early in its life, declining to comment on Fitch's report, the Board had declared that it was not its job to do anything for secondary education and nor did it know anything about it. But it put on record its commitment to favour any scheme which encouraged scholars of the public elementary schools to pursue their education, and its disapproval of the removal of any endowments from the poor even if that might 'raise the cost or degrade the standard of education so obtainable by the middle classes'.[7] By the beginning of the 1890s, the Bristol School Board had built an effective network of institutions, including special centres for blind, deaf, delinquent and truant children, but it had not had to face the problem of significant numbers of children demanding more than elementary schooling, which had prompted the development of higher grade schools in other areas.

The accelerating pace of educational change which was a nationwide feature of the 1890s inevitably affected Bristol. After a hesitant start its Technical Instruction Committee, like most others, was pursuing a fairly narrow and conservative approach in its distribution of funds. One specialist centre, the Cookery School, was launched and evening classes were supported, but most of the money went to existing institutions of higher education and the School Board only ever received just £40 out of the £39,744 distributed by the Technical Instruction Committee between 1891 and 1897.[8] The School Board, meanwhile, had got involved in post-elementary education for its pupil teachers, who from 1889 attended evening and weekend classes at a centrally located board school. In 1896 daytime tuition was introduced at the YMCA, by which time plans for the Board's own permanent centre were well advanced. Despite a rising education rate, there was no strong move towards retrenchment and economy, and the School Board – which for most of the 1890s included representatives of the National Union of Teachers,[9] the Trades Council and the Socialist Society – was generally in favour of educational expansion.

It was the Trades Council which formally brought the higher grade question to the fore. From 1889 Bristol experienced an explosion of trade union activity and industrial unrest.[10] A contemporary said that the city in 1889 was 'a seething centre of revolt. Without organisation, funds or preparation of any kind, various bodies struck for higher wages and better conditions of work', and, during the next year, so many different groups of workers struck successfully that 'the Bristol Labour Revolt' was held up to other workers as a model of good organisation, non-violent action, and speedy settlement. But the dispersal by cavalry forces and police of a big celebratory fund-raising march on 23 December 1892, during which 57 civilians were injured, shocked Bristolians and became known as 'Black Friday'. It increased the determination of trades union and Trades Council leaders to win better opportunities for the working class. Among them were John Wall, the 'shoemaker poet', whose fervour for education was diluted only by his hatred of the deference which organised schooling inculcated into the working class, and Frank Sheppard, a full-time union official and chairman of the Trades Council in 1894, who was to give a lifetime of service to the Labour movement, local government and education.

In 1894, just as the School Board in neighbouring St George was opening its higher grade school, the Trades Council presented to the Bristol School Board a memorial signed by 762 working men, which spoke of the 'desirability of establishing a central Secondary or Higher Grade School, such as exists in Liverpool, Manchester, Birmingham and other large cities of industry at which our young people may continue that education which they have received in their elementary schools'.[11] During the 1895 School Board election, there was much talk of children's educational needs, higher grade schools and educational ladders, and socialist H.H. Gore[12] topped the poll on what was regarded as a very advanced programme: compulsory, free, secular state education, better salaries for teachers, free school meals and open access to school playgrounds and gymnasia. The Ratepayers' Association, with its policy of strict economy, failed to get its candidate elected.

By the time of the next election, boundary changes had brought under Bristol's jurisdiction the neighbouring school board areas of St George, Bedminster, Stapleton and half of Horfield, and, with them, responsibility for an extra 10,000 board school pupils and a large debt. The Bristol School Board's expenditure almost doubled between 1897 and 1900, with the education rate rising again, but it is much to the credit of the Board that it resisted calls for economy and planned the educational provision for its enlarged area in a generous and forward-looking spirit. It did so, of course, with the consent of its electors. In the same year (1898) that the Trades Union Congress met most successfully in Bristol, seven

Progressives (out of their eight candidates), five Tories, one Socialist, one NUT representative and one Protestant Leaguer were elected to the School Board, a pattern which was to be more or less repeated in the final school board election in 1901.

In the last decade of its School Board's life, Bristol moved decisively into the field of higher grade education. It ended up with three schools which it termed 'higher grade': St George, in the district of the same name on the east side of the city; Merrywood, serving the Bedminster district south of the river; and Fairfield Road, located to the north of the city centre. Unlike most cities, where central provision was the priority, Bristol's entry into the higher grade school world was prompted by its peripheral districts. These, the home of an increasing proportion of the city's varied industrial activity, were witnessing a boom in house-building for the lower-middle and working classes, whose needs could not be met by the existing institutions of secondary education clustered in the centre and in wealthy Clifton. Bristol's three higher grade schools are excellent illustrations of both the common characteristics and the possible variations of this new style of education as it flourished in the 1890s, and of the antagonism which surrounded their demise in the first decade of the twentieth century.

ST GEORGE HIGHER GRADE SCHOOL

The birth of the St George Higher Grade and Technical School was in many respects a most unlikely event. The district lies to the east of Bristol on what had always been its more industrial side, running out towards the coal-mining area of Kingswood, where John Wesley had laboured to save the souls of the lawless colliers. St George itself had coal pits, as well as chemical works, the Great Western Cotton Factory, in its heyday one of the largest mills in England, and, on the edge of the district, the Lawrence Hill depot and engine sheds of the Great Western Railway. But most important was the production of boots and shoes, for which east Bristol ranked only a little behind Leicester, Northampton and London; like them, in the 1890s Bristol was to undergo the painful transition to factory production methods.[13]

From the late 1860s, St George had experienced rapid population growth (to 36,000 in 1894), as a result of the building of hundreds of cheap, densely packed dwellings. It was a solidly working-class area, whose wealthiest citizens were small businessmen – shopkeepers and artisans turned employers – and which, moreover, was experiencing such hard times in the early 1890s that a neighbourhood relief fund was launched. Trade was bad, and in 1889 serious floods left many people homeless. Later that year, the newly unionised female cotton workers of St George spearheaded a massive labour effort which attracted national attention. Other unions raised funds, soup kitchens and music hall benefit shows were organised, and the climax was a huge open-air rally on the Downs addressed by national trade union leaders, Ben Tillett, Tom Mann and Will Thorne. Eventually the employers conceded nearly all the women's demands.[14] All this generated a remarkable sense of solidarity in the St George area, and a big lock-out of the boot and shoe workers in 1892 was estimated to have affected 30,000 people. Of all the branches of the National Union of Boot and Shoe Operatives (formed in 1890), the Bristol and Kingswood one has been characterised as the most turbulent, with a propensity for unofficial strikes and socialist-inspired militancy.[15] And after the boundary extension, St George was identified by city-based Socialists as the most promising of the new areas because of the number of residents who were already labour activists and involved in the Independent Labour Party and the Labour Electoral Association.[16]

As part of Gloucestershire until 1898, St George was largely self-governing, with its own authorities for such services as sewerage, paving and lighting, but the area was poorly supplied with amenities like good roads, baths, libraries and parks. It had a School Board of nine members, which by the 1890s was responsible for six elementary schools, but which was constantly struggling to keep up with the ever-increasing school population and a relatively low income from the rates. A penny rate produced only £270 and the School Board was somehow managing to provide each school place for half the national average cost.[17] St George children were not eligible for free places in Bristol's residential charity schools, and the city's other secondary schools were both too expensive and too far away. Early leaving was common and attendance suffered when times were hard, and although the School Board prosecuted some parents, it was very aware that poverty was often the cause. In 1890 over 300 children were being excused the small school fee of 2d per week, and the Board instructed that no child should be sent home if it was known that the parents could not pay. The 1891 legislation permitting free elementary education was unanimously welcomed and immediately put into effect in all the board schools, and 3,000 handbills posted around the district announced the good news.[18] It would seem that the St George School Board had its hands full providing a bare minimum of elementary education.

A contemporary recalled that it was during a visit to the Board's 'best' elementary school, Russell Town, that one of his School Board colleagues commented: 'What a delightful thing to have a higher grade school in this part of Bristol.'[19] Although there were at that time no higher grade schools in the whole of the west of England, his subsequent proposal to the Board met a good response, especially among the six key members – a tailor, a Congregational minister, a coachbuilder, two grocers and a shoemaker who was chairman of the Radical Operatives' Association – who came to be seen as the higher grade school's founding fathers. According to two people who knew them personally, at most one-third 'can have had anything like a liberal education', but they shared a dream of providing 'an avenue for boys and girls of every class to reach the highest posts within the city' and for 'entrance to the best college of Oxford to be open to talent and perseverance'. The School Board did its homework thoroughly, eliciting information about existing higher grade schools, especially Sheffield's, and undertaking visits to Birmingham, Derby and Cardiff. In March 1891 it submitted a preliminary application for a school for 500 children to the Education Department, arguing that 'the population and wealth of the locality are rapidly growing, and the want of such a school is increasingly felt'. The Department gave its consent to the general idea, but clearly did not take the application very seriously, following doubts expressed by the responsible HMI 'as to the capacity of this Board for carrying out the scheme successfully, although it is scarcely possible to express this opinion to them'.

However, the St George School Board busily set about planning and building its new school. It acquired a good site, persuaded the local authority to turn the neighbouring farm into a public park, as the Radical Operatives' Association had long been urging, and offered a prize for the best architect's plan for the new building. This produced, in due course, an imposing red-brick three-storey building. The School Board also had to win over local opinion. The initial news spread quickly around St George, producing 'tumult and affright' that the Board was 'flirting with this outrageous idea'; there was talk of 'the Higher Grade School commonly called the Lunatic Asylum' and 'much adverse criticism, accusations of making the parish a laughing-stock, prophecies of red ruin and desolation, of burdening St George with the most monstrous white elephant it had ever known'. However, the keenest supporters of the idea topped the poll in the School Board election of 1892 (as they also did in 1895 after the school opened), and, as the building progressed, it was recorded that 'all St George ... were manifesting a deep interest in this new and wonderful venture'. No fewer than 595 children applied for the first 125 free places, and tickets were snapped up for the ceremonial opening, which the first headmaster recalled as a packed gathering generating much excitement and cheering. The School Board was disappointed not to attract a national figure to the opening, but a number of important Bristolians came, who were said to have 'looked with envious eyes' on the achievement of their little neighbour.

What made it special was, in the words of one early pupil and teacher, that it was 'conceived and achieved not by the magnate of a wealthy borough but by a group of their own friends and neighbours, men of little showing outside their own world of St George'. A newspaper report labelled them 'certain wise men in the East ... pioneers of popular and secondary education in the city of Bristol'. The school's second and most important early headmaster later paid tribute to the 'brave men who, in the face of all opposition and all kinds of criticism and sarcasm', persevered with their aim of providing 'a generous education to those boys and girls who were not gifted with this world's goods – such as the boys and girls in Clifton and the richer parts of the city possessed'. It was, according to the first headmaster, a 'daring thing for such a small authority to do', not least because a debt of £15,000 was incurred, and he recalled 'many scores of hours' spent in consultation with the School Board members trying to stretch the money as far as possible. St George provides a striking example of how much a small and far from wealthy school board could achieve. Nearly all subsequent commentators have accepted that, while the minority of big urban boards did a good job, the school board system was basically unsound because most boards were too weak or too poor or too apathetic to cater adequately for their districts. Admittedly St George was not a tiny rural board, but it was nevertheless a significant exception to the rule, and its smallness and consequent intimacy seem to have generated remarkable local loyalty to the higher grade school right from the start.

Over the summer of 1894, with the building virtually finished, the staff were appointed, headed by Mr F.W. Westaway, BA, Inter BSc (London), FCS. A nicely printed and illustrated prospectus was circulated, informing parents that the new school would accommodate 250 boys and 250 girls under a graduate headmaster and a fully trained and certificated staff of assistants. 'Great attention' having been paid to heating, lighting and ventilation 'on the most modern principles', the school boasted special rooms for science and art, 'a thoroughly well-appointed Chemistry Laboratory, a large Science Lecture Room, a Workshop, a Dining Room and accommodation of every kind conducive to the well-being of the Scholars'. The Elementary Section, comprising Standards V, VI and VII, studied an impressively broad curriculum, covering literary as well as scientific, craft and commercial subjects. After passing Standard VII, scholars could move on to the 'Science and Higher Section' for a three-year course designed to 'form a sound general education' and to prepare for professional and commercial careers and for various examinations, including London University matriculation and even exhibitions at Oxford and Cambridge. The first two years comprised mathematics, chemistry, physics, geometry, drawing, English, French and Latin, with a third year specialising in particular areas of study (including French and Latin). The fees of 5d per week covered all books and stationery used in school, and 125 free scholarships (25 per cent of the places) were available on the results of an annual examination. The prospectus stressed that it was crucial for pupils to complete their course of study, and that preference would be shown to parents giving an undertaking to that effect, 'as the school is supported almost entirely by grants earned at Examinations'. Everything about this document – the quality of staff and buildings, the curriculum content and structure, the anxiety about premature leaving – is suggestive of careful planning and close knowledge of the likely pupils, together with almost unbounded ambition for what they and the school might achieve.

Despite some last-minute objections from a surprised Education Department in London, the school opened on 19 November 1894. By the end of the first week 300 children had been admitted, and admissions continued over the next few months as they transferred from their elementary schools. According to Mr Westaway, the 'cream' consisted of 13 and 14 year olds drawn from local elementary schools and 'picked out for their past successes and for their positions on the examination list'. During the first two terms equipment, cupboards and science apparatus arrived almost daily, woodwork and drawing lessons were begun, a concert was given in aid of the local poor relief fund, piano and drill lessons squeezed into the timetable, and some evening science lectures were given by the Dean of Bristol, with the headmaster working the lantern. It took several months for a stable staff to settle down. Westaway described them as men and women who 'had in some non-university way gained a distinction in a single subject', and he was 'proud of them all. It was rare for anything to go seriously wrong.' The headmaster took much of the science and mathematics himself, and early on discussed with the top form the possibility of taking two or three Science and Art Department examinations the following May. He found the pupils dying for 'the chance to beat these Bristol schools', and despite being beginners in the subjects and only having six months to prepare, St George School came 'easily first in the whole Bristol area'. Westaway remembered the early pupils being 'wonderfully keen, and ... extremely likeable', and said that once the staff and pupils settled down to 'really solid work', they all 'worked hard, hard'. The Drawing Examiner on an early visit was 'very pleased with everything shown him', and the HMI's first report on the Standards part of the school noted: 'This school has done very good work during the first six months of its existence ... It is a great pleasure to be able to congratulate them on the success which the establishment of this school has met with.'

After just a year Westaway was persuaded to become a sub-inspector for the Science and Art Department, and was replaced as headmaster by Frederick Pickles, a prize-winning graduate of Edinburgh University who had previously taught in higher grade schools and pupil teacher centres. His sister joined the staff too. The school really took shape under their guidance, and while they constantly strove for higher academic standards from both staff and pupils, there was never any question but that St George was a local school, serving the ordinary children of that particular community. Tributes upon Mr Pickles' retirement in 1929 stressed his 'deep and live sympathy for the underdog' and his determination that the school should 'never sacrifice the average pupil to the brilliant'. Just a month into his first term, Mr Pickles declared a half-day holiday to celebrate the opening of the first electric tramway in Bristol, from Old Market to St George, and the school helped to organise a tea for the needy of the district on that occasion.[20] At Christmas, the school's new orchestra put on a concert, which was 'a splendid success. Albert Hall packed. Audience enthusiastic.' A sports' fund was started, football, hockey and cricket matches were arranged between forms and against other schools, all the children had their photograph taken (a novel experience for many poorer children) and the appeal for donations to a library and museum was favourably received both by the children, who 'heartily responded', and by such local notables as Sir W.H. Wills, MP, who gave some books.[21] Almost every one of these initiatives represented an innovation in the neighbourhood, ensuring that St George School's influence extended beyond the classrooms of its pupils into the cultural and social life of the surrounding community.

Meanwhile the serious work of the school continued. Frederick Pickles persevered with his large classes and his inexperienced staff, worrying that 'some of the teachers find it very difficult to get out of the old rut of working for mere results, hence in certain classes there is a lamentable deficiency in thinking power'. But Inspectors Buckmaster and Tutton were 'extremely pleased' with what they saw on a surprise visit in late 1895, the latter observing that 'the school was perhaps the best in his large district', and at the end of that school year, 'their delight at the work accomplished in this first year' was noted. The organised science school which comprised the senior part of the school was developing well too. At the start of the school year in 1896 'many of the boys who thought of leaving are staying on' into the second year of the course, and the first Science and Art Department report could hardly have been more glowing: 'This new school has made excellent progress ... the buildings, equipment, teaching and discipline are alike of an exceptionally high order.' The grant statistics drawn up by the headmasters of 52 of the larger organised schools of science showed that St George was placed first in Great Britain for physics and for 'general work and equipment', and second for chemistry. The quickly established reputation of the school, as well as its novelty, attracted a steady stream of visitors – MPs, members of the Bristol School Board and Technical Instruction Committee, and delegates from other schools and areas – to the extent that the headmaster found that 'this "dropping in" of visitors is becoming rather a nuisance'.

On 1 January 1898 the Bristol School Board took over responsibility for St George Higher Grade School and showed every intention of developing this new style of education. It had already decided that Merrywood Board School should develop into a higher grade school and plans were well advanced for a brand new higher grade school at Fairfield Road. Teachers' salaries were increased, 50 extra free scholarships funded and parents required to sign an undertaking to keep their children at school for a fixed period of time or forfeit £2. St George School itself was flourishing. The various inspectors' reports were extremely favourable: most subjects were 'excellent' or 'well taught', English subjects 'left little to be desired' and the overall standards 'reflect great credit on the School'. Two pupils had matriculated for London University in the first division and 19 students passed the city's pupil teacher entrance examination, and in 1900 St George was recognised as a pupil teacher centre in its own right. In just six years, the school had accomplished an enormous amount, including, in that year, heading the Science and Art Department grant per capita list for the entire country with £6 7s 6d out of a possible £6 10s 0d for each of its 162 pupils, a remarkable record for a relatively small school serving a limited and impoverished area.

MERRYWOOD HIGHER GRADE SCHOOL

Bedminster was another fast-growing industrial suburb of Bristol, separated from the rest of the city by the River Avon. Formerly part of

Somerset, its population more than doubled in the 30 years to 1891, when it reached 54,194, and was predominantly lower-middle and working class. Bedminster men made up the larger proportion of the 3,000 or so miners employed in the Bristol coalfield and the district became home to Robinsons, the big paper bag and cardboard box manufacturer, Wills and the Imperial Tobacco Company, breweries, a tannery and numerous smaller concerns. Workers in Bedminster were not unaffected by the industrial unrest which swept through Bristol during the 1890s, the miners being particularly active. A long strike during which there was a symbolic march to the workhouse, ended only when funds ran out in 1893. A branch of the Socialist Society was formed in that year and in the first municipal election after the boundary extension of 1898, the district elected one of Bristol's four Labour councillors. With a total rateable value proportionately lower even than St George's, Bedminster was a poor area, yet it was noted for its educational aspirations: Patrick Cumin, visiting on behalf of the Newcastle Commission in 1861, had been surprised to find that very few children in the area received no education, and left Bedminster believing that the 'working classes take as much interest in their children as their superiors in rank'.[22]

In 1893–94, the Bristol School Board was planning a new elementary and infants' school in Bedminster.[23] No doubt conscious of the distance between that district and the secondary schools of the city, and probably influenced too by the activities of the neighbouring St George School Board, it was decided to create a big multi-purpose school to serve the whole area, with scope and facilities to develop its higher work should the demand arise. Costing nearly £17,000, Merrywood School was planned for 1,167 children altogether, including 420 in the Senior Mixed (potential higher grade) department. It was to be 'staffed with specially qualified teachers', offering 'a curriculum in advance of that usually found in ordinary elementary schools', with 'classrooms set apart for Standard VII and Ex-Standard VII scholars' and a 'properly-fitted Science Lecture room and Cookery Room'.

Merrywood was formally opened on 21 January 1896 under headmaster William Crank, a non-graduate trained teacher, and Miss Owen. Within six months of the school opening, as anticipated, Mr Crank notified the School Board that he would soon have about 60 children who had passed Standard VII, and he proposed forming a Science and Art Class with a new 'Special Teacher' to teach elementary drawing, first stage mathematics and science, perhaps chemistry or mechanics. He favoured those particular subjects 'because the work in the standards leads up to such a course', which is an interesting assertion that the Education

Department's Standards led smoothly to the Science and Art Department's courses, rather than being as ill-planned and disjointed as was often alleged. The School Board responded swiftly, advertising for a specialist for 'Merrywood Upper Standard School', who should be a certificated master with science qualifications and preferably French and shorthand, and who would be paid £100 rising annually to £150. The Board made a fortunate appointment in James Steger, who went on to gain a London University BSc and become a FCS and, in the 1920s, headteacher of one of Bristol's central schools.

The new class got under way early in 1897 and soon received a vote of confidence from the HMI and congratulations from the School Board, which gave Mr Crank a rise in salary, and speedily agreed to his suggestion that a fuller higher grade department should be developed. From May 1897 the school was to be called 'Merrywood Higher Grade Board School'. It settled very quickly into a successful routine of work. In 1898 the science classes were found to be 'admirably taught', although a chemistry laboratory was urgently needed, and student numbers rose to 75. Further staff were appointed, including a graduate science master who had studied at Jena and Bristol Universities. In 1900 the school's pupils gained 67 first-class and 43 second-class passes in the Science and Art Department examinations, the school was recognised as a centre for pupil teachers, and it was said that in general 'the pupils had no difficulty in getting good situations'.

However, behind this promising facade of development, Merrywood School was on a far less assured footing. In offering a predominantly elementary education, but with undefined potential at the top end, it hit the Education Department's weakest ideological spot. The Department did not like this development but had no alternative suggestions; it had no idea what to do with children of school age (and older) who had passed the Standards. It offered no course of study and no funding, and when school boards found their own solution, it had no more idea what to do with Science and Art classes operating within its schools. It was Merrywood's misfortune to be tackling the problem at the time when the Department was becoming anxious about the implications of its earlier 'blind-eye' policy towards such developments.

The matter first came to the fore in October 1896 when the Bristol School Board asked for a fee of 6d per week (with exemption for poor children) for the new senior class at Merrywood. Over the next three-and-a-half years, all the possible implications received a full airing within the central office. Repeatedly, in this as in other matters, the Education Department found itself in the position of raising objections, scouring its archives for precedents, inviting learned opinions from within the Department, and then conceding the point, with remarks like 'I do not think our case is a strong one' and 'We seem ... to be more or less committed to allowing this.' The Merrywood problem even reached the elevated desk of Sir George Kekewich on three separate occasions. One official warned – rather ominously in view of subsequent events – that 'it will be for the Auditor to consider whether the expenditure of the Board upon the Class described is legitimate', but another thought that as 'the class in question forms but a very small part of the Merrywood Board School', it was probably alright.

In 1899 the Bristol Board sought to bring Merrywood in line with St George by introducing a 5d per week fee with 25 per cent free places on the basis of a competitive examination. Supported by HMI Elliott, it argued that 'many parents ... prefer to send their children to a private fee School, where the tuition is often far from efficient rather than to a School at which education is free'. It observed that children came from considerable distances because of the higher grade character of the school, 'passing on their way Schools which they might attend, and crowding Merrywood'. The Education Department was sceptical and Sir George Kekewich alleged that Bristol's intention behind charging a fee at Merrywood was to make it 'a Social Higher Grade School'. In a way he was right in that one of the School Board's motives for having a fee was to attract the more aspiring and committed parents. But the aim was rather to encourage maximum use of the school's costly facilities and thereby raise standards of achievement, than to exclude children simply because they were poor. Eventually the Department agreed to a fee of 3d per week, with 25 per cent free places, although with the warning that 'this approval may be withdrawn at any time'. However, the approval that Merrywood most wanted – the recognition as an organised science school which it had requested in 1898 – never materialised, and the school had to face the turmoil of the next few years without the added status which that designation would have brought.

FAIRFIELD ROAD HIGHER GRADE SCHOOL

Fairfield Road, the third of Bristol's trio of higher grade schools, was created to serve the fast-growing population to the north of the city centre. This was less a defined suburb than either St George or Bedminster, but rather an area of residential development spreading northwards along the Gloucester Road and taking in the districts of Montpelier, St Andrews,

Bishopston and Ashley Down. The inhabitants were mainly lower-middle class: small shopkeepers and white-collar workers such as clerks, supervisors, commercial travellers and minor officials. There was little manufacturing industry and relatively few unskilled workers. Within reach of the city centre and bordering middle-class Redland and Cotham, this district was not totally cut off from secondary school provision, and Colston's Girls' School and the Merchant Venturers' College, and even the Grammar School and Redland High School for Girls, could claim it within their natural catchment areas.

However, such schools were too costly for many families with educational aspirations, and in 1896 the Bristol School Board decided on a bold solution. There would be a new multi-purpose school in the district of Montpelier for 1,054 children of all ages, including a higher grade department.[24] Objections immediately came from the Bristol branch of the Private Schools Association and from three local vicars, but a Trades Council survey of north Bristol found that only 84 people opposed a new school while 577 favoured the higher grade school idea. The School Board had to resort to compulsory purchase to acquire the site it wanted, a difficult decision for a body dependent on the goodwill of the ratepayers, but one applauded by the Trades Council. After criticisms that the 'elevation was too ornate', the building plans were amended, a loan of £18,000 sanctioned by the Education Department, and higher grade schools in Birmingham and Manchester were visited to inspect their furnishings and fittings. The post of headmaster was advertised at a salary of £275 rising annually to £325, to be responsible for a school of science, a senior mixed department and a junior mixed department. Applicants must be trained, certificated and university graduates – the first time the Bristol School Board had so specified – and preferably have experience of teaching in a higher grade school or school of science. From a field of 48 applicants, Mr J.E. Pickles, MA, BSc (Birmingham), a lecturer at Birmingham Technical School and brother of Frederick and Miss Pickles at St George School, was appointed, with Miss Kate Coburn, BSc, as senior assistant mistress.

The opening of Fairfield Road School was planned for 1 November 1898, with a formal ceremony by Sir George Kekewich to follow, timed for 7.30p.m. so that manual workers could attend. The occasion received full coverage in the sympathetic part of the local press. Sir George told his Bristol audience that higher grade schools 'perhaps in former days were a luxury, but that now they were something like a necessity ... such high class elementary schools ... occupied an important place in the educational organisation of the country'. He was delighted that parents 'were taking a greater interest in the education of their children and desired a higher and better education for them', and that the school boards had stepped in to try 'to bridge the gap'. He even compared their willingness to 'undertake a duty which was not imposed upon them by statute' to his own tendency 'to dabble in matters which were not his business, as they knew his business was concerned with public elementary schools only'. The Bristol School Board could hardly have had higher or more explicit approval for its new venture.

The school, which had ended up costing over £24,000, admitted no fewer than 1,001 children on the first day. The School Board clerk and the Board's inspector were both present to help the teachers deal with the 'immense number of children', and an eye-witness, writing approvingly of the school's laboratories, workshops and drawing-rooms, recorded that the school was filled immediately after opening. The entrance examination for 175 scholarships (100 boys, 75 girls, although in subsequent years the proportions were equal) had attracted so many candidates that extra superintendents had to be employed. By any standards, Fairfield Road School had got off to a very promising start.

However well the new school seemed to be going, it was a matter of financial urgency to gain recognition as an organised school of science. The School Board was so confident that this was merely a formality that it decided to carry the cost (£4,800) of the necessary extra equipment and teaching staff, and authorised Fairfield Road to begin work as a school of science immediately with 78 pupils under instruction in Science and Art Department subjects. But, in December 1898, Sir John Gorst formally refused Fairfield's application, apparently influenced by an approach from the Merchant Venturers about unfair competition from the cheaper school. The Bristol School Board was horrified. Conservative Dr Cook argued strongly that there could be no question of overlapping between the two schools, since Fairfield Road had been 'full from the day of opening and a careful enquiry had shown that not a single student could be traced as having come from any other higher grade school' (that is, Colston's and the Merchant Venturers'). A conference convened to discuss educational provision in Bristol failed to achieve a compromise, the city's MPs were contacted,[25] and the School Board continued to stress to the Education Department that Fairfield was at least two miles from any possible rival institution, and that with 'houses being erected in every direction' in the neighbourhood, 300 children had had to be turned away.

Yet, by the beginning of 1900, the School Board's confidence was seriously undermined. That Fairfield Road – newly built and equipped, well staffed and full of pupils – could not achieve the only recognition which would have given it a future as more than just an elementary school, alerted them to the fact that far more was going on at Whitehall than they, or almost anyone else, yet knew. The Board of Education's behaviour at that time was characterised by procrastination, responses containing inaccuracies and contradictions, and a refusal to meet and talk. It must all have been extremely disturbing to a local authority which had just taken on a big long-term debt in order to carry out what it believed to be a policy favourably regarded by the central authority. This guaranteed that what was obviously a popular and much needed school, like a number of others around the country, started life under a cloud of uncertainty.

A PERIOD OF TURMOIL: THE END OF THE SCHOOL BOARD, 1900–3

The members of the Bristol School Board became increasingly disconcerted by the unexplained manipulation of events by the Board of Education which gradually became apparent. The year 1900 was something of a turning point. First came the Code of that year, which introduced the 'block grant' principle, but actually reduced the grant available to older pupils and pupil teachers in ways which the Bristol Board believed 'will operate to prevent scholars remaining at school'. In the course of a specially convened meeting, the chairman expressed his biggest worry that 'in Bristol, if their older scholars left them to-morrow, where they could go to continue the education they had started in the board's schools'. He quoted Sir John Gorst's opinion that the reduction in income of the higher grade schools 'would not be considerable' and referred to Joseph Chamberlain's promise to the Birmingham School Board that 'something would be done for the higher grade schools'.[26] The Bristol Teachers' Association begged that the regulations be suspended, and argued for the creation of 'a properly constituted Local Authority for the control of Science and Art and Technical Instruction in the City of Bristol', to consist of a quarter drawn from the Technical Instruction Committee, a quarter from the School Board, a quarter representing the voluntary sector, and a quarter of co-opted members.[27] The Bristol School Board was pleased, however, to be empowered to raise the school-leaving age for most children to 14,[28] which meant, of course, that many more children would complete all the Standards and want something more.

The second important new development, the Higher Elementary School Minute, was issued on 6 April 1900. This introduced to English education an entirely new type of school, and one which had few recognisable antecedents within the existing system. It was to offer a four-year course of instruction, with timetables subject to the Board of Education's approval and a 'sufficiency of science instruction, both practical and theoretical', and with an absolute upper age limit of 15. Entrants were to have had their previous schooling in public elementary schools, and must start at the beginning of the course. The new schools were to be strictly separate from ordinary elementary schools, but nevertheless firmly under the umbrella of the Elementary Codes. The Bristol School Board approved much of the Minute but opposed the restrictions on entrants and, above all, the fixing of 15 as the upper age limit. It thereby correctly identified the single clause that made all else in the Minute inappropriate for the aspiring higher grade schools, and left the school boards wondering if this was indeed the Board of Education's resolution of the years of uncertainty. To be on the safe side, the Bristol Board submitted a provisional application for its three schools to be recognised, for while it did not much like the Higher Elementary School proposal, it had no idea what the alternative was. But it very quickly became apparent that the Higher Elementary School Minute was not the eagerly awaited solution. With the Board of Education adding fresh criteria to deter hopeful applicants – including, for example, a maximum size of 300 pupils, much smaller than most higher grade schools – the applications for all three Bristol schools were withdrawn at the end of July.

During 1901 the pace of change quickened and the levels of anxiety and anger rose. Numerous deputations were planned and letters were flying round the country, with the Association of School Boards alerting members to the increasingly antagonistic attitude shown by the Board of Education. Early in the year, the Queen's Court confirmed the ruling made by district auditor T.B. Cockerton after a carefully engineered case challenging the London School Board's expenditure of the rates on non-elementary education. The news of the Cockerton judgment was relayed officially in a circular letter from the Board of Education on 1 March 1901, drawing attention to the 'illegal application of the School Fund to Science and Art Schools or Classes'. The Bristol School Board responded with a strongly worded statement about this 'national calamity', pointing out that the 'Higher Grades are a natural development of the Elementary School system; that their establishment by School Boards was encouraged and fostered by the Government Departments.'[29] Of the three Bristol MPs[30] who acknowledged receipt of the School Board's statement, Mr Charles Hobhouse took it particularly seriously, offering his help, and arguing that 'the case of the Higher Grade School at St George [in his constituency] is so important that some special effort might be made by the Board to preserve its continued existence and activity'. A joint deputation of the School Board, the Trades Council and the Headmasters' Association was organised, and Bristol also agreed to join the deputation planned by the London School Board, which was brusquely informed that 'the Lord President ... does not see his way clear to receive a deputation'.

Next came news of Gorst's Education Bill, which although unsuccessful, made explicit the government's intention to downgrade the school boards. It extended the status quo for a year, until 31 July 1902, but now the Technical Instruction authorities were firmly in control and no new school board developments would be financed. The Bristol Teachers' Association expressed its opposition, and a protest meeting at Broadmead School, which attracted a mostly working-class audience, together with Liberals, trade unionists, Free Churchmen and School Board members, agreed that it was essential for the education of the working class that higher grade schools remained under the authority of the school boards. It strongly opposed specially elected school boards being told what to do by mere sub-committees of local councils. The School Board drafted another petition, asserting that 'a Board which had successfully cared for 60,000 elementary children could be expected to look after 2,000 pupils attending Secondary schools'[31] and calling for a 'really comprehensive measure' of reorganisation. Bristol was not the only area to feel so strongly, and a heated and wide-ranging debate in the House of Commons showed an awareness of the full implications of the legislation.

The publication of the 1902 Education Bill brought forward more desperate protests. The Bristol School Board could see some things to approve, but felt strongly that the school boards had 'immense and valuable experience' and, being directly elected and for education only, were 'more in touch with the needs of their respective districts and feel more of the responsibility of meeting them'. Between March and December 1902, over 80 protest meetings were held in Bristol, national figures like Acland, Asquith and Macnamara came to speak, and Bristolians travelled to neighbouring towns and villages to address meetings. Some of this protest was directed against the religious settlement – the Bishop was mobbed in Two Mile Hill near St George – but the denominational issue was much less controversial in Bristol than in some other areas. However, the implications for democratic control of education were spotted by a variety of bodies. There were protests from the boot and shoe workers, and from the Bristol branch of the National Education League, and a big conference of representatives from trade unions all over the south-west called for secondary education for workers' children up to the age of 18. Among over 100 letters to the local press, one from the Bristol South Women's Liberal Association suggested:

> the Government really did not wish the people to be educated. It was beginning to realise that a power was rising up through the education of the people which, if they did not mind, they would find too much for them.

The Education Bill featured in sermons, editorials, articles, pamphlets and posters, and was a major issue in the municipal elections of November 1902. The Liberals gained ground on the Tory majority, and 'a sitting Liberal who declined to oppose the Bill was defeated by another Liberal'.[32]

During these three years of turmoil, the School Board had to keep its schools running, staffed and equipped, with absolutely no assurance of what lay ahead. The Board spent its last year quietly winding up its affairs, and its last meeting, on 30 March 1903, checking the final accounts and paying warm tributes to its most loyal servants. An evening reception at the Pupil Teacher Centre was attended by many former members, who listened to speeches of thanks and farewell. They could reflect on ten years' successful work in developing higher grade education. The Board had inherited one and created two higher grade schools, and all the signs were that they would flourish conspicuously. No other district of the city cried out for special educational facilities quite as urgently as St George, Bedminster and north Bristol had done, but it is clear that the Bristol Board had plans to upgrade some of its board schools in more favoured locations and had, in 1898, appointed a second inspector to take care of all higher grade work.[33]

In Bristol's decision to commit itself to higher grade education, there are three points of significance. The first is that the Bristol School Board members were not natural lawbreakers. There is no question of them setting up schools in deliberate defiance of the central authority, or of doing so surreptitiously, or to gain prestige or bigger grants. They were far from playing any sort of pioneering role, and they made sure that their higher grade work was as legal as it could be. They were in constant communication with all the right authorities, their applications for loans were approved, the various inspectors reported favourably, and Kekewich personally showed his interest in their major enterprise, Fairfield Road. The work was always to be financed mainly by Science and Art Department grants, and Bristol could prove that in the case of a well-established and successful higher grade school like St George, far from being an illegal charge on the rates, the non-elementary part of the school actually earned a little more than it cost. Until quite late on, the fact that responses from London were often belated, unhelpful or contradictory was seen as evidence of inefficiency at the top rather than any secretive attempt to hamper the progress of higher grade education. There was therefore all the more reason for the School Board to be dynamic and positive.

The second main point is that Bristol's higher grade schools were quite definitely a response to a need. Despite the efforts of an unusually united and enlightened group of educated people, and the city's network of old endowed schools and newer proprietary ones (none of which seemed to be suffering unduly from the higher grade school competition, despite the dire warnings of their heads and governors), the supply of secondary schools did not meet the demand for post-elementary schooling. Each of the School Board's higher grade schools came about in different circumstances and assumed a different form, demonstrating a flexibility and responsiveness to local needs which was to be conspicuously lacking in the Board of Education's work after 1902. And, in spite of the fees, the parental undertaking, homework requirements and so on, these large, neighbourhood, all-age schools were full and growing; it is safe to predict that, given a favourable future, they would have succeeded in keeping an ever widening social range of children and families interested in pursuing education to higher levels.

The third judgment is that the Bristol School Board seems to have gone about its new task sensibly and professionally. School boards were increasingly in communication with each other, seeking advice and exchanging ideas, and the Bristol Board forestalled a number of possible problems by consulting or visiting others which had preceded it in higher grade school development. There were, of course, some criticisms of the School Board's higher grade school policy, mainly on the grounds of cost, but the general tone of newspaper opinion was of appreciation for the service rendered to the city by the School Board, coupled with concern over the muddle and restrictions in which it had to operate. As far as one can judge, Bristol's higher grade schools were efficiently and enthusiastically run, well staffed, and full of children studying a wide range of subjects to a variety of levels. In 1903 the oldest of these schools was just nine years old, but they had already established a clear identity in the city, filling a gap which no other body could or would occupy, and from there, 'reaching out into territory hitherto monopolised by the middle and upper classes'.[34]

NOTES

1. This section draws on J. Latimer, *The Annals of Bristol in the Nineteenth Century* (Bristol: W. and F. Morgan, 1887); J. Latimer, *The Annals of Bristol in the Nineteenth Century (concluded) 1887–1900* (Bristol: William George, 1902); B. Little, *The City and County of Bristol* (London: Werner Laurie, 1954); N.G.L. Hammond (ed.), *Centenary Essays on Clifton College* (Bristol: J.W. Arrowsmith, 1962); Hill, *Bristol Grammar School;* E.T. Morgan, *A History of the Bristol Cathedral School* (Bristol: J.W. Arrowsmith, 1913); M.G. Shaw, *Redland High School* (Bristol: J.W. Arrowsmith, 1932); J. Wright and Co.'s *Bristol and Clifton Directory* (Bristol: J. Wright, various years); Kelly's *Directory of Bristol* (Bristol: Kelly's, various years).

2. S. Fletcher, *Feminists and Bureaucrats: A Study in the Development of Girls' Education in the Nineteenth Century* (Cambridge: Cambridge University Press, 1980), p. 86. Fletcher depicts, F.G. (later Sir Joshua) Fitch as the oustanding man among the Endowed Schools Commission's five Assistant Commissioners; a former elementary schoolteacher and London University graduate, Fitch was principal of Borough Road Training College and a leading HM Inspector.

3. 'Whisky money' was the term commonly applied to the surplus funds originally raised to compensate publicans whose licences had been withdrawn, which the Local Taxation Act of 1890 placed in the hands of local authorities to use at their discretion either in relief of rates or to support technical education. Stimulated by Technical Instruction Acts in 1889 and 1891, many local authorities chose the second option and Technical Instruction or Education Committees were the main beneficiaries.

4. The Merchant Venturers' Society was an ancient mercantile organisation which had acquired great wealth and influence in the city, especially the Clifton area. Its membership often overlapped with the City Council and had a long tradition of philanthropic enterprise.

5. Certain names (Percival, Fry, Winkworth, Wills, Fox) crop up repeatedly in connection with educational activity in Bristol; their cohesiveness was presumably why they were able to oppose Fitch so effectively. H.E. Meller in *Leisure and the Changing City, 1870–1914* (London: Routledge & Kegan Paul, 1976), looked at relationships within the Clifton group centred around the Reverend Percival (Headmaster of Clifton College), which she saw as a paternalistic interdenominational elite.

6. Early agreement on Lewis Fry's syllabus had removed religious controversy from the board schools.

7. Bristol School Board, Minutes, 2 February 1872.

8. Bristol Technical Instruction Committee, Minutes, (1891–1903); and L.H. Clare, 'Change and Conflict in Bristol Public Education 1895–1905' (University of Bristol MLitt thesis, 1975).

9. One of the NUT's most vocal national leaders, Dr T.J. Macnamara MP, was a former Bristol board school headteacher. R. Betts, 'Dr Macnamara and the Education Act of 1902', *Journal of Educational Administration and History*, XXV, 2 (1993).

10. Described by S. Bryher, *An Account of the Labour and Socialist Movement in Bristol* (Bristol: Bristol Labour Weekly, 1931), pp. 16, 19–20, 38–43; see also S. Mullen, 'The Bristol Socialist Society 1885–1914', B. Whitfield, 'Trade Unionism in Bristol 1910–1926', and E. Malos, 'Bristol Women in Action 1839–1919', all in Bristol Broadsides (Co-op) Ltd, *Bristol's Other History* (Bristol: Bristol Broadsides, 1983).

11. Quoted in F.K.D. Wood, 'The Beginnings of Municipal Secondary Education in the City and County of Bristol (1895–1919)' (University of Bristol MEd thesis, 1968), p. 10.

12. Hugh Holmes Gore was a solicitor, a Christian Socialist, and a former pupil of Clifton College, who lived in the slums and dressed in robes and sandals. 'Universally respected' as a supporter of the Shaftesbury Crusade and the Dings Boys' Club, he was known as 'the workers' candidate', and in 1894 had come within 100 votes of defeating Sir W.H. Wills in a parliamentary by-election in East Bristol. W.M. Eager, *Making Men. The History of Boys' Clubs and Related Movements in Great Britain* (London: University of London Press, 1953), p. 292; and Bryher, *Account*, p. 12.

13. Drawn from Little, *City*, Ch. 10; and A.J. Pugsley, *The Economic Development of Bristol* (Bristol: Bristol Times and Mirror, 1922), pp. 25–7, 37. It is thought that the boot and shoe trade originated as a pastime for disabled miners; Bristol specialised in hobnailed boots.

14. Bryher, *Account*, pp. 16–19. Every day for over a month, about 1,500 women and girls marched with arms linked from the factory gates through the city to Clifton, and on Sundays, wearing white aprons and shawls, they gathered outside various churches and chapels eliciting middle-

class support. Eventually, hours were cut (to 6.00a.m–5.30p.m.) and three paid days' holiday (Christmas, Easter and Whit) granted.

15. Malos, 'Bristol Women', p. 116; and A. Fox, *A History of the National Union of Boot and Shoe Operatives 1874–1957* (Oxford: Blackwell, 1958), pp. 138, 164, 201.

16. Bryher, *Account*, p. 65.

17. A.J. Pugsley, *The Door of Opportunity: Being an Account of Higher Education in East Bristol and Especially St George Secondary School* (Bristol: Pugsley, 1944), pp. 1–2, 7.

18. St George School Board, Minutes, 12 February 1890, 19 February 1890, 27 July 1891, 30 July 1891.

19. This early history of St George School is constructed from: PRO Ed.21/6162; St George School Board, Minutes; Bristol School Board, Minutes; Bristol School Board, School Management Committee, Minutes; Old Georgians' Society, 'St George Higher Grade School 1894–1947' (two boxes of documents and newspaper cuttings collected by W.T. Sanigar); Pugsley, *Door of Opportunity*; *The Georgian* (school magazine, from 1905), including *St George Secondary School 1894–1944 (Jubilee Number)* (1944); and St George Higher Grade and Technical School, Log Book.

20. Earlier in 1895 had occurred the biggest national lock-out of boot and shoe workers, causing acute distress and suffering until the workers gave in after six weeks; by the winter 3–4,000 operatives in east Bristol were unemployed and dependent on the revived relief fund for starving families. The same pattern of industrial dispute, unemployment and emergency relief was to be repeated in the winter of 1898. Mullen, 'Bristol Socialist', p. 51; Fox, *History of the National Union*, pp. 227–30.

21. Wills also financed a public library for the St George area.

22. *Royal Commission to enquire into The State of Popular Education in England (Newcastle Commission)* (1861), I, p. 35, III, pp. 61–2, 65.

23. This early history of Merrywood School is drawn from: PRO Ed.21/6128; Bristol School Board, Minutes; Bristol School Board, School Management Committee, Minutes; Wood, *Beginnings*. Merrywood itself has no surviving records, and it is therefore impossible to build up as complete a picture as for St George.

24. This early history of Fairfield Road School is drawn from: PRO Ed.21/6128; Bristol School Board, Minutes; Bristol School Board, School Management Committee, Minutes; Wood, *Beginnings*.

25. Sir W.H. Wills asked a question in the House of Commons and Lewis Fry approached the Science and Art Department.

26. Chamberlain was by that time in a highly equivocal position over education. For many years one of the most radical educational voices in the Liberal Party and for the nonconformists, and always extremely proud of the achievements of the Birmingham School Board, he now found himself allied to a party which held diametrically opposite views on the subject. His 'conversion' to the 1902 Act by Morant was yet to come.

27. Bristol School Board, Minutes, 30 April 1900, 28 May 1900.

28. This was by virtue of permissive powers contained in the 1900 Act. In Bristol, the Standard of total exemption went up from VI to VII and of partial exemption from IV to V.

29. Bristol School Board, Minutes, 1 March 1901, 25 March 1901.

30. Bristol had four MPs at that time: West, Sir Michael Hicks-Beach (Conservative, Chancellor of the Exchequer in Lord Salisbury's government); South, Walter Long (Unionist); East, Charles Hobhouse (Liberal); North, Sir Frederick Wills (Unionist).

31. Chairman Jarman, a Baptist minister, was so incensed by a particularly waspish criticism from Sir John Gorst that he declared, 'there is only one word in the English language that is a fitting reply to a charge like that. It is a word of three letters; a word I will not use.' Bristol School Board, Minutes, 20 May 1901; Wood, *Beginnings*, p. 39.

32. Bristol School Board, Minutes, 28 April 1902; Clare, *Change and Conflict*, pp. 174–8; *The Times*, 3 November 1902. After the Act came into force, only 250 out of 72,000 Bristol ratepayers undertook passive resistance.

33. Anglesea Place School on the edge of Clifton added French, business training and bookkeeping to the curriculum, and at Castle School, which had extra facilities like a swimming pool and had earlier accommodated the pupil teacher classes, a new headmaster was brought in with a brief to amplify the work of the upper classes and encourage the attendance of ex-Standard children.

Bristol School Board, School Management Committee, Minutes, 21 September 1897, 14 September 1898; and Special Committee, Minutes, 8 July 1898.

34. Clare, *Change and Conflict*, p. 7.

4

BRISTOL: EDUCATION COMMITTEE AND SECONDARY SCHOOLS, 1903–10

On 1 April 1903, the Bristol Education Committee assembled for the first time. Consisting of 21 city councillors and ten co-opted members, it was twice the size of the School Board, but included just nine members with school board experience, two of whom were the women whom it had, by law, to co-opt from somewhere. Like the City Council, it initially had a Conservative majority, and it chose as its chairman Dr (later Sir) Ernest Cook, a local scientist of some note, who during his seven years' experience on the School Board had generally shown a cautious attitude towards the extension of educational opportunity.[1] Avery Adams, the long-serving Clerk to the School Board, was appointed Secretary to the Education Committee after a move by the Conservatives to bring in the former Secretary to the Technical Instruction Committee was defeated. Overall, the political complexion of the new education authority was significantly different from the old one, whose increasingly radical composition has been noted. Furthermore, it has been shown that big discrepancies between the city council wards built into the new system a 'serious constitutional weakness', which meant that the Education Committee, like its master the City Council, was 'by no means as democratic as it should have been'.[2]

It did, however, share with the School Board great uncertainty as to the intentions of the Board of Education. The 1902 Education Act required only that the new local education authorities should 'supply or aid the supply of education other than elementary', and no one could have known at that stage how directive the central authority was to become in shaping secondary education. An early indicator was the new Pupil Teacher Regulations, which made all recognised secondary schools eligible places of instruction for pupil teacher scholarship holders, a change which not only seriously undermined the status of Bristol's Pupil Teacher Centre, but permitted pupil teachers to attend schools about which neither the Bristol Education Committee nor the Board of Education knew much at all. It was the first sign of one of the recurring themes of the early years of the new arrangements: endowed and proprietary schools, whose virtual immunity from inspection and public control had become a major cause for concern during the 1890s, were very readily accepted as efficient by the Board of Education. Those in Bristol achieved recognition without difficulty,[3] and in all cases correspondence was carried on primarily between the respective governors and headteacher and the Board of Education. The Education Committee was thus assigned a role in the background, finding itself in the somewhat embarrassing position of having to request basic statistical information about fees, numbers of pupils and teachers' qualifications from schools over which it was supposed to hold some authority.

The results of this fact-finding exercise occasioned the establishment of the major Coordination Sub-Committee, whose guiding principle was firmly stated to be 'that existing facilities should not be lessened, nor the cost to the students increased'.[4] Welding together the assortment of educational institutions proved to be a formidable task. It was not helped by the mass of regulations, memoranda and reports which emanated from the Board of Education, turning the essentially permissive legislation of the years 1899–1902 into something very different. However, the members of the new Bristol Education Committee meeting in 1903 must have felt that at last, after four or five years of extreme uncertainty and frustration, the central authority had expressed its confidence in their capacity to organise the education best suited to their city. Among their more significant responsibilities were the three higher grade schools, whose past battles for official acceptance were to prove to have been mere rehearsals for what lay ahead.

ST GEORGE COUNCIL SECONDARY SCHOOL

The oldest and most successful of the three higher grade schools, St George had the strongest claim to be upgraded to secondary status.[5] Inspection reports were good, grant earnings continued to rise, and the school recorded its tenth success in London University matriculation, and its fifth Inter BSc In 1903, plans were drawn up for a new art room, physics laboratory, domestic science centre, dining room and gymnasium, and Mr Pickles, whose salary was raised to £400 per annum, lobbied hard for more generous scholarship provision. Following the Secondary School Regulations of 1904, Bristol Education Committee submitted a revised application for the recognition of St George, setting out the details which so qualified it. The school then numbered 566 children, of whom 260 were in the secondary school course, and Mr Pickles had devised an entrance examination which would be a 'better test of mental capacity'. New appointments had been made, so that the teaching staff in 1904 comprised 12 graduates (nine men, three women) and seven others (two men, five women) mainly in craft and practical subjects. St George School worked for 44 weeks a year and still charged a fee of 5d per week.

The Board of Education objected to this last piece of information, arguing that such a low fee was 'open to serious objection on general educational grounds' and that £3 per annum was the minimum acceptable. It was willing for pupils of 'intellectual promise' to be exempted after an examination, but stated that these should 'in no circumstances exceed 25% of the total in the school'. Bristol Education Committee replied in strong terms. Without St George School, they said, the education of many public elementary school children over the last nine years 'must have ceased at a much earlier age', and a substantial rise in the fee would undoubtedly keep out 'a large proportion of eligible scholars whose parents are unable to pay the higher fee'. This would be an 'educational calamity' since St George was the 'only school in Bristol giving a course of Secondary Education at a fee within the reach of the industrial classes whom it was intended to serve'. The Committee affirmed its commitment to encourage 'children to prolong their school life, and to increase the number of those pupils passing from Elementary to Secondary Schools', a standpoint which it felt 'should have the unqualified support of your Board'. The Board decided to wait for the results of the school's first full inspection, scheduled for February 1905.

Four HMIs spent three days at St George Higher Grade School and their consequent report, like others of its kind, contained much factual information about the school, as well as expressing a number of the ideals about secondary schooling held by the Board of Education and its inspectorate. On the factual side, the pupils consisted of 245 boys and girls, mostly aged 13, 14 or 15, and nearly all from Bristol. In the categorisation labelled 'Class in Life', the largest single group came from artisan homes (94), followed by clerks (60) and retail traders (37), with merchants and bankers (26), professional and independent (16), farmers (5), deceased (5) and elementary teachers (2) completing the total. This represented a heavier weighting towards the lower end of the occupational list than most higher grade schools.

The building was found to be more or less adequate, if rather dirty and neglected,[6] although the absence of an assembly hall, library, reading room, swimming bath and gymnasium was commented upon, as was the fact that 'there are no racquet or fives courts'. The HMIs' mention of those two sports vividly illustrates the social gulf between them and the St George area. Of most concern, however, was the fact that the school library, the playground and the lavatories were shared by all pupils. There had been 'no attempt to separate the Secondary from the Elementary School classrooms, it being necessary in some cases to pass through the classrooms of the one School to reach those of the other'. The HMIs looked forward to the time when the buildings would be used exclusively by a secondary school of 300–350 children. This determination not only to create separate secondary schools but to prevent all contact between their pupils and elementary children was to be reiterated obsessively over the next few years, and was one of the 'new' features which most education committees had to learn from scratch. Close links between elementary and higher grade schools and the 'end-on' nature of the resulting education were intrinsic to the old system, and the local authorities found it hard to grasp why it was so damaging for older pupils to mix with younger ones, who were very likely to be relatives, neighbours or friends.

Turning to the staff, the HMIs found that, although the headmaster's qualifications and experience were considerable, 'it must be noted that he has not been connected with any Secondary School, and can hardly be expected to give his School the impress of Secondary School traditions and ideals'. The rest of the staff were well qualified and enthusiastic, but too scientifically biased and experienced 'almost exclusively in Higher Grade Schools'. The suggested solutions were to raise the headmaster's salary so that the school could 'secure the services of a first-rate Secondary School Head Master', and to recruit to the staff in future 'a more literary element and as far as possible Public School experience', a comment which is in line with what Tropp has described as 'a general tendency for inspectors to urge the introduction of teachers with direct knowledge of grammar or public schools (preferably Oxford or Cambridge graduates). They were most insistent on this in the higher grade and municipal secondary schools.'[7]

Often appearing in HMI reports on former higher grade schools, this general desire to transform the teaching staff contrasted sharply with the acknowledgment of a high standard of actual teaching. At St George, this was 'of a very high order of merit ... the teachers are familiar with modern methods, are much in earnest and on the whole successful in interesting their classes to a unanimous degree'. The HMIs criticised the excessive amount of science teaching and urged that more time should be given to English and French, and also to Latin, since in a school of 250 there must be 'many' wanting to learn Latin or Greek; again, the disparity between the priorities of the inspectors and the realities of life in St George, even for its most capable children, is striking. In the absence of Latin, English, in which 'some very good work is being done', would have to be the basis of the grammatical and literary training of the pupils and must therefore 'be severe, classical, and, if such a word may be used, scientific'. Among lessons visited, history was 'admirably taught', geography was 'excellent in every detail', French 'decidedly good', chemistry of a 'truly advanced character', physics 'likewise excellent', mathematics 'little fault to find' and moral and religious instruction 'in all respects satisfactory'.

The HMIs' recommendations included more care with writing, which helps to 'mould the character of a child', and more attention to mending, darning and patching in needlework, which was both useful and 'has a moral and educational side also'. A more suitable science course should be devised for the girls, rather than the one which 'is largely a duplicate of the boys' course'; the inspectors had been surprised to see fourth-year girls working on advanced electrical measurements and felt that, unless they were planning to become telephonists, their time would be 'better spent on domestic Science or Hygiene'. This compilation of curricular recommendations reveals some very muddled thinking on the part of the inspectors, centring especially on their obvious uncertainty about what kind of child went to a municipal secondary school and why. Drawing on what they knew to be important in a public or high-school education and on what they believed to be the needs of the lower-middle and working classes, they produced a peculiar amalgam of the classics plus darning, and fives plus hygiene.

In conclusion, the inspectors returned to their opening theme. While acknowledging that the discipline of the school and the conduct of the scholars were faultless, and that the teachers were 'a loyal and dutiful body ... who do their utmost to make the school the best of its kind', they were nevertheless unhappy. There was 'a great amount of public spirit in the School' and yet 'the general tone can hardly be regarded as that of a Secondary School', nor was it 'easy to see where the traditions and ideals of a Secondary School could come from'. As if anticipating the likely bemused response to this, they attempted to explain themselves by saying:

> the Secondary School spirit is more easily recognized than defined; if it is a spirit that is produced on the one hand by the teacher's readiness to give full weight to the importance of the individual pupil, and on the other the pupil's generous recognition of his duty to sacrifice himself for his School, it is safe to say that there is not enough of that spirit at the St George's Secondary School.

Translated into practical recommendations, this meant shortening the school day, since 41.5 hours per week was too much; introducing that 'excellent thing', a compulsory school cap for boys and badge for girls; starting the day with a morning assembly for the whole school; and rather more vaguely, 're-organisation of the school on public school lines'.

The St George School staff were not happy with the inspection report. Mr Pickles found them 'much depressed at certain references made to them' and told the Higher Education Committee that he had 'tried to my best to cheer them up, but I cannot remove a certain uneasy feeling'. It must indeed have been disheartening for the staff to be so warmly applauded for their skill and dedication by the sternest of critics and yet to be told repeatedly that only some other kind of teacher could really do the job properly. They had nearly all gained the highest academic and professional qualifications accessible to them, and the fact that the school consistently earned grants so high that the Board of Education came to regard them as excessive, must have added weight to their belief that they were effective teachers. There was no way, as the Board perfectly well knew, that such teachers could acquire loftier literary (that is Oxbridge) qualifications or public school experience, any more than could the pupils in their classes, the aspiring teachers of the future. So they were all in essence being told that although they were the cream produced by their kind of education and among the most successful members of their communities, they would not be welcome in their own school in the future.

Surprisingly, the question of raising the fees was not mentioned by the inspectors and soon after, in response to a House of Commons question from Dr Macnamara, the Board of Education confirmed its continued sanction of the 5d-per-week fee. Perhaps the visiting HMIs had been influenced by seeing for themselves the poverty of the neighbourhood. St George School was thus one of a tiny handful of schools in the country to resist the minimum £3-per-annum charge and to continue to express its fee in pence per week.[8] In June 1905, the really important decision arrived: recognition as a secondary school for the year 1904–5, at the higher rate of grant payable to former Division A schools. For the first time in its life the school had an official status.

However, the HMI assigned to the Bristol region, Mr Theodosius, nursed an unusually strong antagonism towards the higher grade schools and continued to pose real difficulties for St George. In a long private letter to Chief Secondary Inspector Fletcher in May 1907, his frustration poured out. 'Frankly', he opened, 'there is no case whatever for St George's getting such an enormous grant except the fact that they have had it ever since they were Cockertonised', and continued 'it was publicly boasted some years ago that this school with its fee of 5d a week plus the Board's grant contributed £100 a year to the rates of Bristol. How such a state of things could have been allowed to exist, I cannot understand, but probably the Board knew nothing about it'. Certainly, St George School's consistently high level of grant (£1,500 in 1906–7) was notable – and a source of great pride to the school – and even Theodosius had to concede that the level of work had 'considerably improved'. However, he was angry that the Education Committee 'cling to their policy of promoting their Elementary teachers' so that not a single teacher in the three municipal secondary schools had experience outside an 'elementary' school. He suggested cutting the school's grant to make the Education Committee find the money to finance 'more expert staff'. Clearly, relations between the HMI and the Bristol Committee were very strained.

Fletcher thought that some of the issues raised by Theodosius deserved a wider airing, and the Bristol situation became the stimulus for a major appraisal of the way in which the new secondary school system was settling down. In a sort of early 'Black Paper', which was printed and circulated to all HMIs,[9] Theodosius argued that Bristol was experiencing 'a breakdown in the "educational ladder" at the top'. He opened with a resounding tribute to the 'older grammar schools of every grade', which 'never let a really brilliant boy escape notice' and then ensured that 'every nerve was strained to bring his work to university scholarship standard', even though that meant that 'the work was frequently done to the neglect of the less intelligent boys'. What he wanted to see was the first grade secondary schools – which in this context he identified as Bristol Grammar School, Redland and Clifton High Schools for Girls - taking first pick of the talented 12 year olds in public elementary schools. The 'superior culture' of those schools' headteachers should enable them to devise a suitable examination, which, with a redistribution of scholarships, would ensure that 'the best children might be caught before they entered a municipal school'.

The elitist views expressed by Mr Theodosius were extreme even for the times and not all his HMI colleagues concurred. One responded, 'I do not see ... why it should be supposed ... that these Schools are unable to provide for children of exceptional capacity the opportunity of advanced education'; another did not agree 'that there is ... only one educational ladder, viz: that leading to Oxford or Cambridge' and even wondered if some of those who had been to Oxford or Cambridge might have been better off elsewhere. These men seem to have caught something of the mood of optimism for the potential of municipal secondary schools, as well as recognising that the old grammar schools and Oxbridge did not have a monopoly of good education. Their comments contrasted markedly with Theodosius's views and it does seem that Bristol was unfortunate in being assigned him as its HMI. The proportion of Bristol children receiving aided secondary education was low (4 per cent compared with a national figure of 7.8 per cent), and to assert that only Bristol Grammar School, with a total of about 300 places, was capable of providing real secondary education for boys was an extraordinary notion. The strength of opposition to his views among other HMIs was sufficient to restrain the Board of Education from any dramatic action in the direction of the formal grading of secondary schools. Fletcher and Headlam, who had indicated that they felt some sympathy with Theodosius, consoled themselves with the hope that better scholarship provision would help to match the cleverest children with the 'best' schools, and the 1907 Free Place Regulations were very much in line with that viewpoint.

St George School stopped being recognisably a higher grade school in 1907 and started to look more like the kind of secondary school Theodosius envisaged. Firstly, all elementary pupils had transferred to the new Rose Green Elementary School, so that St George Council School, with accommodation reduced to 300, would 'in future be used entirely for secondary school education purposes'. Mr Pickles had resisted this as a 'risky experiment' which was potentially 'disastrous', and he remained convinced that elementary and secondary schools 'must be in organic connection'. Secondly, all new entrants had to sit an entrance examination in English grammar and composition, arithmetic, easy geography and English history. This annual entrance examination, which applied to all three municipal schools, was a big step towards turning them into the grammar schools which became familiar in the middle of the century, and institutionalised a much more rigid selection mechanism than had been found necessary before. The higher grade schools hardly ever turned away pupils. Many of the pupils had been brought on through the schools' own elementary departments, or they could be given special attention to bring them up to standard, and the desire to study seems to have been a sufficient qualification for entry. If, as regularly happened, there were more candidates than expected, the normal solution was to create an extra class, find a room somehow and appoint an extra teacher, not to devise a test designed to discard the surplus.

Thirdly, all parents had to sign an agreement promising to keep their children at school until they had completed the four-year course. This apparently desirable object exemplified the great difference between the comfortable middle class attitude to education and the uncertainties which dominated the lives of the majority of the population. Presumably, parents of all sorts who were able and willing to keep their children at secondary school for four years did so anyway, and making them sign an agreement did nothing to enhance either their ability or their willingness. The sometimes expressed suggestion that it made parents take education more seriously may have had some significance in homes where money was not a problem, but is not very convincing in view of the financial sacrifice which most parents had to make to prolong their children's schooling, even if scholarships were won. As late as 1944 one affectionate chronicler · of St George was arguing that, because of the agreement, 'many a conscientious parent has refused to bind himself in view of economic uncertainty'.[10] An added deterrent was that only at the end of the four years would their children have any qualifications to present to the outside world. The 1904 Regulations ruled that no pupil should sit examinations until the age of 15, and already the range of examinations formerly taken in higher grade schools was being reduced, with the universal School Certificate examination still a long way off.

In the summer of 1908, only 49 candidates came forward to sit the entrance examination for St George Secondary School, compared with 168 the previous year. Mr Pickles reluctantly admitted nearly all of them, although 'the usual high standard of work exacted had to be lowered to bring some of these candidates into the Pass list', and he was convinced that the removal of the elementary part of the school, which he had so strongly opposed, was a crucial factor. He also acknowledged in the school magazine of 1907 that the 'lengthened school course will mean much self-sacrifice on the part of many parents in East Bristol'. A contemporary felt that the loss of the elementary school was a 'severe blow', particularly because it was so useful in avoiding the 'violent change' from elementary to secondary school. These observations contribute to an unavoidable impression that the character of the school was transformed. By a series of gradual and often quite subtle changes instigated by the Board of Education, the vital organic connection between elementary and post-elementary schooling was severed, and St George ceased to be the school of its own people. There had been every indication that the developing higher grade school would draw more and more people through its doors, people who had never considered that post-elementary education was for them or their children; in sharp contrast, the selective secondary school held them at arm's length, constructing a number of obstacles sufficient to deter all but a determined minority.

In November 1908 St George School was subjected to its second general inspection. At that time the school was 314 strong (131 boys, 183 girls), of whom an unusually high number (52 boys, 83 girls) held scholarships. Parents comprised a handful of professional and independent people, 86 retail traders, 52 commercial managers and 156 of the lowest category which the Board of Education characterised as 'Services (domestic and other), Postmen, etc., Artisans'. Again the majority of children were aged 13 and 14, although 34 were 16 years old and eight were 17 years or more. The buildings were satisfactory but the school badly needed a playing field of its own, and the Committee was urged to erect wooden paving on the street outside, since the noise 'adds much to the nervous and physical strain on both teachers and pupils'. The inspectors really were ill at ease in busy urban areas like St George!

The report noted that the curriculum had changed 'considerably', with less – but still too much – physics and chemistry, more domestic economy and cookery for the girls, and the introduction of Latin to the four upper forms. The HMIs found it rather quaint that the teachers were using a Latin textbook designed for younger children, and were keen that 'some of the more subsidiary subjects such as Drawing and Manual Work might be dropped or partially discontinued' to allow time for more Latin and for starting it with younger children. In the meantime, English lessons must include more grammar, 'for purposes of discipline', and French should concentrate on 'severe drill in systematic grammar', such as the teaching of auxiliary verbs and conjugations to first-year pupils. A library should be set up to help in 'raising the literary tone of the School', and despite several new appointments to the staff, they lacked 'severe intellectual training'; still 'the most pressing want is a master of high literary attainment'.

The inspectors were also disturbed that at 11 guineas, the average cost per head was too low, and argued that a higher fee which covered all schoolbooks need not affect the 'large number of children from poor homes, to whose parents the purchase of the necessary schoolbooks is a very considerable burden', because they could win scholarships. The scholarship/free place argument had already won firm favour as a conscience-salver amongst those whose incomes saved them from having to compete, but people better acquainted with actual circumstances could see the flaw. As Mr Pickles eloquently explained in the school magazine in a piece which might still be instructive in some quarters, for poor children to win scholarships was:

> almost an impossible achievement, so long as a competitive examination is the only test of merit. They often have no books of their own, little or no opportunity for private study, the home atmosphere is perhaps against them, and the necessary word of advice or encouragement often remains unspoken.

In fact, the consistency of Mr Pickles's concern for the poorer child was remarkable and was not deflected by the changed status and character of his school. In 1905 he had said that 'it would be much better for England if it were recognised once and for all that Secondary education is neither for the rich nor the poor *per se*, but for the capable children in whatever rank of life they may be found'. In 1907 he imagined that 'some day, I suppose, it will be recognised that the poorer a district and the more unfavourable its environment, the better its schools and teachers should be'. On his retirement 20 years later, Mr Pickles was proud to estimate that, of the 70 St George pupils who had gone to university, 'not five of them would have reached there had it not been for the school', although he had never made that the main business of the school. As his first graduate pupil said on the same occasion, Mr Pickles possessed a 'deep and live sympathy for the underdog', and 'never sacrificed the average pupil to the brilliant ... He was inspired by a courage due to his vision of the possibilities of education' and was determined to maintain St George School's position as 'the chief educational centre for East Bristol'.[11] In the light of this story of the first 15 years of the school's life, his work of extending educational opportunities for the children of the St George area was clearly achieved in spite of the central authorities, rather than because of any help or encouragement from them.

FAIRFIELD ROAD SECONDARY DAY SCHOOL

Fairfield Road School presented a different challenge to the Board of Education. Unlike St George on the unfashionable eastern side of the city, and Merrywood over the river to the south, Fairfield was located in an area which both geographically and socially was of interest to the older secondary schools. Less than five years old at the time the Bristol Education Committee took over from the School Board, its senior section had never achieved the school of science status for which it was built and was consequently losing funds. Bristol's application for the recognition of Fairfield Road as a 'Division A Secondary Day School' was therefore despatched in May 1903 as a matter of urgency.[12] According to the first headmaster of the secondary school, his predecessor had already 'very wisely' drafted a number of students up into the senior classes to create a secondary school nucleus and strengthen the school's claim. But the Board's refusal was prompt and abrupt, following the dismissive comments of Science Inspector Buckmaster that 'unless any Higher Grade Board School doing good work of its kind can be considered a "Secondary School", then this school is not eligible'.

A three-man deputation sent from Bristol to appeal to the Board of Education was told by the head of the Secondary branch, the Hon. W.N. Bruce, that there were two main objections. Firstly, he had received complaints from the Merchant Venturers' Technical College about 'overlapping and undue competition' and insisted on consulting its governors and those of Colston's and Redland Girls' Schools (neither of which was actually recognised as an efficient secondary school at the time). Secondly, Bruce believed that in view of the 'large number of girls in the School [103 out of 166] and the class from which the students generally were drawn ... the needs of the district would be better served by recognition of the school at Fairfield Road as a Secondary School Division B'. His reservations about the Division A/Division B differentiation of secondary schools were referred to Morant, and thence to Sir William Anson, who adjudged that 'this seems to be a case in which the interests of the students will be sacrificed to the financial advantages of the A grant ... The case illustrates the need for a reconsideration of our scheme of grants to Secondary Schools.' Little did the Bristol deputation know that in seeking to retain Fairfield's original character, it had helped to seal the fate of all schools specialising in science.

In due course the Merchant Venturers' School responded that 'there is no evidence that more Secondary instruction, either free or at a nominal charge, such as would be supplied at Fairfield Road School ... is needed here at present', while the governors of Colston's Girls' School argued that the difference in fees (£1 per annum at Fairfield as opposed to their £6) would 'damage it seriously and perhaps permanently', and 'involve them in a ruinous competition'. They believed that their school was 'of the kind in which (it may be assumed) your Board wish candidates for

Pupil Teachership to pass their preliminary time', in contrast to Fairfield, where however good the instruction, 'its tone and mental atmosphere could hardly fail in a large measure to remain those of a public elementary school'. The Education Committee put together an impressive reply to these objections, which even Bruce conceded seemed to constitute 'a very fair case'. It pointed out that, since both Fairfield Road and Colston's Girls' Schools were full, it was impossible for Fairfield to 'rob them of a single student', and in its opinion, the two schools met the needs of different classes of children. Fairfield Road catered for the 'class above the very poor, but yet not able to pay the fees charged at those two Institutions, especially where the family consists of several children of school age'. The Committee expected that the rapid growth in population in north Bristol would provide plenty of pupils for all the schools. Colston's could cater for those who could pay its fees, and who 'prefer the more liberal education of more varied scope ... in addition to the more limited amount of Science ... besides securing the "tone and mental atmosphere" ... which prevail'. At Fairfield, on the other hand, 'there is no demand for classical education ... and a training chiefly literary would not be calculated to best fit the students for the business they may have to follow'. Many of the boys, it was said, went into engineering trades, building, plumbing, carpentry and joinery, and a number of girls planning to become pupil teachers specialised in cookery and domestic science.

Early in 1904 the Board of Education brought together all the interested parties for a major conference. It seems to have been a fairly heated encounter, described with phrases like 'much dispute', 'insisted strongly', 'laid great stress' and 'strongly opposed'. The Education Committee presented a strong case based on the calculation that ten secondary school places per 1,000 of the population over 12 years of age 'was no more than an adequate provision', and that Bristol was therefore 1,250 places short of the 3,500 required. It was very difficult for the spokesmen from the other schools to dispute this, either factually or in principle, and Buckmaster[13] noted that 'the others did not seem inclined to contest' these figures. The Division A/Division B issue was still unresolved, with the Board of Education repeating its belief that the B course was more suitable for pupil teachers, and the Bristol delegation was sent away to agree a fee which the objectors did not regard as unfair competition.

The Education Committee remained convinced that better-off parents, seeking different things in the education of their children, would continue to patronise a variety of institutions, but, after much heart-searching, did agree to a slight increase in Fairfield's fees, to a maximum of 9d per week.

Buckmaster insisted that 'the minimum fee for a Secondary School is £1 a term', and indicated that he did not like fees quoted in terms of pence per week because it smacked of elementary schools. Therefore the ruling went out from the Board: no recognition for Fairfield Road School unless the fees went up to £3 per year. The Education Committee found the refusal 'more than a great disappointment', but a further approach directly to Morant produced an ultimatum: unless Bristol agreed to a £3 fee with 25 per cent free places, and a parental guarantee to cover the full four-year course, recognition of the whole school might be withdrawn. There was nothing more the Education Committee could do. On 1 July 1904 it agreed that Fairfield Road should become a school without the special science bias for which it had been designed, and at an annual cost to parents of over three times as much as the Committee wanted, payable for four years.

At last Fairfield Road Secondary Day School could get under way, although planning was done in a frantic hurry over the short summer holiday. Mr J.E. Pickles having left to become Education Secretary in West Bromwich, a new head – Augustus Smith, a London University science graduate and trained teacher[14] – was appointed. An illustrated prospectus was hastily produced, letters of explanation sent to existing parents, a form of parental undertaking devised and the examination to select ten new scholarship holders organised. A body of pupils, comprising 54 from the old Science and Art Classes, three-quarters of whom retained their free places, 65 from Standards VI and VII and 45 from outside the school, was cobbled together in four classrooms, and the curriculum organised to provide two years of general education followed by two advanced years of either more scientific or more literary work.[15]

However, 1905 brought problems. The Board was extremely displeased to find that the plan was for Augustus Smith to be head of both schools, with two acting headteachers in the senior and junior departments under his general superintendence. Assistant-Secretary Mackail[16] said that if he had known about it in time, he would have 'advised a refusal of sanction of the arrangement', while Morant thought the Board could refuse to recognise Mr Smith as headmaster of the secondary school beyond the current session 'and thus perhaps get a better Head for it'. No doubt Morant's wishes were known to the HMIs when they visited Fairfield Road on the occasion of the school's first general inspection in February 1905. Theodosius and Tutton were so upset by what they saw that they immediately submitted an unofficial advance report to the Board of Education. They had found that both Fairfield and St George were still known as higher grade schools to Bristol people and both were 'secondary in little more than name', a statement which was underlined twice. They cited as evidence from Fairfield the fact that the elementary school shared the same entrance, stairs and playground, the class of children was the same, the headmaster and staff were 'almost without secondary school experience', and 'the atmosphere of the two types of school is the same ... the children of the Secondary school regard themselves as being in the higher forms of the Elementary'. At both schools the headmasters, 'with the best intentions in the world, are groping in the dark after secondary school ideals of which they have only the vaguest conception'.

The HMIs' secret report ruffled so many feathers at the Board of Education that a conference of the heads of the office, the highest decision-making mechanism at the Board, was convened. Mackail commented to Bruce that the 'case of these two Bristol schools (with which you are only too familiar) has now come to a point where it is necessary to take a definite line', and Morant passed it on to Anson with an observation which rings almost like a battle cry: 'St George's School and Fairfield Road School will be important cases for our main fight as to the standard of Secondary Schools. Mr Theodosius's papers ... are profoundly interesting and instructive.' In the event, the heads-of-office meeting was less dramatic than the build-up to it implied. Strong disapproval of the joint headmasterships was expressed, but Mr Smith would be allowed to remain at Fairfield as long as the school was found to be efficient from year to year. However, it was agreed to 'put strong pressure' on the Education Committee to separate the buildings without delay, since reports 'clearly show how unsatisfactory is the joint use of buildings by Elementary and Secondary Schools'. This information was to be conveyed to the Education Committee as soon as the report of the general inspection was available.

This report arrived in June 1905. It noted that Fairfield Road Secondary School consisted of 62 boys and 97 girls, mostly aged 13, 14 and 15, and that the fathers of nearly half of them (73) were clerks. Of the rest, 29 were artisans, 17 'professional' and 16 retail traders. In assessing the buildings, the inspectors were obsessed by their dislike of elementary and secondary schoolchildren and teachers mixing. The secondary school was said to consist 'merely of the few classrooms on the ground floor which happen to be unused by the Elementary School', and although the specialist science, art and practical rooms were good, the boys' and girls' dining rooms were 'used by the children of both schools. This cannot be considered a satisfactory arrangement'. The cloakrooms, washroom and offices (lavatories) also had to be shared, as did the playground, 'with the result that the noise, which seems incessant, is almost intolerable'. As there was only one staff room, all the teachers used it, 'which is undesirable'. They were adamant that the accommodation for the secondary school, which has 'neither the position nor the dignity which a Secondary School should have', must change. They recommended moving out the whole elementary school, leaving the building to the secondary school with a preparatory department for 300–400 children altogether; this was in a building approved for and currently used by 1,200 children.

Turning to the staff, the headmaster was said to have 'his heart entirely in his work and devotes himself enthusiastically to all the interests of the School, he is popular with boys and masters'. Fairfield Road was, of course, a co-educational school with a mixed staff. But the HMIs felt that any secondary school head 'ought to have had Secondary School experience, and should as a rule have had a somewhat broader academic career than is implied in the diploma of B.Sc.'. One wonders how the University of London would have reacted to its degrees being described in that way! They concluded by saying that a secondary school headmaster 'is expected to bring to the School a high type of tradition'. The last five words were inserted in place of the deleted 'the highest public school traditions', a phrase which says a great deal about the attitudes of the inspectors, and also arouses curiosity as to why someone at the Board of Education changed it. The senior assistant mistress exerted an 'excellent influence' and the rest of the staff were 'exemplary', displaying great devotion, enthusiasm, keenness and 'an excellent spirit'. They were particularly commended for giving 'every support to games'. But their qualifications were rather one-sided towards the science side, and there was 'no one with any special classical training' (originally 'distinction') who might be responsible for the Latin syllabus, a deficiency which should be rectified in future appointments.

The curriculum was 'suitable', although a six-hour day was too long, and 'somewhat more time than is necessary' was allotted to science, mathematics and drawing. Less than three hours of Latin and just over three hours of French per week were 'very short, especially in the case of Latin'. The syllabus in that subject 'shows a complete want of experience' and the senior pupils (who were in their first year of Latin) 'ought to be in a position to read Caesar by the Summer Term'. Other than that, most of the individual lessons were very favourably commented upon, discipline was 'good – questions of punishment hardly arise', and the conduct of the pupils was 'most satisfactory'. But the inspectors closed their report by returning to their opening concern:

> [everything about the school] its buildings, its organization, its government, its staff, in the attitude of teacher to pupil and pupil to teacher, are the spirit and atmosphere of an Elementary School; nowhere could the Inspectors discover the elasticity, the individualism, the personal initiative or sense of responsibility that may reasonably be looked for in a Secondary School.

The secondary school must have the building to itself so that it could make 'a fresh start'.

We do not know if the Fairfield staff were as dejected as their counterparts at St George after their first general inspection report, which contained the same message of praise for their work and regret that they were in the school at all. It seems, despite the criticism and the continuing uncertainty about the direction in which the school was to go, that they had great faith in the job they were doing, which generated a mood of buoyancy in the new school. Certainly, Mr Smith was optimistic in his contribution to the first edition of the school magazine at Christmas 1905, feeling that 'we are adopting the spirit and character of a good Secondary School, and are establishing traditions that we hope will make "Fairfield" a name of which old scholars, parents, and citizens will be proud'. He was delighted that the Old Boys were planning a rugby club and that last year's Standard VII girls, many of whom had moved on to 'various situations' and were 'reluctant to sever their connection' with the school, had organised an Old Girls' Club.

By the time of its second general inspection in November 1908, Fairfield School had grown to 269 pupils (120 boys, 149 girls), holding 39 scholarships (many fewer than at St George), and the bulk of them were 14, 15 and 16 years old with 27 older than that. Although they were 'the same class of children' and nearly all from public elementary schools, they were staying longer, which created something of a problem because Fairfield was recognised only for a four-year course up to the age of 16. Most older pupils were intending teachers operating under different regulations, but those who happened to be still at school after the age of 16 had no official status, and 325 attendances towards the end of the school year were 'disallowed' by the Board. The largest single category of parents was commercial managers (92), and there was still a considerable number of retail traders (40) and of the lowest category of artisans and service jobs (52). But in both the top group, 'professional and independent' (55), and the next, 'merchants and manufacturers' (34), there was a significant proportional increase on 1905, suggesting a gradual change in parental perceptions of the school. Most of the school's leavers went into commercial life or elementary teaching.

Again, despite praise for the 'energy and enthusiasm' of the staff, there was strong criticism of the lack of 'scholars of a high order'. There were too many changes of staff, some caused by 'breakdowns from over-work' and some by 'dissatisfaction with the conditions of work', particularly the poor salaries and short holidays. Again, however, the present staff were praised for their 'energy and enthusiasm'. Latin was making fair progress in the school, and the HMIs were pleased to note the introduction of a monitorial (prefect) system, a school choir and magazine, a former pupils' association, excellent lunch arrangements and better organisation of games. These all helped to generate a 'better corporate spirit', and overall there had been a 'very considerable improvement' which could be extended further when the 400 elementary children moved out.

Everyone concerned had come to accept that this last change would have to happen. Mr Smith had found it an increasing worry to juggle his admissions each year to fit the accommodation, regardless of the keenness or suitability of the candidates, and there were terms when he could take only a handful of new pupils. He was under pressure to keep more of his pupils through to the third and fourth years of the course, numbers in the fourth-year class were indeed growing, and he favoured admitting them younger, at 11. By 1907 the secondary school could expand no further and suitable children were being turned away. The Education Committee was eventually able to satisfy him and the HMIs when it opened the new Sefton Park Elementary School in January 1910. It took 400 juniors from Fairfield Road, together with the infants who had already moved out to temporary accommodation, and from that date Fairfield Road was exclusively a secondary school.

One interesting feature of this story of the early development of Fairfield Road School is the evidence which points to an articulate and self-assured parent body. On a number of occasions, parents communicated directly and effectively with the Board of Education in ways which suggest a perhaps surprising level of knowledge and concern. For example, one parent, objecting to buying homework books for his higher grade school son, protested that he paid his rates and 'everything seems to be done to close the Schools against the Working Classes'. Another, just a few days after the start of the term when fees of £3 per annum were charged for the first time, complained:

> Fairfield Road School was built for elementary education and for the
> people in the district … and in accordance with that idea there was

no opposition at the time of its erection, as the voters were given to understand it was for elementary and secondary tuition.

A third, in 1907, wanted to know 'under what Law my son at Fairfield "Higher Grade School" is threatened with expulsion if I will not sign a paper binding myself to keep him at that school for four years', and how it was that he could be 'turned out of a school that I have to pay for through the rates'. The whole business seemed to him 'so absurd' and 'really amounts to persecution', and he threatened to involve his MP if necessary.[17]

None of these parents criticised secondary education as such or its development within their school, but they did object to its taking over from elementary education, and to what they perceived as an infringement of their rights. The style of education with which, in not much more than a generation, they had become familiar, was being changed and taken further from them, and they did not like it. When they complained to the highest authority, they found that their rights were much more vaguely defined than when elementary codes and regulations covered virtually every eventuality; the Board seemed to take the line that if the school and the local authority were behaving in a way that the Board basically approved, then the parents would just have to fit in. The transition to the new style of secondary school involved an unmistakable change of character at Fairfield as elsewhere, and at least a proportion of parents were left feeling angry and alienated in a way that never seems to have accompanied the evolution of higher grade schools.

MERRYWOOD SECONDARY SCHOOL

Of Bristol's three higher grade schools, Merrywood was in the weakest position to withstand the critical eye of the Board of Education after 1903. The School Board's policy of allowing the higher grade part of the school to evolve in its own time and providing resources as the demand arose meant that for official purposes it was the least developed of the three. Like Fairfield it had failed to achieve the all-important school of science status, but Merrywood had one saving grace: it was located in a densely populated district which everyone agreed needed something more than ordinary elementary education, but which no 'existing' school could adequately serve.

By the end of 1904, the Bristol Education Committee was ready to turn the senior department of Merrywood into a secondary school.[18] It had moved 300 infants into temporary premises in a nearby chapel, and planned some structural alterations at Merrywood to accommodate 420 boys and 450 girls, approximately 250 of whom would comprise the secondary school. Following a deputation from Bristol, the Board of Education accepted on principle a mixed secondary school at Merrywood, subject to a number of conditions. Firstly, the Board 'expressly reserve the right to re-consider the position' should any existing secondary school complain of 'undue competition'. Secondly, the building must be clearly divided for secondary and elementary schools, with joint use of facilities permitted only temporarily, since the 'parents of boys attending the Secondary School might very likely object' to the common playground for secondary and elementary boys. The officials at the Board seemed unable to grasp the fact that the secondary and elementary children very likely had the same parents, or that Merrywood was a co-educational school. The secondary school should cater for about 200 children, with all its own specialist facilities, and it must have 'a staff of its own, entirely separate from the Elementary School', including its own headmaster. Those older children not planning to proceed to the secondary school – the feasibility of long-term planning was assumed – must be provided for in the elementary school. And finally 'provision must be made for organised games ... this is an essential element in the life of a well-equipped Secondary School', and particularly important at Merrywood which suffered the 'grave inconvenience' of a playground shared with the elementary school.

The Education Committee proceeded to implement the Board's requirements as far as possible, creating within the same premises an elementary school for 550 and a secondary school for 200, the latter having seven classrooms, chemistry and physics laboratories, a science lecture room, cookery and art rooms and a central hall. But an interesting complication arose when F.R. Arscott, a commercial traveller living near Merrywood School where he had four children, launched a campaign against its conversion into a secondary school. He favoured instead the building of a new 'central school'.[19] He contacted his MP, Walter Long, got together a committee of parents, and distributed 5,000 handbills advertising a public meeting at the Temperance Hall in Bedminster. Five hundred ratepayers turned up, of whom only 14 voted in favour of the conversion. A protest resolution was also received from the Bristol and District Radical Operatives' Association, which was always strong in Bedminster. Morant became interested, asking to be 'kept informed of this case', especially after Mr Arscott put his finger on a real weakness in the Board's case. He had read in the *Daily Telegraph* that in London the legality of turning buildings constructed for elementary education over to secondary use had been questioned, and that a Bill was being considered to regularise the position. Did not the same apply to Merrywood?

Nobody at the Board of Education knew how to answer this, until eventually the President and Morant came up with an extraordinary solution. The Board would continue for the time being to give grants to secondary schools and pupil teacher centres functioning in 'elementary' buildings, although it was of the utmost importance that 'this Department should not seem to give any form of sanction … to any Institution conducted on an illegal basis'. The obvious parallel with the Cockerton judgment on the higher grade schools did not escape Morant, but he was confident that 'a careful statement … as regards the possible illegal use of the building', stating that the Board's sanction of the school did not legalise it, would smooth over the difficulty. This remarkable exercise in sophistry demonstrates so very clearly how the Cockerton problem could have been handled had the Board of Education wanted to save the higher grade schools. It is also reminiscent of the ease with which endowed school buildings were put to uses different from those specified in their deeds. The Board now had a new weapon to brandish, particularly useful in its crusade for segregated, self-contained secondary education. It caused considerable consternation to the Bristol Education Committee just at the time when it was finally getting its schools sorted out; there was nothing it could do to change the original purpose of the buildings, and it can only have served to throw back into question the hard-won secondary status of the higher grade schools.

'Merrywood Secondary School', still unrecognised, opened in January 1906, and, after a visit in March, HMI Theodosius recommended – with conspicuous lack of enthusiasm – that it should be recognised by the Board of Education. The file then trailed around the Board's offices for four months while various objections and doubts were raised. In response, Bristol promised to obtain a playing field, took steps to ensure that 'the Head Master has now no connection with the Elementary School and for all practical purposes the Departments are quite separate and distinct', and reluctantly agreed to raise the fees to £3 per year, the minimum acceptable to the Board. It did not, as instructed, appoint a new 'properly qualified' headmaster, preferring to place its confidence in the existing head, William Crank, a trained certificated teacher with 30 years' experience.

Merrywood's first general inspection took place in May 1907. There were 102 boys and 137 girls on roll, 31 of whom had scholarships, and they were predominantly 14 or 15 years old. Only 19 had come from sources other than public elementary schools; 93 of their parents were 'commercial managers, etc.', 61 were in the lowest 'services, artisans etc.' category and 48 were 'retail traders'. In general the inspectors felt that Merrywood was 'in the nature of a continuation school', depending almost wholly on entrants from public elementary schools. They thought that once the elementary school moved out, the building would be a 'thoroughly good' secondary school, with excellent science rooms and a playing field a few minutes' walk away. The cost per head was 'far too low' at £9 10s 0d, and the Education Committee was urged to offer higher salaries, without which 'it will be useless to look for that high standard of specialists which no Secondary School should be without'.

The inspectors found that Mr Crank 'devotes himself unsparingly to the work', and was a headmaster of long standing, although 'none of this experience has been gained in a Secondary School'. His staff of 16 were all certificated but included only four graduates, and the teaching was thought to be 'mechanical and wanting in the inspiring power' which was achieved by real specialists with 'high academic qualifications'. They were 'a devoted and loyal body, and spare no pains in their efforts to bring the School to a high level of efficiency, giving most generous support to all school institutions'; the keen support for games, the introduction of a prefect system, the beginnings of school and former pupils' societies and the rare use of punishment were all pleasing to the HMIs. But, although most of the lessons observed were competent or better, the general standard of work was 'at present low ... nowhere is the work really bad, but nowhere does it rise above a level of uniform mediocrity'. In addition, French, as the only foreign language, must be made more systematic and grammatical, in order to serve its function as an 'instrument of general literary training'.

It was on receipt of this report in Bristol that a major misunderstanding came to light. Both the report and an accompanying letter said that the elementary school must move out of the Merrywood premises, but the Bristol Education Committee thought they had met the requirements by separating the two schools within the building, and told the Board of Education that it was 'under a wrong impression'. HMI Theodosius was furious. He said that Bristol's letter represented 'a complete change of front', that 'the Education Committee will do nothing for these Municipal Secondary Schools unless the Board insists' and, with a hint of vindictiveness, advocated that the additional (and variable) grant should be 'withheld altogether'. Hard as they tried, the officials at the Board of Education could find nothing in the papers requiring all the Merrywood elementary children to move out, only a letter of 1905 clearly acquiescing in the two schools' joint use of the building. A cautious voice advised, 'we do not seem to be in a position to take up a very strong line'. Theodosius was disbelieving, and proposed a technical fiddle involving changing the official status of the site, but the disgruntled HMI had to be informed that the Board had nothing to back up his mistaken conviction.

By the time of the second general inspection in October 1910, the inspectorate in general was taking a less critical line, so the Education Committee escaped further harassment. On that occasion, the teachers were said to work very hard, to have 'responded cheerfully to criticisms' in the past, and to be 'well above average ... in teaching power'. There was keen competition for the 200 places and a 'happy increase' in the number staying longer at school before moving on to higher education or commercial or industrial life. And there had been improvements in games and corporate life, with the children being better trained in initiative and self-government. Merrywood thus became one of a small – and diminishing – number of combined elementary and secondary schools, at least in urban areas, which succeeded in preserving the organic connection between the two so valued by the higher grade school headteachers. It was one of the very few to defy the Board of Education's obstinate stance on this issue.

BRISTOL PUPIL TEACHERS' CENTRE

One aspect of education which was radically altered in the first decade of the twentieth century was the training of pupil teachers. At the beginning of the decade pupil teacher training lay firmly in the same sphere as higher grade school education, with which it shared a number of characteristics. It had long been the main route by which working-class children could advance their education and social position, and had been developed primarily by the school boards. The higher grade schools fitted smoothly into the system, with significant numbers of their pupils moving on to training, some of their staff members helping out with lectures, and the schools themselves offering good teaching practice experience.

Along with most of the larger school boards, Bristol had taken advantage of the Education Department's acceptance in 1880 of the merits of grouping pupil teachers for central classes given by special instructors. From 1889, evening and Saturday morning sessions were being held at centrally located premises; a quarterly examination screened the hopeful candidates, and pupil teachers from voluntary schools were charged £2 per year. The success of the classes – in 1898, for example, 27 out of 45 students were placed in the first-class of the Queen's Scholarship examination for admission to training colleges and only one failed[20] – encouraged the Bristol School Board to plan its own permanent centre. A new building in Broad Weir, incorporating a special basement science centre from which the city's peripatetic science demonstrator operated, was opened in 1899 and admitted 440 pupil teachers, 320 from board schools and 120 from voluntary schools.

The Centre made a promising start despite a few initial problems, two of which derived from the strongly feminine nature of the pupil teacher world. No fewer than five women teachers were appointed in quick succession and either never arrived or left very soon after, and the Manchester graduate who eventually accepted the post of assistant mistress had to consult her parents first. There was also concern about the poor performance of girl pupil teachers in parts of the examination, particularly geography and history, for which the Board of Education's emphasis on needlework and cookery was largely responsible. The Bristol School Board had never been very enthusiastic about the merits of cookery,[21] and was persuaded by one of its members, Miss Townsend, to instruct the heads of all elementary school to arrange for girls to study geography instead of extra needlework and to do drawing with the boys.[22] By the end of 1900, numbers sitting the entrance examination had trebled since 1895, and the Centre was instructing 643 pupil teachers, an unusually large number.

However, it was the misfortune of the pupil teacher centres to enter what looked like being their most flourishing period just as they came under threat,[23] alongside the higher grade schools and the school boards themselves. The Regulations of 1904 spelled out the Board's long-term plans for pupil teachers: that from the age of 12 to 16 they should receive a 'sound liberal general education' in the company of non-pupil teachers, that is in secondary schools. The committee looking into the coordination of education in Bristol was concerned that, like many other areas, the city lacked secondary school places for girl pupil teachers, unless 'ordinary paying pupils of Secondary Girls' Schools take up the teaching profession in Elementary Schools in much larger numbers than they have done hitherto'. Such a development would have pleased Morant but it was to be at least another decade, during which the profession experienced a dire shortage of recruits, before elementary school teaching became a respectable occupation for middle-class girls. So the Bristol Education Committee decided to keep up its Pupil Teacher Centre, which was reaching a 'high level of efficiency' according to the HMI in November 1904, and it made plans to improve the facilities, increase the number of students and employ six permanent teachers, most of them graduates.[24]

The Bristol Centre was then the largest in the country, only three others (Bolton, Islington and St Pancras) having more than 200 students.[25]

These plans represented a serious misinterpretation of the intentions of the Board of Education, which in 1906 recommended that the Pupil Teacher Centre should close. The local authority prevaricated, but eventually was bullied into line. In 1907 it experimented with 20 of the new bursaries for teacher training,[26] and the Pupil Teacher Centre was closed in 1910, although not without something of a local outcry because 'the Centre provided for the poorest pupils an entry into the teaching profession' which free places at secondary schools did not wholly replace.[27] In any case, for some years the intending young teachers in secondary schools mixed little with the other pupils, generally being placed in separate and self-contained classes with their own teachers, facilities and playground.[28]

The transformation of the pupil teacher system thus becomes another instance of the way in which an apparently commendable educational reform can be viewed in a very different light upon closer examination. It had certainly not been anticipated by those at the local level, who took some time to realise that changing the nature of the teaching profession was a high priority at the Board of Education; indeed, it has been suggested that Morant's main interest in reforming secondary education stemmed from his desire to achieve that goal.[29] From the students' point of view, the chief differences compared with the higher grade/pupil teacher centre system, were: they studied little science, or even none at all; with or without a bursary, they had to maintain themselves for much longer before they started earning; and instead of being the senior pupils of the institution in which they had studied for much of their school lives, they were often treated as unwelcome and second-rate intruders in the older established secondary schools. Morant did not bring about a dramatic improvement in the general education of such pupils. Instead, he so ordered things that the teaching profession attracted different recruits – and for a while very few of them – thereby reducing opportunities for poorer children and cutting away the working-class roots of the teaching profession.

THE NEW EDUCATION SYSTEM IN PLACE

From its early optimism in 1903, Bristol's new education authority had to learn a great deal about its role and powers in a very few years, particularly in relation to secondary education. The 1902 Education Act refrained from saying anything and the 1904 Regulations tell nowhere near the full story. The Cockerton judgment and the abolition of the school boards created a vacuum into which the Board of Education and its inspectorate could move, tailoring all secondary schools to their own preferred pattern with little regard for local wishes. Bristol, like other new education authorities all over the country, was brusquely acquainted with the details of that pattern as, under pressure, it discarded many of the characteristics which it had assumed to be intrinsic to publicly aided secondary schooling. A striking feature of that period of change was the contrast in the tone adopted towards the local education authorities on the one hand and the endowed and independent secondary schools on the other. From the first, the Board reserved the right to communicate directly with the managers and governors of non-municipal schools, and a sense of mellow rapport is rarely lacking from the correspondence. The views of the local education authorities were ignored, or rather, not even solicited. There seems to have been very little contact between the Bristol Education Committee and the voluntarily provided secondary schools, and the attempts of the former to coordinate its secondary school provision were greatly hampered by the privileged access which the older institutions had to the Board of Education.

One of the more curious features of the Board's policy towards the new secondary school system was the almost complete absence of statistical or demographical information. It relied on a 'rule of thumb' approach on the numbers question, being much more interested in the quality of schooling available than the quantity which might be desired. The only time that the number of secondary school places required in Bristol was raised, nobody questioned the Education Committee's suggested target of ten places per 1,000 of the population. But despite Bristol's success in turning all three of its higher grade schools into secondary schools, this proportion was not achieved and the Committee was shocked in 1913 to discover that only 4 per cent of the city's children were able to proceed to secondary schools, a figure considerably lower than the national average. Given that there were no guidelines on numbers, the clause in the 1902 Act which stipulated that local education authorities 'shall have regard to any existing supply of efficient schools or colleges' could be used to great effect. Unlike 1870, this 'gap-filling' exercise had no finite statistical limits, but was subject to personal judgments and prejudices. Two Bristol examples graphically illustrate this.

In 1899 the Christian Brothers started a Roman Catholic boys' school in one room of a private house in Berkeley Square, charging fees of between £2 and £6 per year.[30] By 1903 they were educating 54 boys between the ages of eight and 17 and sought recognition for the establishment as a Division A secondary school. Visiting HMIs found the rooms to be 'very stuffy' and 'much smaller than I generally recommend for recognition', with desks extremely close together. There were only five boys in the third year or advanced part of the Board of Education's four-year course, although, because there were only three teachers, those boys had to be taught with boys still in the elementary part of the course. The teachers were all trained by the Christian Brothers' Society in Ireland, without degrees or experience of English secondary schools, and the teaching was 'too much of the nature of lecturing'. Despite this catalogue of imperfections, recognition as a secondary school was recommended: the 'precise character' of the recognition (A or B) could be delayed until later, and grants were even awarded retrospectively. The school was therefore assured of its future promptly and without fuss, and with what might be regarded as almost an excess of the sort of flexible common sense which any new school needs. The HMIs obviously felt comfortable at the school and at the time of the first general inspection in 1906, having noted all sorts of things wrong with the school, firmly declared, 'this School is of the Grammar School type'.[31]

Another place where the HMIs felt thoroughly at home was Colston's Girls' Day School.[32] Speedily recognised as a secondary school (Division B) in 1903, it greatly impressed the unusually large team of six HMIs who visited in 1905. They found it 'difficult to exaggerate the high standards of excellence', enthused about the headmistress, her loyal staff, the 'exceptional cleanliness, tidiness, and brightness' of the buildings, the 'uniformly excellent' lessons, and the 'refining influence' the school had on its pupils. With a fee normally of £6, the parents were predominantly clerks (118), retail traders (81) and professional and independent people (55), with very few artisans (13). A number of girls were admitted from public elementary schools, which 'puts some strain' on the school, but 'the special care and watchfulness of the Head Mistress' ensured that 'the very high tone of the School is maintained … it is astonishing how rapidly scholars who may have been brought up in other surroundings, assimilate to their environment'. One of her rewards seems to have been a most sympathetic response from the central authorities to her suggestions. Thus she was influential in the various disputes over Fairfield Road, contributing to the lobby which succeeded in imposing some key changes on the school against local wishes. And her application to become a recognised centre for pupil teachers was speedily acceded to, despite strong protests from the Education Committee, not least at the £4,000 it was required to lend the school to build a facility which Bristol already possessed.

The brief telling of the stories of the Christian Brothers' College and Colston's Girls' School exemplifies how local education authorities could be relegated to the role of insignificant bystanders while the endowed and independent secondary schools sorted out their own affairs with the Board of Education. Notification of decisions often reached the Education Committee only after they had been made, decisions which could have far-reaching implications for the educational structure of the city over which it was supposed to hold responsibility, as well as incurring financial liabilities.[33] On the other hand, the promptness and consideration which such schools invariably encountered at the Board point strongly to a special relationship, which meant that trust deeds could be changed, poor buildings overlooked, and practical difficulties ignored. It was as if the Board willed that certain schools should become secondary schools, whatever the problems, and one suspects that the schools themselves were never in any doubt about their future. The looseness of the terms 'existing' and 'efficient' is thus underlined. The definition of 'efficient' was virtually meaningless at the time the Act was passed, and the description 'existing' could be applied selectively. All the older endowed and proprietary secondary schools clearly 'existed', and were thus given a privileged position which many of them scarcely merited on other grounds, and which bestowed on them a status, almost a mystique, which has not yet been dispelled. Newer institutions were at a very grave disadvantage and – then as now – in trying to solve the problem of what to do with the children the selective schools do not want, have always been faced with the unenviable choice of trying to emulate these schools or resigning themselves to a lower status.

The central authorities after 1902 attempted both ploys with the higher grade schools. Bristol's Mr Theodosius was a prominent example of the kind of HMI who really wanted the higher grade schools to be downgraded in status, and used that as a threat whenever his wishes were challenged. Then, when it became clear that they would become secondary schools, he nagged them into adopting the traditional features of the older grammar schools and shedding many of the characteristics which had made them unique. This was reinforced by changes in the administration of the schools, as Theodosius pressed for a separate governing body for each secondary school, who would receive the central grant for that school as a capitation grant direct from the Board of Education. His recommendation was to become standard Board of Education policy by 1907 – a sort of forerunner of the direct grant status created by the 1944 Education Act, and, after the abolition of that, of grant maintained status. And perhaps the reasons were not so different too:

having found some local education authorities both determined and opinionated about their own schools, the Board decided to try to remove all secondary schools from their clutches and place them in the hands of bodies who would be more amenable to influence.

The endowed and independent schools were also much more likely to be of the 'right' social class. The picture of Colston's Girls' School struggling to 'assimilate' its elementary school entrants is a classic statement of the merits of social and behavioural manipulation, and shows that that is how the inspectors believed elementary school children and the secondary system ought to be brought into correlation. The children should be admitted in manageable numbers and then changed or 'refined', rather than allowing the development of their own schools, out of which they would emerge better educated, but still recognisably of the social class and background from which they started. The higher grade schools had few weapons against such an ideological onslaught. They were dependent on public funds, their inventors no longer existed (although the new education committees often proved to be loyal defenders of the schools they had 'inherited'), their governors and headteachers had no special rapport with the people who mattered, and their main beneficiaries were neither influential nor rebellious. The evidence from Bristol shows that at least some local people cared very much that 'their' schools were being changed, but in the realm of secondary education they had no statutory rights on which to take a stand, and it was impossible to convince antipathetic officials of the special merits of a style of education so different from the one that had nurtured them. The Education Committee resisted central pressure as much as it could; it quickly developed the same kind of proprietorial and protective instinct towards the municipal secondary schools as the school board had had towards the higher grade schools, and its successes in resisting the removal of the elementary school from Merrywood and in maintaining the low fee at St George rank as notable victories, rare amongst any local authorities.

But, in the end, the Education Committee, the heads and teachers, and prospective parents were all forced to accept that, if St George, Fairfield and Merrywood were to exist at all as secondary schools, it would have to be on the Board of Education's terms, and they had to fight every inch of the way even to achieve that. They never became quite like the older grammar schools,[34] but they certainly resembled them more closely than they resembled their own earlier versions. As higher grade schools, their complete accessibility to all children, and their ability to devise a worthwhile education for a wide variety of pupils, however long they stayed and whatever their aspirations, gave them a unique slot in the city's educational provision which the new-style secondary schools did not even try to fill. One student of the subject has asserted that 'Bristol never seriously attempted to provide "Secondary Education for all"', but that the realisation in 1913 of its poor performance in secondary school provision spurred it into considering other alternatives. In 1917 a Junior Technical School was opened, and in the 1920s three 'central schools' were set up in the north, south and east of the city. But they were given second-rate buildings and, to prevent competition with the secondary schools, pupils were not allowed to take scholarship examinations or transfer schools. Although the central schools were successful within the confines assigned for their operation, they never really prospered or developed a distinctive identity, and serve to prove that the elementary education system could have no satisfactory or enduring apex once its natural progression had been curtailed.

The secondary school, one Bristol commentator has observed, was 'an implant, based on middle-class models, grafted unnaturally on to a working class system'[35] and in Bristol, as all over the country, there was a high rate of refusal even to try for scholarships or free places. A preliminary examination was introduced in 1912 to encourage parents to consider the possibility of secondary education for their children, but up to a half of those who 'passed', chose not to sit the final examination, perhaps not surprisingly, when there were ten successful 'preliminary' candidates for every subsidised place.[36] Such children were undoubtedly the biggest losers in the reorganisation of education after 1902, and there is now a growing body of evidence, particularly from oral sources, which shows that many of them found the later part of their schooling extremely frustrating and depressing.[37] The evidence of disaffection and truancy among older 'elementary' schoolchildren presents a startling contrast to the impression gained from reading the log books of the higher grade schools, with their minimal punishment, excellent attendance and hard-working, committed pupils.

As elsewhere, elementary schools quickly adjusted to the demands of a competitive scholarship examination, although in Bristol public criticism of the special coaching they laid on brought a ban from the Education Committee, which merely encouraged teachers to coach pupils for a fee out of school hours.[38] One Merrywood pupil recalled being promoted from his Standard VI class of 62 children to the new secondary school in 1905. He was there for just one morning before it was discovered he was too young, and he was assigned to the elementary school hall, where two classes, comprising Standards VI, VII and Ex-VII, were accommodated. There, the curriculum (for his last 18 months of schooling) was 'devoid of frills such as Woodwork, Science and French, so it is only to be expected that I have very little to remember'. He left school early, on his thirteenth birthday, and commented: 'Had we been allowed to continue in "Higher Grade" the last year or two would certainly have given us a wider education. Those of us who were caught in the transitional period could be said to have been deprived.'[39]

This boy was, it must be remembered, just a tiny part of the 96 per cent of Bristol children in that situation, and it was a situation which lasted for rather longer than the word 'transitional' usually implies. Although many of them would not have continued their schooling beyond the statutory minimum, under the higher grade school system they could have done so. The new-style secondary schools, with their higher fees and extra costs, their selective admission and four-year 'academic' curriculum, and their physical and cultural separation from the elementary schools, very effectively closed off any further education for the majority of the population. It became abnormal for ordinary children to continue their education, thereby producing a range of expectations which were to be relayed down through generations of parents who lacked the resources or the will to challenge the educational package delivered to them by the politicians and civil servants who so ably represented the early twentieth-century elite.

NOTES

1. A product of the old Trade School which became the Merchant Venturers' College, Cook was an analytical chemist and the founder of the Clifton Laboratory, a private scientific research and teaching establishment. W.T. Pike, *Bristol in 1898–99: Contemporary Biographies* (Brighton: W.T. Pike, 1899), p. 280. A commentator on the latter end of his long chairmanship (he retired in 1931 at the age of 76) observed that the Conservative Education Committee adopted solutions which 'reflected Cook's own Victorian views of thrift and the party's traditional caution with money'. D. Harrison (ed.), *Bristol between the Wars: The City and its People 1919–1939* (Bristol: Redcliffe Press, 1984), p. 105.

2. Clare, *Change and Conflict*, p. 228. Two Liberal wards of 8,500 people elected six councillors; five Tory wards of 8,500 elected 21.

3. By the autumn of 1903 Bristol Grammar School was recognised as a Division B (more literary) school, and Colston's School and the Merchant Venturers' Technical College as Division A (more scientific and generously funded). Others were approved during the ensuing months, some after a little more hesitation.

4. Bristol Education Committee, Higher Education Sub-Committee, Minutes, 14 April 1904.

5. This section about St George School is drawn from: PRO Ed.35/860; Bristol Education Committee, Minutes; Bristol Education Committee, Higher Education Sub-Committee, Minutes; St George School, Log Book; Old Georgians' Society, 'St George Higher Grade School 1894–1947' (two boxes of documents and newspaper cuttings collected by W.T. Sanigar); Pugsley, *Door of Opportunity*; *The Georgian* (school magazine from 1905), especially *St George Secondary School 1894–1944 (Jubilee Number)* (1944).

6. Mr Pickles repeatedly noted in the log book problems with the caretaker, including several appearances of his drunken wife. He managed to replace them in 1905.

7. Tropp, *School Teachers*, p. 191.

8. According to the Board of Education, *Statistics 1910–11* (1912), there were just two schools with fees not exceeding 1 guinea per annum, and a further ten (nine of them Council Schools) with fees between 1 and 2 guineas.
9. PRO Ed.12/139 Grading of Secondary Schools 1907–11.
10. Pugsley, *Door of Opportunity*, p. 38.
11. For much of the time, Mr Pickles had the solid assistance of Alderman Frank Sheppard, an early stalwart of the Labour movement in east Bristol who became the city's most distinguished socialist and first Labour Mayor (in 1917–18). His association with St George School lasted nearly 50 years. Bryher, *Account*, p. 46.
12. This section on Fairfield Road School is based on: PRO Ed.35/846 and 35/847; Bristol Education Committee, Minutes; Bristol Education Committee, Higher Education Sub-Committee, Minutes; Fairfield School Magazine (from Christmas 1905).
13. Buckmaster, Chief Technical Inspector at the Board since 1904, drafted a detailed report of this meeting in PRO Ed.35/846. In 1908 he was demoted by Morant, who launched a savage attack on him, accusing Buckmaster of evasion and untruths and publishing his own devastating version of events. Eaglesham, 'Centenary', p. 9.
14. A man of 40, with 15 years' experience as an elementary school headmaster and part-time lecturing experience at the Pupil Teacher Centre, the Merchant Venturers' College, the Clifton Laboratory and the University College, Augustus Smith must have seemed to the Education Committee the ideal person to raise the standards and status of Fairfield Road at this critical point in its history.
15. This seemingly sensible solution to the Division A/Division B dispute was initially encouraged by the Board of Education, but cancelled within a year.
16. Eaglesham wrote: 'A scholar to his finger-tips, Mackail's interest was reputedly less in administration than in his classical researches ... Latin must be compulsory for all. This view Mackail strongly maintained.' E.J.R. Eaglesham, 'Implementing the Education Act of 1902', *British Journal of Educational Studies*, 10, 2 (1962), pp. 155–7. To Corelli Barnett in *The Audit of War*, p. 225, Mackail was 'sublimely oblivious, or dismissive, of Britain's urgent educational needs as an industrial society'.
17. This boy can be traced through the school's admissions registers; he did complete a four-year course (1906–10) with the help of a two-year scholarship awarded in 1908, and left to become a maker of scientific instruments.
18. This section on Merrywood School is drawn from PRO Ed.35/855; Bristol Education Committee, Minutes; Bristol Education Committee, Higher Education Sub-Committee, Minutes. As before the records relating to Merrywood are less good than for the other two schools.
19. The term 'central school' was little used in Bristol at that time, being the terminology of a later generation, and it is impossible to know quite what the Bedminster parents had in mind.
20. Bristol School Board, Minutes, 24 January 1898.
21. The School Board had refused to build a cookery room at St George Higher Grade School, and left it to the Technical Instruction Committee to establish a central school of cookery in Great George Street with branch schools around the city.
22. Bristol School Board, School Management Committee, Minutes, 14 January 1897, 13 July 1898; Bristol Technical Instruction Committee, Minutes, 29 July 1891.
23. Early in 1902, the judgment in the case *Dyer* v. *London School Board* made pupil teacher centres financed by the rates illegal; later in 1902, the Education Act empowered local education authorities to train their teachers.
24. Bristol Education Committee, Higher Education Sub-Committee, Minutes, 16 November 1906, 21 January 1907.
25. Board of Education, *Statistics of Public Education in England and Wales, 1903–4–5* (1905).
26. Bristol Education Committee, Higher Education Sub-Committee, Minutes, 2 November 1906, 21 January 1907.
27. Wood, *Beginnings*, p. 49. As Tropp has shown in *School Teachers*, pp. 186–7, the bursary system followed by training college postponed earning until the age of about 20, which was a formidable deterrent to working-class entrants to the profession.
28. In older secondary schools they were segregated for reasons of social prejudice; in municipal schools, they were a separate group because they were the only pupils entitled (and financed) to remain at school after the age of 16. Ellen Hallett, a bursar at Fairfield Road School before the

First World War, could not recall any other senior pupils: the bursars were the 'sixth form'.

29. By L. Holcombe, *Victorian Ladies at Work: Middle Class Working Women in England and Wales, 1850–1914* (Newton Abbot: David & Charles, 1973), p. 37.

30. This paragraph draws on PRO Ed.35/830; Bristol Education Committee, Minutes; and Bristol Education Committee, Higher Elementary Sub-Committee, Minutes. Halevy, *Imperialism*, pp. 185–9, described the striking growth of Roman Catholicism at this time – up to 1,000 conversions a month, including the son of the Archbishop of Canterbury – and noted that regarding their schools, the Catholics 'were even more determined than the Anglicans to preserve their denominational character'.

31. St Brendan's ('Christian Brothers') College eventually moved from Berkeley Square (still basically two neighbouring houses) in 1960, when the school numbered 600.

32. This section is drawn from PRO Ed.35/844 and 35/846; Bristol Education Committee, Minutes; Bristol Education Committee, Higher Education Sub-Committee, Minutes.

33. As well as the Christian Brothers and Colston's Girls', financial help from the local authority was sought within the first three years by Bristol Grammar (manual instruction workshop), Redland High (science laboratory), the Cathedral School, and the Private Schools' Association.

34. As well as practical differences, they never challenged the older schools in terms of prestige. Bristolians making choices about secondary schools later in the century recall that St George, Fairfield and Merrywood sat around the bottom of the list headed by Bristol Grammar School. Almost by accident, Fairfield retained its 'grammar school' label.

35. Clare, *Change and Conflict*, p. 252.

36. Wood, *Beginnings*, p. 7. George Creech recalled that from his class of 60, only 12 opted to take the Bristol junior scholarship examination, two of whom passed, and that financial considerations were the main reason for the rest dropping out.

37. See especially S. Humphries, *Hooligans or Rebels? An Oral History of Working-Class Childhood and Youth 1889–1939* (Oxford: Blackwell, 1981), or his shorter 'Radical Childhood in Bristol 1889–1939' in Bristol Broadsides, *Bristol's Other History*, pp. 5–29, both of which draw heavily on the Bristol People's Oral History Archive, comprising over 200 interviews.

38. Wood, *Beginnings*, p. 6.

39. A.C. Hone, quoted in Clare, *Change and Conflict*, Appendix I.

5

THE NATIONWIDE FATE OF THE HIGHER GRADE SCHOOLS AFTER 1902

In this chapter the discussion is widened from the confines of Bristol to discover how higher grade schools, and the educational principles they embodied, fared in other parts of the country. Bristol's three higher grade schools survived in different guises, and with what some would say was enhanced status, but they did so at the expense of several of their key distinctive features. From being the best that the public education system could offer, they were obliged to occupy the lowest level in an educational structure designed for quite different purposes. Reference has also been made to certain features which were peculiar to the Bristol situation, so the important question remains as to how far that city's experience was typical. Were other local education authorities more in accord with Board of Education policy, and were they therefore allowed greater control over their own schools, or were they subjected to the same kind of official harassment? Did their higher grade schools manage to become secondary schools, and if so, did they have to change much? And what of those which took a step down in status, to become higher elementary or even ordinary elementary schools? Did children and parents view the new-style schools in a similar light, or did the Board of Education accomplish a fundamental revision of educational and social attitudes?

The focus is primarily on the higher grade schools which became municipal secondary schools. They were the majority and secondary school status was what many people at local level believed to be, if not the proper destiny for the schools, at least a just recognition of their achievements; anything else would have meant a downgrading and a betrayal of their efforts to date. A recurring theme is the difference in attitudes which existed between the central and the local authorities. Along a whole range of considerations, from major issues of principle to trivial practical points, the priorities and models from which the Board of Education was working emerge as startlingly divergent both from the needs of ordinary children and the preferences of local education authorities. The rumbling disconsonance between the central educational authority and a number of the local ones was an ever-present accompaniment to the emergence of England's publicly aided secondary school system. The bitterness with which some of the more controversial issues were enjoined proves how deliberate was the construction of the 'typical' maintained secondary school; if at first the Board of Education was behaving more or less from instinct, the ensuing struggles forced it to act more consciously. There may not have been much self-doubt or re-examination of the issues at the Board, but it was at least obliged to develop an increasingly explicit rationale for its policies.

RESHAPING THE MANAGEMENT OF SCHOOLS

A guide to current educational legislation produced in 1903 declared that 'all the active work of education will, under the Act, now be done by Education Committees ... selected by popularly elected bodies, with the addition of co-opted members'.[1] While the assumption contained in the first phrase soon proved to be illusory, the rest was an accurate statement of one of the few definite, mandatory aspects of the 1902 Education Act. The structure and composition of each new education committee had to be approved by the Board of Education and the pages of the *School Government Chronicle* in the early part of 1903 were full of the submission and resubmission of schemes. These produced, as a typical education committee, a large body (30–40 people), of whom at least two-thirds were councillors and the rest co-opted, including two statutory women and, on the Board's insistence, representatives of universities or other institutions of higher education in the area.

A smooth transition from the previous administration in terms of personnel was not a priority either for the councils drawing up the schemes or the Board approving them. A handful of school board members generally did crop up on the new education committees, but many more were discarded, and some notable figures refused to serve on principle. Thus, Birmingham education lost the services of Reverend McCarthy, who likened the dissolution of the school board to the assassination of Julius Caesar, and while wishing the education committee well, avowed his intention to stand apart and 'still fight as strenuously as ever in the ranks of Liberalism'. His retirement was honoured by remarkable tributes from local teachers, the Midland Education League of which he was chairman, and Sir George Kekewich who attended a special farewell dinner.[2] And in Leeds, G.J. Cockburn was so insulted by the city council's picking and choosing whom they fancied from the school board that he 'could not bring himself to accept the invitation'. His long letter of reply consisted of an uncompromising attack on the new education committee, alleging that it was no more than an instrument for doing the government's dirty work, and that the power of electors had been 'reduced to a farce'.[3] He did have the satisfaction of seeing Leeds swing so overwhelmingly to the Liberals in the 1904 municipal elections that *The Times* wrote: 'Not for a quarter of a century ... has such a defeat been sustained by the Conservatives. The education question considerably influenced the result.'[4]

The majority of education committees took two early steps: a survey of existing secondary education provision, and the appointment of a director or secretary of education. The first often proved to be a redundant exercise because local authorities had overestimated their control of the situation in relation to the Board of Education's direction of affairs. It also tended to be an unexpectedly long and complicated affair, although those authorities fortunate enough to obtain the services of Michael Sadler[5] received invaluable advice. The second was an unsurprising development of the school board practice of relying heavily on a clerk or secretary, who had become far more than a clerical or legal subordinate; many holders of the post were extremely knowledgable and influential figures in local education circles. It was obvious that the new local education authorities, with much larger responsibilities, would need similar assistance, and the role was likely to grow in importance because the majority of committee members did not necessarily possess any expertise on education but did have other council commitments.

However, this unexceptional trend took the Board of Education, and Morant in particular, by surprise. It seems to have been expected in those quarters that the school board clerks would disappear with the school boards, and that the clause in the 1902 Act which said they should be compensated was designed to get rid of them rather than recognise their merits. Instead, not only the job, but in a number of instances the same individuals, reappeared in the new system, often with enhanced responsibilities and powers. Possibly, it has been suggested, local authorities were keen to save the cost of compensating them,[6] although salaries were generally raised at the time to quite high figures, such as

£500 per annum plus expenses in Warwickshire, or, in Leicestershire, £500 for the director and £400 for the secretary.[7] Internal Board of Education documents reveal that Morant deplored this development and did his utmost to minimise the importance and influence of the new local education officers. Throughout his tenure of office, the Board of Education's correspondence with the directors' professional association was full of a hostility which was surpassed only by his disparaging treatment of certain individuals.

A further important deterrent to local education authorities was that if they did take the big decision to provide and maintain secondary schools, the Board of Education expected them to relinquish virtually all control of the institutions to semi-autonomous governing bodies. The 1904 Regulations laid down that recognised secondary schools must be conducted by a body of governors approved by the Board, and explained that the 'Board attach importance to direct communication with the Governing Body, and to preserving for the Governing Body as much responsibility, independence and freedom of action as is consistent with effective control'. This requirement was not rigorously pursued at first, but in 1907 the Board ruled that all grant-aided secondary schools must have an approved 'instrument of government', and the following year produced a model 'instrument', which attempted to move control of secondary schools a long way from the hands of elected local representatives. The local education authorities opposed this trend on several grounds. It represented a break with the familiar school board practice of them having sole responsibility for their own schools, and it challenged what they believed to be their legitimate right and duty, as authorised by Parliament, to make provision for the educational needs of their areas. It also, of course, made for formidable practical difficulties to let assorted governors decide the needs of individual schools at a time when most local authorities were trying to organise their overall resources. Nearly a century later, the introduction of grant-maintained status had exactly the same impact in those areas where it became a popular option.

The pattern which many of the early education committees arrived at was for sub-committees, sometimes with co-opted local representatives, to look after the interests of institutions of secondary and higher education. The Board criticised this format over and over again and was extremely reluctant to compromise, and there often ensued protracted negotiations picking over the minutiae of the organisation and personnel. Worcestershire made moves in the right direction, but Yardley School's local committee of ten, with its nominees from the Yardley Charity, did not please the HMIs because its powers were 'very limited' and 'in no way defined'. Birmingham was less compliant, unanimously dismissing the Board's model instrument as 'unnecessary for Council Secondary Schools, seeing that they are under the control of public representative authorities'.[8] The most solid resistance came from Leeds, whose Director of Education, James Graham, thus earned himself a place high on Morant's personal blacklist. Not only did Leeds submit an unacceptable instrument of government and then refuse a wholesale revision, but Graham rallied his fellow directors, eventually forcing Morant to climb down, much to the delight of the 45 local education officers who wrote to congratulate Graham.[9]

The disagreement over governing bodies thus became both a cause and a result of the poor relations between the local education authorities and the Board under Morant. Because he did not trust the education committees to run secondary schools of the desired type, he pressed for independent governing bodies in direct contact with the Board. This had the added advantage of giving headmasters the autonomy typical of the public schools, along the lines argued during a dispute at Nottingham High School by Reverend Percival: 'local interference has two bad effects, it disheartens and paralyses the Master, and it makes both parents and boys unduly critical'.[10] To relinquish control in that way was totally unacceptable to the local authorities, who believed that they had arrived at a rather more satisfactory sharing of responsibilities. But all that they achieved by resisting the Board's advice and arguing their own case was to confirm Morant in his belief that they were unsuitable authorities for secondary school management.

A NEW IDENTITY

Chapter 2 began with a firm assertion that the higher grade schools had an identity which was well understood by local people, that is the administrators, teachers, pupils, parents, residents. It is now a well-established fact – and some additional evidence has appeared in the preceding pages – that the central authority also accepted them as a recognisable type, and had adjusted its rules and practices to accommodate, and even encourage, their development. However, when the political tide turned against them, it was relatively easy and very convenient to proceed as if the higher grade schools were nothing unusual, no more than a bungled attempt to solve a problem which the Board of Education was itself now ready to tackle properly.

In this context, 'properly' meant the dissemination of the values associated with the traditional English secondary school, whose 'raison d'etre' was the mastery it was assumed to have developed in forming the character of young middle-class men. Academic work, lessons, the classroom, were only a part of the whole experience which secondary education should comprise, and schools needed to have the facilities and the organisation to cater for the other constituent parts equally effectively. The boarding school education which most of the Board's officials had received not only allowed, but required, the greater organisation and socialisation of any residential, closed community, and they sought to carry many of those principles into the urban day schools for which they were now responsible. One suspects that a sizeable part of their often unexplained hostility to elementary styles of education lay in the fact that pupils failed to experience education in its wider sense: to have their ideas and values influenced, their characters moulded, their relationships with their peers shaped. It would be different for the pupils of the new secondary schools. They would have a recognisable ethos, maybe a poor imitation of the great independent schools but unmistakably in the same tradition, and if that represented a significant divergence from elementary school traditions, so much the better.

The problem of what to do with girls was solved by the emergence of the English girls' high school as shaped by the Girls' Public Day School Company and increasingly imitated by the endowed sector. Taking as its guiding purpose the formation of character by means of a 'liberal', arts-biased education, with a special emphasis on high spiritual and moral values and service to the community, this emerged as the most important and influential prototype of the new 'serious' secondary schooling for middle-class girls. The schools, staffed by some of the earliest products of the London and Cambridge colleges of higher education – characterised by one contemporary as 'highly educated, exerting great moral force, and ruling with justice and kindness'[11] – were committed to extending the intellectual capacities of their girls, although not necessarily to the limits of those capacities. In a number of ways, girls' schools of the high school type were built around the assumption that 'the normal work of a woman is to be the maker of a home, to be a wife, and above all a mother'; as Sara Burstall, the influential Head of Manchester High School for Girls, warned:

> one must always remember that the girl has her home and her home duties and joys. She must not be taken away from family life, from being with her father and brothers at the close of the day and at weekends, from going out with her mother and helping her.[12]

The ethos which the Board of Education sought to create in the secondary school system for both males and females had a built-in exclusivity, readily understood by those who had experienced it, but difficult to describe to anyone else. The early inspectors visiting the new aided secondary schools laboured to identify and label the characteristics which seemed to them reminiscent of their own schooling, and developed an affection for the term 'corporate life' as an umbrella title. 'Corporate life' is, of course, an intangible quality, which has been recently rediscovered in OFSTED inspection reports on the Spiritual, Moral, Social and Cultural dimensions of schooling: a not dissimilar attempt to define school ethos, similarly blighted by loose and subjective definitions. Then, as now, certain activities were taken as evidence of its existence, and the HMIs soon took to devoting a separate section of their reports to each school's progress in that area. Indeed, the term crops up so repeatedly in inspection reports on the new aided secondary schools that it seems at times to be the single most important yardstick against which they were measured for suitability although, significantly, it was often omitted from reports on more traditional secondary schools, as if taken for granted. So, every new secondary school was encouraged to start the day with a religious service (an apparently simple change which had important implications for the design of school buildings), and its existence and quality were always commented upon. A school magazine was regarded as a good sign, preferably with a badge and Latin motto on the front cover, and the same badge should appear on that 'excellent thing', a compulsory school cap. In addition, favourable mention was always made of any chess, literary, debating or musical clubs, of old boys' societies and reunions, of prefects, monitors and a house system, and of the wearing of gowns by members of staff.

However, top of the list was undoubtedly games. The relationship between corporate life and organised games was assumed to be so close that they were often juxtaposed in the same sentence as if meaning the same thing. For instance, in two Birmingham schools it was noted that 'care has been taken to develop a sense of corporate life' at Waverley Road through good use of a hired playing field, and George Dixon's acquisition of a games field 'cannot fail to strengthen the vigorous corporate life which already flourishes in the School'. Worcestershire, on the other hand, had its plans for Yardley School on the edge of Birmingham rejected, on the grounds that 'the area of the proposed site is insufficient to provide room for organised games'.[13] Education committees thus had little choice but to buy or rent fields and to provide gymnasia and other facilities. Bradford gradually added the necessary buildings to its eight municipal secondary schools, in several of which the HMIs deemed that 'a gymnasium on the spot is a pressing necessity', and the pupils of two of them were commended for raising the money to build 'a serviceable pavilion' at their loaned playing field.[14] It seems almost that commitment to organised games was the sole test of credibility for an aspiring secondary school. Approval was conferred on local authorities which secured a playing field, to teachers who supervised games, and to pupils (especially boys, girls were less significant) who participated enthusiastically.[15] It was assumed that rugby football and cricket were the main sports, or, as Mark Grossek put it, 'those outdoor antics which, under the Union Jack, accompany education unfailingly'.[16]

He also had vivid memories of the impact that going to a grammar school had on his appearance and general manner. As the son of a tailor, he was probably better dressed than many elementary schoolchildren, but he found quite a difference at the Whitaker Foundation School, where the boys all wore clean white collars and some even cuffs, and there was no daily search for dirty necks and ears. 'I should have to "tog up"', he concluded, changing his collars more often and wearing his best clothes every day, and, above all, flaunting his new school cap with its badge, which was the surest sign that 'I had made a distinct advance in the social scale.' With some exceptions,[17] the wearing of anything distinctive to elementary schools was abnormal; there seems to have been no particular embarrassment or social stigma attached to wearing shabby clothes, charitable 'boot funds' were often administered by education authorities, and teachers were accustomed to checking (daily) that pupils were not lousy or suffering from ringworm. The adoption of school uniform in the new secondary schools was a means of proclaiming a common identity, both to the schools' own pupils and to the outside world.[18] It was also one of the more significant 'hidden' costs of the new-style secondary education. After 1902, the few scholarship pupils at a grammar school must have really stood out in their own neighbourhoods, and there could be disadvantages to sporting a distinctive appearance. In comfortable Bournemouth, which had a profusion of private schools, the opening of the municipal secondary school in 1901:

> caused a good deal of jealousy among boys who remained in the elementary schools and the first pupils found themselves ... in danger on the way home of assault by stone-throwing from boys of other schools. In fact the local press reported that a policeman had to be stationed to prevent a free-fight developing, and the Mayor dealt severely with the first offender brought before him.[19]

Mark Grossek recorded that gone too were the days of eating ice-cream or toffee in the streets, or joining in street games, it being necessary to become 'altogether more genteel', which included 'improving my speech' to match the nice accents of his new classmates.[20] Similarly, Walter Southgate realised at about the age of 14 that there was a whole different language from that of the cockney street, and it required of him 'great effort and concentration to drop the accent'.[21] The discarding of their local accents seems to have been obligatory for scholarship pupils all over the country. It was a particular concern of London's Chief Inspector, especially in the case of intending teachers, and at Thornton Grammar School in Bradford the English teachers were said to have made great efforts 'to correct the provincial accent'.[22] This was another of the ways in which grammar schools imitated public schools, which had already established 'public school English' (the forerunner of 'received pronunciation') as 'one of the foremost indicators of social class in Britain'.[23] It must have furnished one of the easiest ways of discriminating those who had been assimilated, albeit superficially, into middle-class life from those who stood completely outside it.

Normally the municipal secondary schools remained a little different in ethos from the endowed ones, and there is evidence[24] that working-class children did settle more readily into them, not least because there were proportionately more of them. Despite changes, the municipal schools hung onto their closer affinity with lower-middle-/working-class people in ways that the Board of Education constantly criticised. A teaching staff experienced in the public elementary school system, children drawn predominantly from public elementary schools, too many on scholarships, a tolerant attitude towards pupils who had to leave prematurely: all these were causes for complaint by the HMIs. The pressure on heads and local administrators to make their schools more like the middle-class institutions which attracted approval and prestige must have been enormous, and over the years nearly all 'grammar' schools moved irresistibly in that direction. Malcolm Muggeridge, from his early century experience of a South London borough secondary school, characterised it as 'limping along after the older-established grammar and public schools, cordially detested by them, but aiming at turning out a similar product'.[25] It is not unusual to find decades later, when access to all maintained secondary schools was through the 11-plus examination, or even today, after most of them have become comprehensive schools, that the former endowed schools in an area still retain a certain mystique, ranking higher in parental esteem than the schools with municipal origins.

CURRICULUM

The 1890s had been a lively time for curricular issues, when, for the first time, science and technical subjects achieved sufficient academic respectability and a strong enough foothold in the education system to alarm those who doubted their value. By then, almost all types and levels of educational institutions had been obliged to take cognisance of the development, albeit for differing reasons and with varying degrees of enthusiasm. Those provided mainly out of public funds – technical colleges, evening classes and civic university colleges – were the most positive expressions of this new trend. The higher grade schools, while offering a broad span of school subjects, were most clearly distinguished from other institutions of secondary education by their systematic teaching of science and technical subjects. This was partly because they were dependent on Science and Art Department grants, and partly out of a genuine belief that such subjects were both intellectually valid and particularly useful to their pupils; the enjoyment and competence in science subjects shown by higher grade school pupils have already been noted in Chapter 2. The liberalisation of the Science and Art Department's requirements from 1895 indicated that the trend was away from the exclusive sponsorship of science and technical studies, and, by 1904, when the main Secondary School Regulations were drawn up, the higher grade school curriculum had advanced a long way from the early days of the organised schools of science.

It might be thought that, if those Regulations had been genuinely looking to achieve the balance, flexibility and responsiveness to local needs which the Board of Education said it valued, there would have been room for a proportion of more scientific secondary schools, especially as the classical curriculum was safely ensconced in the prestigious schools over which the Board had no control. Instead, the 1904 pronouncement that central grants were primarily designed to 'give impartial encouragement to all well-considered local effort towards developing a general system of Secondary Schools through many channels and in varying directions' was soon proved to have no substance at all as far as curricular choice was concerned. Science and technical subjects were constantly under attack, while the merits of Latin, Greek, modern languages and English were regularly and thoroughly expounded.[26] Excellence in the latter range of subjects was to be a goal for all secondary schools; excellence in the former was commented upon unfavourably, as if an aberration from the past. Schools were put under intense pressure to seek Division B status, as if that represented the 'proper' curriculum for a secondary school, and those that speedily gave up their science bias were applauded.

On the other hand, the anguished pleas from various local authorities that the ending of Division A status would seriously reduce their grant, met with little sympathy at the Board, where their correspondence was annotated with remarks like 'this somewhat extraordinary letter', 'a piece of intentional stupidity', and 'so much in the nature of conjecture that I should prefer to leave it alone'.[27] It has been impossible to find an example of any HMI giving a firm vote of confidence in the science and technical teaching of a school which prided itself on its work in those areas. The good qualifications of the science staff and the high standard of the pupils' achievement were often commented upon, but the advice was always to reduce the amount of time, the scope of the work, or the level of achievement. Hence, in Birmingham, George Dixon School, whose future as a secondary school was extremely uncertain in 1903–4, was persuaded to cut the amount of physics in its advanced course, and Waverley Road School was told that its chemistry laboratory was too big. At Leamington's pupil teacher classes, 'too much time is devoted to Elementary Science'.[28] The staff at St George School decided in 1904 'to drop Science Examinations altogether after this year and adopt an academic Examination' and physics was removed from the girls' timetable.[29]

As far as girls were concerned, it was assumed by most middle-class educationists that a significantly different style of curriculum was desirable. This was tied up with the simple practical problem of fitting a full range of subjects into the very short working week favoured by most girls' high schools. In most, science was the chief specialism to be sacrificed and a good many resembled Clapham County School for Girls, which notionally taught physics and chemistry throughout the school, in a room equipped with one gas point, one sink and water tap, and some methylated spirit lamps.[30] The Board did its utmost to accommodate unscientific girls' schools which wished to be recognised under the Secondary School Regulations. The first and most famous set of Regulations, in 1904, announced its intention to pay:

> due regard to the differences inherent in the nature of the two sexes, to the different aims towards which their school life should be adjusted, and to the effect on character of the exercise of the various faculties during the critical years of life

It offered a less rigorous hours-per-week requirement for science and mathematics in schools which met for fewer than 22 hours per week. A number of girls' schools objected even to this much – such as Winchester High School which fitted one hour's 'science' into its 16-hour week – and so, by 1906, science and mathematics could be given up altogether, in exchange for courses in housewifery. The next year it was indicated that simply being a girls' school would be accepted as a good enough reason for not doing Latin, otherwise regarded as the most important distinguishing feature of a secondary school curriculum.[31]

Inspectors were always impressed by schools which had apparently solved the 'science for girls' problem by teaching them nature study leading on to botany, or by turning cookery and housewifery into 'domestic science'. They seem to have been completely in accord with Sara Burstall's opinion that science should consist of studying the density of milk, the temperature of frying fat and the composition of soap and soda.[32] Although some high school headmistresses were said to 'strongly object' to this waste of school time, others were gradually persuaded to develop courses, especially for less academically inclined older girls, for whom 'there is nothing very definite to do' and who 'are not intended to earn their own living'. Thus, Manchester High School's 'technical' course comprised 14 periods per week (half the total) of cookery, laundry, hygiene, domestic science, dressmaking, housewifery and household mending, and some London schools followed Clapham High School's lead in offering a certificated 'brides-to-be' course.[33] Municipal secondary schools, on the other hand, were reluctant to devote precious school time to domestic subjects and the female members of inspection teams were often far from impressed by the quality of teaching. In fact the HMIs became thoroughly ambivalent about the desirable content and level of domestic subjects, on the one hand urging a more scientific approach to elevate the standards of education for middle-class girls, and on the other falling back on their old affection for the simple, plain work that was held to be suitable for the lower classes. At Waverley Road cookery followed a good syllabus which made it 'utilitarian as well as educational', whereas at St George School the 'fancy needlework seen struck the Inspector as being of questionable taste' and mending, patching and darning, which have 'a moral and educational side', were 'not sufficiently encouraged'.[34] Needlework, proclaimed the Board of Education in 1909, appeals 'directly to the natural instincts of girls ... it should be looked upon as a matter of shame that any girl should reach woman's estate without a practical knowledge of what use she can make with her needle'.[35]

By contrast, manual instruction for boys, which had been positively encouraged by HMIs up to about 1900, experienced a steady erosion of time and status by a combination of official pronouncements and HMI pressure.[36] It was one of the favoured targets for pruning, as the HMIs nagged away at enhancing the allotment of time, the qualifications of the staff and the levels of achievement in literary subjects, especially Latin. It should be remembered that the higher grade schools taught English, including literature, as well as modern foreign languages, and a few also offered Latin, generally as a voluntary subject for older pupils. But, not surprisingly, their performance in those subjects was not what the typical HMI was familiar with, and it was absolutely taken for granted that a secondary school could not exist as such unless it taught Latin seriously and continuously. Its presence on the timetable, the content of the syllabus, the competence of the teachers, and the progress of the pupils were always commented upon, usually at some length and with forceful exhortations to enhance its place in the school. Hence, the 1904 report on George Dixon Girls' School was pleased to find that Latin was replacing commercial subjects, and the boys' school was encouraged in 1909 to extend Latin throughout the school at the expense of German. At Thornton Grammar School in Bradford, standards in French were so low that 'it would be better if it were dropped from the curriculum and the time given over to Latin', while at Waverley Road School Latin was reported to have got off to a good start, although the sixth formers, grappling with this new and unfamiliar language, were said to be 'timid', as if they 'feel themselves on perilous ground and ... hesitate for fear of making a false step'.[37]

There, as at all similar schools, the biggest criticism was the absence of a specialist classics teacher, which gave rise to the Board's recurrent concern that the municipal secondary schools lacked a 'background of scholarship', regardless of their achievements in science or other subjects. A charitable interpretation of the Board's stance on the curriculum would say that its members honestly believed that secondary education was meaningless if it did not introduce pupils to the intellectual discipline of learning classical languages. We can now say with confidence that they were wrong, but even in the context of the early twentieth century, England's Board of Education was addicted to the literary style of education in a way which no other country quite shared. Science was downgraded in all types of schools, technical colleges were neglected and provincial universities guided in other directions, and evening-class enrolments dropped sharply after 1902 with the re-imposition of fees and the introduction of 'grouped' courses. Shut off from and disdainful of other approaches to learning, the Board did not much mind if excellence in science and technical subjects remained peripheral to the prestigious parts of the education system. Nor was it too worried that sections of the population who looked to post-elementary education to supply them with the skills and qualifications which could advance their occupational and social prospects, felt excluded from pursuing their education in the new state secondary schools.

STAFFING AND ORGANISATION

The Board of Education's unswerving loyalty to a particular educational model was, if anything, even more graphically illustrated with regard to the staffing of the new secondary schools. There are clear hints that the inspectorate genuinely expected newly constituted secondary schools to be staffed by 'proper' secondary teachers, and were surprised when local authorities retained the services of the higher grade school teachers and heads who had built up their schools to a level which made it possible for them even to contemplate becoming secondary schools. The Board of Education could see nothing to recommend in a close working relationship between local authority and headteacher, and seems to have assumed that the 'potentate' style of headship familiar in public schools was what all secondary school heads should be like.[38] Its belief in headmasterly autonomy did not extend to heads whose ideas conflicted with its own; in such instances the typically close cooperation between municipal school heads and their employers was seen by the Board and the HMIs almost as a conspiracy to pervert the development of true secondary education.[39]

Yet the selection of staff was the responsibility of the local authority, and even the Board did not generally presume to interfere in individual appointments. Therefore HMIs had to find other ways of expressing their disapproval. They bemoaned the unattractively low salaries and short holidays offered in municipal secondary schools, repeatedly recommended the appointment of teachers with 'a background of scholarship' or 'high literary attainment', and pressed for the separation of elementary from secondary children, on the assumption that the headteacher would stay with the elementary part of the school. It is difficult to find a municipal secondary school where the inspectors were happy with the staff they found. Over and over again teachers were commended for their dedication and competence, but told explicitly that they were unsuited to the job. Thus, at Birmingham's Waverley Road School in 1907, staffing changes were essential, even though the teachers were 'adequate in number' (27 for 445 children), the teaching 'seldom fails to be clear and effective', the discipline was such that 'there is little punishment or detention and little need for any: the teachers are well able to encourage their pupils to do their best by other means', and the headmaster and senior mistress were well regarded.[40] At Yardley School, one of eight new secondary schools planned by the Worcestershire Education Authority, the assistant mistress was 'of the Elementary School type', and the 'very limited' experience of the rest of the staff was 'much to be regretted', since it was 'quite impossible for a staff to create the tone and atmosphere of a Secondary School unless a majority of them have experienced as teachers what is meant by these almost indefinable terms'.[41] The Board's frustration was given full vent in its 1906 report, by far the most critical to date. Its general condemnation of the municipal secondary schools included references to their teachers, who were 'underpaid and often overworked', unfitted for the work and inadequately qualified; an 'improved standard of teaching power' was at the root of the necessary changes in such schools.[42]

Accompanying the Board's persistent criticism of municipal secondary school teachers was the 'complete transformation of the method of recruitment' to the teaching profession which it effected between 1902 and 1914. This is well documented elsewhere,[43] and has generally been applauded as one of Morant's main achievements. But there is, of course, no way of knowing whether the new system actually produced better teachers; a number of contemporaries were convinced that it did not, notably the NUT which was otherwise attracted by the better educational opportunities and consequent enhancement of status.[44] Nor is it possible to know whether young teachers were better served in pupil teacher centres than by being spread around several, very varied institutions of secondary education, some of which were less than welcoming and segregated them into separate classes and playgrounds. Again the NUT was vocal in its criticism of this practice of segregation, which it found to exist in 75 out of 85 schools surveyed in 1907. Many of the traditional girls' high schools made their first uneasy acquaintance with elementary school girls in the guise of pupil teachers, and even in the municipal secondary schools, intending teachers were often isolated because they could well be the only senior pupils.

The 1904 Regulations for Pupil Teachers came out in favour of single-sex institutions, against too much science teaching, and agreed that 'the tradition and habit of social differentiation would make it difficult (at all events for some time to come) to draft Pupil Teachers to any large extent into many schools of the old grammar school type'.[45] The new requirement of an extended secondary education and the consequent postponement of earning functioned as a considerable deterrent, even when scholarships and bursaries were available. Recruitment from rural areas plummeted, and it can be argued that for families who were obliged to regard education as a practical investment rather than a cultural experience, the new system forced choices of a vocational nature on even younger children (that is at 11 or 12, when deciding whether to go to secondary school), which was the exact opposite of the change the Board professed to want.[46] The net result was to produce an 'alarming decrease' in recruits, which forced authorities to employ increasing numbers of 'supplementary' (unqualified) teachers.[47]

It took at least a generation to attract middle-class girls in any numbers into elementary teaching, and rather longer to convince their teachers of the merits of training for secondary school teachers. In both boys' and girls' schools, there was a strong strand of opinion which favoured heads and governors having considerable discretion in the selection of staff, so that they could seek out those qualities other than degrees or diplomas, which 'cannot be so easily formulated or tested, but which are ... far more vital'.[48] This kind of attitude, that 'the teacher is heaven-sent', infuriated one critical contemporary, who complained bitterly that 'so much nonsense continues to be talked on the subject, usually by men and women who ... think more of a good bat or a good degree than of the necessary training'.[49] There was, it should be said, a fairly strong current of opinion which disdained – and sometimes caricatured – the ineptitude of the untrained Oxbridge graduate teacher. To A.P. Laurie, for instance:

> secondary schoolmasters are merely amateurs as compared with the trained elementary teachers ... It is remarkable that the secondary schoolmaster is convinced ... that he can teach by the pure light of nature, and that teaching is the one profession for which no special training is required.[50]

But the Bryce Commission came out in favour of public school teachers being drafted into higher grade schools, and the Board of Education's enthusiasm for the same idea became a highly contentious issue. The spokesman for the higher grade school heads was not at all impressed, asserting that 'I am quite sure we do not want these men unless they are teachers. We have no room in our busy schools for amateurs or improvers, all must be good and competent workmen.'[51] Even *The Times* declared:

> Let the Grammar School bring itself to that state of efficiency which has

been forced upon the Higher Grade School by the hostile criticism it has
had to meet and the public inspection to which it has all along been
submitted. Let the Grammar School train its teachers.[52]

This kind of thinking no doubt fortified the local education authorities
who, like the school boards before them, felt a commitment to those
young teachers whom they had sponsored and whom they regarded as
their most successful and deserving products. They were resistant to the
idea of displacing them from the best jobs they could offer in order to
make room for 'outsiders', as well as being keen to integrate the
functioning of all the institutions of the public education service, so that
the national teacher-training system serviced the provided secondary
schools as well as vice versa. Meshing together the two types of
secondary schoolteacher proved to be a slow process. Occasionally
inspectors recommended to a badly staffed older grammar school the
employment of trained, ex-elementary teachers in order to 'put the school
on its feet', but on the whole, that type of teacher found it very difficult –
and probably made little effort – to penetrate the endowed/public school
world. The traffic was definitely intended to be one-way in the opposite
direction.[53] Furthermore, the Board did its best to maintain the distinction
between the two types of teacher by explicitly discouraging teachers in
training from tackling degrees, and intervening to reverse the laudable
efforts of training colleges and university departments to coordinate their
courses and share responsibilities for all education students. The patchy
but slowly growing lobby for secondary school teacher-training made
almost no impression on the Board of Education, which continued to
regard the trained teacher, even if a graduate, as an unwelcome intruder –
or at best, a junior colleague – in the new secondary school system.

The whole question of staffing is a powerful illustration of the Board's
narrow approach to the new secondary school system. It seems that as
higher grade schools earned recognition as secondary schools, the Board
envisaged a virtual clear-out of the staff, with perhaps a few remaining to
take care of the diminished science and technical side, but under the
guidance of heads and senior teachers who knew what a 'real' secondary
school was like. According to the NUT's historians, it became 'very
difficult for elementary teachers to teach in secondary schools, or for
working class children to learn in them',[54] and it was almost entirely due
to the obstinacy of local authorities that trained teachers maintained a
presence on secondary school staffs. The Board was not without influence
in trying to achieve its goal, but its inspectors could find very little that
was definably wrong with the vast majority of municipal schoolteachers;

and no doubt they were looking! This strongly points to the conclusion that the local education authorities were correct in believing that their secondary school teachers were up to the job they were doing, and that the Board of Education was at fault in refusing to recognise excellence in others or to accept that there were valid alternatives which could offer much to the new system.

PREMISES

Chapter 2 showed what pride the school boards took in the physical setting they provided for their higher grade work. Their successors, the education committees, naturally expected to continue using the relatively new buildings, which often represented their major capital investment and heaviest debt, and to construct new schools along similar lines as they became necessary. Generalising somewhat, we may note that the typical higher grade/municipal secondary school was located in the heart of urban areas to serve the densest concentration of population; it occupied a comparatively small site, so that buildings were tall and substantial rather than elegant, and playground space limited; it was extremely functional, with facilities fully used by the maximum number of pupils during the school day, as well as at other times; and it happily accommodated children from the age of 4 or 5 upwards with flexibility and a remarkable capacity for instant 'growth'.

By the turn of the century, a number of urban grammar schools had succeeded in moving out of city centres to more spacious premises with playing fields, located in the middle-class suburbs which supplied, and paid the fees of, their pupils. Increasingly, the only secondary schools likely to be operating in areas of dense population were those maintained by public authorities. One senses at the Board of Education an underlying distaste for these solid brick buildings in their urban settings. Visiting HMIs seem to have been ill at ease, viewing as an intrusion into the hallowed realms of secondary education the noise and bustle of the city streets, the proximity of industrial and commercial activity, and the ubiquity of the ill-educated lower classes. Sneyd-Kinnersley, for example, arriving in Manchester in 1903 to take charge of the north-west inspectorate after pleasant spells of duty in Anglesey, Norfolk and Chester, hated the city's smoke, gloom, rain, noise, traffic and stone pavements.[55] Like Bristol's St George School, George Dixon School in Birmingham was advised to build a new pavement to 'deaden the noise of the heavy traffic', and Wyggeston School in Leicester was told that the acquisition of a 'better site in a more open part of the town should be considered as one of urgency'.[56] In rejecting the chosen site for the new Yardley School on the edge of Birmingham, the inspectors complained about the number of surrounding roads, the nearby brickworks and the excavations of the Great Western Railway in the neighbourhood. Worcestershire's Director of Education found all these objections 'trivial and baseless', particularly as the new railway station would positively benefit the school by enlarging its catchment area, and angrily exclaimed: 'I have yet to learn that it is an objection to a Secondary School to be bounded by roads on three sides.'[57]

The Board was not so foolish as to expect that all secondary schools could enjoy the rural settings, stylish architecture and spacious facilities of the great public schools, and there were far too many run-down old endowed school buildings and newer small (particularly girls') schools operating in private houses to make detailed regulations feasible. But it seems to have taken the view that if secondary schools had to be located in uncongenial urban settings, at least they should be insulated from their surroundings as far as possible. Out of favour went the 'typical' higher grade school building, which was very much part of and accessible to the local community. In came the more spacious grammar school, the building itself spread over a larger ground area, with specialist rooms under-used, and with several acres of playing fields, all enclosed by a wall or fence to keep out anyone who did not belong to the school, as well as, for much of the time, those who did. Secondary schools became single-purpose, single-sex, single-age group institutions, a development which can be seen as an admirable clarification of their purpose, but which also represented a dramatic narrowing of the role which higher grade schools, simply by their physical presence, had played within their neighbourhoods. They also, it has been suggested, became more uniform in design, due to the constraints imposed by the Board's insistence on such facilities as a central hall to permit morning assemblies, a suitable entrance for visitors, and the separate accommodation of boys and girls.[58]

One of the commonest causes of disagreement was the way in which the Board nagged all local education authorities to make their municipal secondary schools more spacious by reducing the number of pupils. Schools which had been built and approved for 600 or 1,000 pupils, and functioned successfully as such, were told that they had room for only a half or a third of that number. The Board insisted on counting only ordinary classrooms in its calculations, which meant that at, for example, Waverley Road School in Birmingham, it discounted the chemistry and physics laboratories, the lecture theatre, the cookery, woodwork, metalwork and art rooms, and the gymnasium, which together had accommodation for upwards of 270 children, as well as the assembly hall, which could hold 340. The school was thereby reduced to a maximum of 420 pupils. Birmingham also had problems over its George Dixon School, for which it was more than happy to construct a fine new building. There was an eight-year tussle with the Board before the school was finally settled, during the latter stages of which it was informed that secondary school recognition was unlikely on the grounds that the new building lacked a library, museum, sixth-form room and adequate provision for games.[59] Despite the Board's best endeavours, it was a continuing trend for council secondary schools to contain more pupils than endowed ones, although the residual affection for small, cosy schools remained powerful, and it was many years before local authorities repeated what was common experience for a number of nineteenth-century school boards: the running of viable schools of 1,000-plus pupils.[60]

The importance of organised games in creating the grammar school ethos has already been referred to, and it is impossible not to be struck by the Board's obsessive preoccupation with playing fields. It crops up in every single application for recognition and in every single subsequent inspection report, often as the first and most persistently urged pre-requisite. And it was always couched in terms of the inestimable value to corporate life, with all its implications for character building, team spirit, group loyalty and healthy competition. It seems to have had almost nothing to do with physical health or fitness; it has been suggested that concern for the welfare of pupils, which was important in elementary schools, 'did not extend to secondary schools, whose pupils were expected to be ... sound in wind and limb'.[61] One of the chief causes of the Board's irritation with Worcestershire Education Committee was that the latter 'makes little effort' to acquire playing fields for its planned secondary schools. The first proposed site for Yardley School was rejected because it 'does not afford room for organized games such as cricket, football and hockey', and an arrangement with the Yardley Charity Governors, a wealthy trust which had been involved in planning the new school, to create a public recreation ground was unacceptable unless the school had sole use of it. Eventually the school acquired a field about a mile away, which more or less satisfied the Board, and Yardley thus became one of the many secondary schools which tramped its pupils long distances, so that they could receive their weekly dose of organised games.[62]

The principle that each school should have its own exclusive playing field was extended to other specialist facilities. School boards took it for granted that good laboratories, cookery rooms, workshops and swimming baths should be used by the maximum number of people, and that duplicating facilities was a waste of money. They seem to have been ingeniously efficient at fitting pupils, pupil teachers and teachers on courses into whatever facilities were available in the schools or colleges in their area. This does not seem to have posed any particular problems, but it has taken our education service most of the rest of the century to return to the idea that it is enormously wasteful to provide specialist facilities to which only a few hundred children have access, and which are locked away both from them and from the rest of the community for much of the time. By contrast, the pseudo-monastic educational experience of the Board of Education's officials told them that a secondary school was a self-sufficient unit, providing for all the needs of a residential community, and virtually closed to the outside world. When they came to apply this almost instinctive preference to urban day schools, it could be harnessed very conveniently to achieve two practical targets dear to the Board's heart: the complete physical separation of public elementary from secondary education, and the separation of the sexes. Both were to become enduring features of England's secondary school provision.

FEES AND CLASS OF PUPIL

The question of the fees charged to pupils constituted one of the issues on which the higher grade/municipal secondary school tradition differed most fundamentally from the whole of the rest of secondary education. In the absence of proper state support or generous private endowment, most secondary schools had had to charge fees, but it was also true that by far the easiest way to ensure social selectivity was to make it expensive. Certainly, the endowed schools showed no inclination to reduce their fees as a result of state support. By contrast, municipal secondary schools and local authorities were always unhappy about raising fees, and they maintained a larger proportion of free places than the older secondary schools, thereby making the statistics for all aided schools look quite respectable.

The Board of Education issued a clear challenge to the more progressive higher grade schools in the 1904 Regulations, which specified that 'unless local circumstances can be proved to require exceptional treatment the Board will not recognise a school in which no fees are charged'. Subsequently, in dealing with reluctant local education authorities, the oft-quoted rationalisation was that fees must be sufficient to ensure 'efficiency', which was, of course, defined and measured by the Board. The draft of the 1905 Regulations included the statement that 'a fee of a substantial amount is desirable', and offered a number of justifications: to guarantee schools' financial stability; to 'emphasize the fact that the education provided is of a superior kind and consequently of a greater value to the scholars'; to convey the message that 'good education cannot be bought cheap; it must be paid for'; and to ensure that low-fee schools did 'not compete injuriously' with other secondary schools in the same locality.[63]

What became the accepted minimum secondary school fee of £3 per annum (expressed as and payable termly), was a compromise which pleased no one. It represented a doubling or even a trebling of higher grade school fees where they existed, and the local authorities knew that it was just too high for many of their parents, especially when it was accompanied by a four-year commitment. Dr Macnamara, one of the NUT's MPs, wrote in 1905 that 'the working-class parent will throw up the sponge in despair' at the £3 fee.[64] On the other hand, there was a strong and persistent lobby within the Board of Education that was never happy with so low a figure, and was constantly trying to edge fees upwards. Even some endowed schools did not escape the pressure. Wyggeston Boys' School in Leicester had, in the absence of a higher grade school in the city, developed an unusually good record of liaison with the local authority, and took considerable pride in the number of its former elementary school scholarship pupils who won Oxbridge exhibitions. In 1903–4 the Board of Education ruled that 'the range of fees ... is extremely low for a School of the type in which Greek is taught' and pressurised the Wyggeston Foundation – which did not need the money – to raise the fees to £12 per annum.[65]

It was with pleasure that the Board noted in 1906 that of the 685 secondary schools it recognised, only 4 were 'wholly free' and only 28 had fees of less than £3 per annum, while 46 charged £3.[66] Many of the remaining 607 had sought official recognition primarily for the financial reassurance it brought – in other words, the poorer schools – and the vast majority of unrecognised secondary schools retained their independence by charging higher fees. Taking the picture as a whole reinforces how completely the Board of Education succeeded in maintaining the middle- and upper-class dominance of secondary education, in the face of what they saw as a challenge from below. And the pressure was for fees to rise; for example, from £1 2s 0d to £1 11s 6d per term at Leamington Secondary Day School in 1905, and from £3 to £4 per annum at all Birmingham's municipal secondary schools in 1912.[67] By 1911, just one recognised secondary school (Todmorden Secondary School in Yorkshire) still charged no fees, and only 50 (45 of them council maintained) charged 3 guineas or less; 5 to 6 guineas was the most popular range (137 schools), except for foundation schools which favoured 7–10 guineas, while nearly all the Girls' Public School Trust schools charged 17–18 guineas.[68]

The Board of Education was interested in the relationship between fees and the socio-economic class of pupils entering aided secondary schools, and heads were required to categorise their pupils ready for the HMIs. Although the Board kept changing the categories, it is clear that before 1907 the socio-economic background of municipal secondary school pupils was little changed from higher grade days and significantly 'lower' than that of endowed secondary schools. Municipal school parents in the 'professional and independent' category rarely exceeded 10 per cent, and could be as few as 5 per cent (Hanson Boys' School, Bradford) or 3 per cent (St George School, Bristol), whereas endowed schools could expect at least 20 per cent of their parents to be from that background. There was an even bigger difference in the next group, 'merchants and manufacturers', who made up around 40 per cent of endowed school parents but only 10 per cent of those connected with municipal secondary schools. The biggest category for all former higher grade schools was the lowest one, 'service (domestic and other), postmen, etc., artisans', who numbered between 35 per cent and 50 per cent of parents, followed by the next lowest, 'commercial managers', at around 25 per cent.[69] Analyses of the information contained in the early Admission Registers of higher grade/municipal secondary schools confirm that, for a while at least, the schools continued to be patronised primarily by lower-middle and upper-working-class families.

Until 1907, most of the municipal schools offered larger numbers of scholarships than the Board of Education thought desirable: 27 per cent of the 445 pupils at Waverley Road School, 45 per cent at the newly-established Yardley School and 64 per cent at St George School in Bristol. After that date, the free-place system and teaching bursaries guaranteed that poorer children were not completely excluded from secondary schools, but few authorities displayed a genuine dedication to that principle by offering maintenance awards as well. Books, uniform, dinners and travel were all costs to be considered, as well as four years' loss of earnings. To its shame, the London County Council between 1908 and 1911 used this as a weapon against about 100 scholarship children whose 'moral, hygienic and physical qualities' gave offence to some secondary school teachers; arguing that the ending of maintenance support would have 'a bracing effect' on the children, it engineered the withdrawal of most of them.[70] The West Riding, one of the 'best' authorities for awards, had to bow to government financial pressure in the 1920s and 1930s with the result that 'thousands of the best brains of the Riding would find themselves unable to remain at school'.[71] Evidence of this sort of behaviour undermines the tendency among historians to echo the Board's own interpretation that the free place system made secondary education accessible to children of all classes. Of course, having free places was better than not having free places, but they can hardly be claimed to have 'placed advanced instruction within the reach of the ... very poor',[72] or to have 'enormously facilitated ... the passage of children from the elementary school to higher institutions'.[73]

Nevertheless, the alarm that was felt by influential people at the Board's acceptance of Labour plans for a free-place system is highly significant. The Board had, after all, chosen a model of secondary schooling which was expensive and in some ways wasteful of resources, and it constantly berated local authorities for trying to offer their own version more cheaply.[74] And yet the prospects of giving a slightly fairer chance to poorer children and of raising intellectual standards within the secondary schools were not welcomed. Sir William Anson was worried that the free-place system would not only spoil the secondary schools, but would 'very often fatigue and embarrass the unfortunate children who were sent up to occupy these places', and the Headmasters' Association argued that there ought to be fewer free places, for fear of turning 'innumerable good artisans and domestic servants into very inferior and wretchedly paid clerks'.[75] Even ten years later, Fisher was telling the House of Commons that working people should not want more education 'in order that they may rise out of their own class, always a vulgar ambition'.[76] While one should not ignore those free-place children who coped and succeeded, they do not disguise the fact that a pseudo-meritocratic test was ruthlessly applied to the 90–95 per cent of the nation's children who could not afford the advantages the other 5–10 per cent took for granted.

LENGTH AND NATURE OF SCHOOL CAREER

One of the more remarkable features of the higher grade schools was their flexibility in responding to the needs of a wide variety of pupils. It was a feature forced upon them by the circumstances in which they operated, but the skill with which they made a virtue of necessity was one of their chief strengths. The range of abilities and aspirations which they successfully accommodated, often in the same class at the same time, with minimal absenteeism and disciplinary problems, was worthy of note. At Nottingham's People's College, for example, within the space of a few weeks the headmaster was lamenting the pressure on boys to leave early and start work, and rejoicing in the award of a three-year science research scholarship to a former pupil. By 1905, when the People's College was about to close its doors to older pupils because the Board of Education did not believe Nottingham needed a third municipal secondary school, its former pupils boasted nine PhDs, mostly gained abroad in science.[77] Looking back from a time when mixed ability classes and special needs children are seen as making major demands on secondary school teachers (although the length and general shape of school career are now fixed), one wonders how the early teachers coped. The Board of Education's sponsorship of a four-year course of general education as the kernel of secondary schooling represented a major switch to standardisation from the variety and flexibility those teachers handled as a matter of routine.

The Board also felt no need to provide or endorse any means of examining pupils during or at the end of the prescribed course, and it expressly forbad the taking of external examinations before the age of 15. Its attitude reflected a growing dislike of examinations among certain sections of the educational world around the turn of the century. By the 1890s, there was something of a reaction to the mid-Victorian enthusiasm for written examinations, which were increasingly seen as 'an unholy combination against general understanding and moral culture'.[78] Most heavily criticised of all were examinations as they had functioned within 'payment by results' systems, of which the Science and Art Department's was cited as the most recent and bureaucratic example. This reaction roughly coincided in time with the emergence of an alternative method of 'certification' for high-status occupations in the shape of a public school education *per se*, which was a safe way of discarding overt patronage, and, it has been suggested, prevented the development of more systematic, skills-based methods of recruitment.[79] On all counts, examinations lost out as an appropriate accessory to the education envisaged by the Board of Education in the new secondary schools.

The Board's resistance to examinations showed an ignorance of how important it was for many children to get a quick and tangible return from their extended schooling. Examination qualifications were becoming the single most important vehicle for social and occupational mobility, and the commercial and scientific/technical qualifications of the higher grade schools, constructed in intensive one- or two-year courses, had been ideal in that respect. Walter Southgate, the clever son of a very poor quill-maker, was unable to pursue his education except through evening classes, but at least his Standard VII merit certificate, with its four distinctions, got him a respectable job in a City law office, and his brother became an electrical engineer.[80] An analysis of the recorded first jobs of 662 leavers from higher grade/early municipal secondary schools shows that only four took up unskilled work; all the remainder entered occupations which required training or further education, carried some status, and offered above-average security.[81] For the many children like them, the school system was failing if it did not measure their attainments and record them in a tangible form. The higher grade schools were well acquainted with that harsh fact of life, and although the multiplicity of examinations on offer may have looked rather a muddle, they did guarantee that each year's study by each child was potentially of use to him or her in the labour market.

The older secondary schools, where access to professional occupations through university education was traditionally held to be a high priority, were not immune from the same kind of pressure from pupils and parents. The 'premature' departure of 15 and 16 year olds from such schools was an acknowledged problem, and the Bryce Commissioners had visited a number of endowed secondary schools with no recognisable sixth form. So, despite the Board of Education's resistance to the idea, the new secondary schools were compelled to bow to pupil and parental pressure on the question of examinations, and look to outside bodies. Most popular were the Oxford and Cambridge Locals, especially the junior level, together with some drawn from assorted bodies like the Royal Society of Arts, the College of Preceptors and the London music colleges. They made up a more theoretical package than the examinations used in higher grade schools, although in a number of subjects the modernisation of content and methods dates from this period.[82] Somewhat ironically, in at least one London endowed secondary school, tests seem totally to have dominated the supposedly examination-free years leading up to the Cambridge Junior Locals. Mark Grossek's most vivid memories of his disappointing three years at the Whitaker Foundation School were the masses of wearisome learning by heart 'without a word of explanation' from the teacher; the repetition in chorus, which 'reduced everything to a dead level of boredom'; and the endless tests – 'more tests than teaching' – which he was amazed to find the boys marked themselves, since 'most of our teachers … disliked extra jobs, and avoided them whenever they could'.[83]

Early leaving continued to plague the new secondary schools as much as it had their predecessors, both higher grade and endowed, and, although the average school-leaving age was moving gradually upwards, some 30 per cent of pupils left before they were 15.[84] The municipal school heads were generally sympathetic, and local authorities normally refrained from imposing the financial penalty to which they were entitled. The Board of Education and the HMIs, on the other hand, were highly critical of this laxness and inefficiency, seeing it as clear evidence that the wrong children were being admitted to secondary schools. The Board's apparently commendable attempts to increase the normal secondary school career showed so little understanding of the real causes of early leaving, that it did nothing to solve the problem but merely ensured that a proportion of children left school with nothing to show for their efforts and expense.

An interesting sidelight on this point is that one of the HMIs' more consistent early complaints was that the former higher grade schools all worked too hard: hours were too long, holidays too short, and the pressure of work too great. As a general rule, a 9a.m.–5p.m. day for 44 weeks of the year was normal, which fitted reasonably well into the working pattern of most lower-middle and working-class families. The middle-class expectation of schooling was nothing like so demanding. The whole perception of adolescence could afford to be more leisurely, the speedy acquisition of marketable qualifications was much less important, and there was an underlying assumption that, unlike their working-class contemporaries, middle-class children (particularly girls) benefited from spending time in their homes with their families.[85] So, one finds the inspector at George Dixon School in 1902 criticising the heavy timetable, the 'undue exertion' of pupils and teachers, and the excessive six-hour day, five-day week, and the Birmingham Municipal Technical Day School was strongly recommended in 1907 to reduce its hours.[86] Given that secondary schools were increasingly likely to be located in middle-class suburbs, the spare hours of scholarship holders tended to be filled with travelling or hanging around during the fairly long lunch break, because it was too far to go home. This was particularly true in London; Mark Grossek at the Whitaker Foundation School (hours 9.45a.m.–1.00p.m., 2.30–4.30p.m.) recalled leaving home at 8a.m. to walk to school (in order to save the train fare), with 2d per day to buy his own lunch – a daunting regime for a small boy.[87]

In fact academic standards, as they came to be understood, were not to the fore in the early days. The right style of curriculum was very important, as was the notional possibility of entrance to the old universities, but beyond that, schools were not expected to furnish proof of achievement against any measurable standard. Only scholarship pupils were examined on entrance, which was in itself a big change from the normal elementary/higher grade school practice of accepting successful completion of a certain Standard as sufficient evidence of suitability to take the next stage. Secondary schools generally ran their own entrance tests – rather ineptly, it seems – with scholarship or free place candidates being required to reach a higher standard than fee-payers. Manchester Grammar School, for example, ran two examinations a year, one for foundation scholars and one for 'feepayers and the less able'.[88] Although HMIs were supposed to certify that all pupils in grant-aided secondary schools were 'eligible' and 'suitable', the definition seems to have been intentionally loose, and was certainly interpreted that way.

The Board of Education was simply not in a position to expect more, given its rationale of secondary education: the development of character, with intellectual training of a general nature, for those who could afford to pay for it. Whereas higher grade schools had never excluded pupils who could not pay for their education, secondary schools did not turn away any who could. Mark Grossek's opinion of some of his classmates at the Whitaker Foundation School – 'a dull, stolid lot', including some 'loutish young troglodytes ... for whom the word dunce seemed almost too flattering a description. Not even at Gibraltar Street [his board school] had I come across so close an approach to mental deficiency'[89] – may or may not be typical. But it was generally true that for at least the first half of this century, the average grammar school was not distinguished by its intellectual excellence.

GIRLS IN SECONDARY SCHOOLS: UNEQUAL EDUCATION

Although the figures suggest that more girls received a secondary schooling after 1902 than before,[90] it can be argued that the Board of Education's shaping of twentieth-century secondary education did even more of a disservice to girls than to boys. As well as prejudices to do with curriculum, staffing, socialisation and social class, girls were presented with a form of schooling which embodied limiting features based on stereotypical perceptions of gender roles. The nineteenth century has often been credited with the origins of equal educational opportunities for women, with tributes paid to the sterling efforts of certain pioneering individuals in gaining access to public examinations, in founding the first 'proper' secondary schools for girls, and in forcing an entry into the university world.[91] However, girls' secondary schools affected a very small number of pupils drawn from a narrow stratum of society,[92] with little provision, or desire, for contact with the lower classes or the public elementary school system. It seems that the daughters of the professional middle class were the first to patronise the new girls' day schools, and although some of the schools were soon priding themselves on the mixture of social classes they accommodated, others aimed explicitly at social exclusiveness, with investigators being struck by the intense snobbishness they encountered at girls' schools. They were competing for parental patronage with up to 15,000 private schools – many of them very small (as few as half a dozen pupils) in order to preserve a refined, family atmosphere – which catered for the estimated 70 per cent of girls receiving any so-called 'secondary' education.[93] The new schools had to be prepared to accept girls at any age, quite often in their mid-teens for a year or two's 'finishing', to be very tolerant of erratic attendance and half-hearted academic efforts, and to make much of their decorous, lady-like standards and avoidance of competitiveness and 'over-pressure'.

Evidence of two significant inequalities emerges from the shaping of the girls' secondary school curriculum after 1902. First is the limiting, less serious approach to girls' education, shown by the low priority given to science and mathematics, the flexibility over Latin, and the enthusiasm for girls doing practical subjects which, according to the Board, merited only a low status in boys' schools. Secondly, there were different assumptions based on the social-class background of the pupils. It is curious how obsessed the upper and middle classes were with the physical and emotional frailty of their females, particularly when they took it for granted that their domestic servants were capable of long hours of heavy hard work, and their main worry about working-class factory girls was their robust energy and irrepressible sexuality.[94] But obsessed they certainly were, and various 'experts' continued to feed their anxieties. The Chief Woman Medical Adviser to the Board of Education told a university audience in 1908 that 'as regards mental work, great care should be taken to avoid any undue strain. Lessons requiring much concentration and therefore using up a great deal of brain energy, Mathematics, for instance, should not be pushed', and a well-known woman gynaecologist warned in 1911 of the 'failure in function' which was often associated with 'the "neuter" type of girl [who] tends to resemble that of a half-grown lad, she is flat-chested, with a badly developed bust, and her hips are narrow'.[95] The voices of more enlightened authorities like Dr Elizabeth Garrett Anderson struggled to be heard, and official reports continued to favour lots of untaxing domestic subjects and the postponement of examinations, and to urge that due attention be paid to the 'periodic disturbances to which girls and women are constitutionally subject [which] condemn many of them to a recurring if temporary diminution of general mental efficiency'.[96]

Such concerns inevitably affected the organisation of girls' high schools. They were nearly all day schools, and in order 'to offer the advantages of a solid education without taking girls too much away from their homes', they worked only in the mornings, school hours being normally from 9.00a.m. to 1.00p.m. This was generally regarded as the best time for 'brainwork', and had the advantages of getting the girls home in daylight and avoiding the undue social mixing which would occur during a midday break.[97] It produced a working week of about 18 hours, which, with 13 weeks' holiday a year, meant that in the course of a year the typical high-school girl worked about half the number of hours of her higher grade school contemporary. There was, in addition, an assembly to start the day and a mid-morning break for 'light luncheon', followed by drill. Even so, the schools worried greatly over the delicate constitutions of their staffs and pupils. The long summer holidays were said to be vital for the mistresses to recover their strength, and it was strongly recommended that they should be given an 'ample supply of couches for reclining' in their common rooms, as well as 'more allowance in the matter of absence due to illness'.[98] Their fragile health was held by Sara Burstall to justify fully their receiving lower salaries than male teachers, although a more enlightened contemporary thought it was about time that comparative health tables were drawn up, to show 'what the difference between the sexes actually amounts to. Women have suffered far too much in the past by guesses at their inefficiency in one field or another.'[99] It was certainly true that most women secondary teachers were relatively badly paid, and a number of underfunded schools were only able to keep going because of the financial self-sacrifice of their teachers.

The schools were also constantly aware of the criticism that they put their pupils under too great a strain. Miss Burstall advised that 'girls need more rest; they are more susceptible to injury through nervous strain during the years of secondary education; they should not do as much work in a given period as boys', and she particularly deprecated the taking of external examinations, blaming Miss Buss of North London Collegiate for introducing that 'grave error' into girls' secondary education merely to imitate the boys' schools. Equally out of favour were science and mathematics. The former was only useful – indeed essential – as a preparation for domestic duties and the care of children, and the latter:

> should be kept at a minimum for girls; it does not underlie their industries as it does many of the activities of men ... an excess of it, the subject

being useless to them and disconnected with their life, has a hardening effect on the nature of women.[100]

It is easy to make fun of this kind of over-solicitousness,[101] and one sometimes wonders how far it was a publicity exercise to appease reluctant parents and resistant males. The women heads and teachers, more than anyone, must have been aware of what has been observed as the remarkable robustness and energy of the typical high school girl, who had a formidable appetite for work and such an attachment to school activities and games that it was difficult to get her to go home. One late-nineteenth-century feminist reckoned that the high schools were producing 'a new type of girl, self-reliant, courageous, truthful, and eager for work ... sometimes blamed for want of grace ... but lacking helplessness and silliness'.[102]

The high school furnished a model of girls' secondary schooling which appealed strongly to the middle-class males in Morant's Board of Education. Indeed, it would be truer to say that it positively captivated that particular audience, which had been brought up and educated in a sexually segregated world, and in virtual ignorance of adolescent girls or female institutions of any kind.[103] Headmistresses were treated almost with reverence by the Board's representatives who, when visiting schools, seem to have been so bowled over by the atmosphere of lady-like restraint and demure obedience that they effectively suspended all critical judgment. It is noticeable how often inspectors commented favourably on the girls' part of a mixed higher grade school which they otherwise criticised heavily, or singled out for praise the senior mistress and her assistants, while the male teachers were inadequate and in need of replacement. At Birmingham's George Dixon School, for example, the inspector commended the 'quiet and pleasant' teaching and the 'excellent feeling' in the girls' 'school', on the same visit that he found the boys' department so wanting that the question was not whether it was a good secondary school but whether it could be a secondary school at all.[104]

The model of girls' secondary schooling promoted after 1902 differed markedly from the higher grade school tradition. It endorsed the anxieties of middle-class parents, particularly those in urban areas, about their daughters mixing with the wrong kind of children of the same sex, let alone the opposite sex.[105] The mixing of social classes which resulted from the admission of scholarship girls from elementary schools had been the subject of special enquiries by some of the Bryce Assistant-Commissioners, who found that such girls were well up to standard academically, if sometimes a little mechanical and drilled, but did need time to settle socially into their new schools. There was some support for intermediate or middle schools to help newcomers to adjust to the different social environment, and a strong belief that their assimilation could only be managed – and rendered acceptable to fee-paying parents – if very small numbers were involved. Sara Burstall developed this point in 1907, when she warned of 'a certain risk to an ordinary girls' high school in receiving all at once a large number of scholars from public elementary schools', although she did concede that 'to have a limited number ... is a real advantage. These girls have a spirit of earnestness and hard work which is of the greatest value to the tone of a form'.[106] Visiting HMIs were usually interested to observe how a school was coping with this perceived problem, and impressed when girls from poorer homes were being successfully moulded to the school's image. Commiserations were extended to Colston's Girls' School in Bristol (which in 1905 recorded just 13 artisans' daughters among its 337 pupils) because the 'large influx of scholars from the Elementary Schools puts some strain upon the middle of the School'. But thanks to the headmistress's 'special care and watchfulness', the school was exercising 'a refining influence' on these unfamiliar creatures, whom the HMIs observed assimilating to their surroundings with astonishing rapidity.[107] Even more strongly than in boys' schools, the process was seen as a difficulty for the school rather than the pupil, and it was the latter who had to make all the adjustments.

Such attitudes ignored the lessons learned by the higher grade schools, which had unique experience of what happened when children of different sexes, ages and backgrounds mixed together at school. Their experiments with co-education were reported to produce no major problems and a number of benefits, as various witnesses told the Bryce Commission: 'highly satisfactory; the physical and moral results are good' or 'the mixture of the sexes in schools ... answers exceedingly well'.[108] Most of the new education authorities were happy to continue this pattern of school provision if it efficiently satisfied the demand for secondary school places. But to the Board of Education, the 'best' examples of the secondary school model from which they were working were all single-sex, and so new additions were more likely to acquire status and attract the right kind of parents if they were of that type. Various of its representatives expressed unease at the idea of adolescent girls and boys mixing at school, and showed an almost obsessive interest in the 'offices' or lavatories, cloakrooms and places for the girls to hang their hats. The Board insisted on improvements to the building which Yardley School planned to use for only one year, because there was no separate cloakroom for girls and the access to the offices was in full view of the boys' playground,[109] and the People's College in Nottingham was told that 'it is not at all desirable that boys and girls of 14 and 15 years of age should be taught together'.[110] Instead, girls' schools were advised to avoid locations near factories, hotels, theatres, restaurants, public houses, offices or warehouses, or anywhere 'where large numbers of youths may be about at the dinner hour',[111] and it became a normal – and constraining – part of secondary school design for new buildings to be 'rigidly symmetrical', with separate entrances and sex-specific facilities at opposite ends.[112] A firm attachment to single-sex schooling, which still has its devotees,[113] was thereby built into the new secondary/grammar school system. Although it is difficult to disentangle cause and effect, it seems that co-educational grammar schools have tended to rank lower in terms of prestige than single-sex ones in the same area[114] – and, significantly, nearly all secondary modern schools were co-educational.

In fact, the most valuable asset of secondary school girls of whatever social class was that they did not seem to know that they were supposed to be so delicate. Despite the narrowing constraints of curricular requirements and social pressures, they seized their new opportunities with relish. In that respect, the early part of the century *was* a significant time for the advancement of women, and middle-class girls were almost certainly better off being educated in high schools than by any of the alternatives which their parents would have considered utilising. However, one still feels a lingering irritation that the schools were not more adventurous, possibly leading the way in changing attitudes as they became more established and admired. Some middle-class women were prepared to take a very radical stand on women's political rights in the first decade of the century,[115] but in education the 'pioneers' took a much less challenging line. They seem to have nurtured their cosy relationship with the Board of Education, leaving their less influential educational contemporaries to feel the brunt of the Board's repeated interventions, always in the direction of curtailment and inequality. The insistence of the senior policy-makers on a limited, domestically based role for women was out of touch with the reality of their own times, and bequeathed to the girls' part of the secondary education system a number of enduring problems. It need not have been so. Interpretations which argue that the early twentieth century was a time of great progress for women's education, or that, given Victorian conventions about gender, women educationists had to compromise in order to achieve as much as they did,[116] fail to take account of the higher grade school tradition of girls' education. To a later generation, the achievements and expectations of higher grade school girls are strikingly sensible, 'modern' and egalitarian.

THE ORGANIC CONNECTION WITH ELEMENTARY AND FURTHER EDUCATION

One of the fundamental guiding principles of the early twentieth-century Board of Education was its assumption that for the new secondary schools to succeed, they had to be as unlike and distanced from the elementary system as possible. Morant was one of the strongest exponents of this almost instinctive belief. Time after time the message was repeated to the former higher grade schools seeking to raise their status, although it tended to be another of the preferences for which the Board found difficulty in articulating reasons. It was one of the features of the new system which the local authorities and their headteachers were slowest to understand. The organic connection between elementary education and what followed it, whether higher grade, school of science, pupil teachership or technical college, was so much an integral part of the local authority system that it was hard to see how it could be otherwise. It was not just an issue of principle, but a routine, practical feature of the organisation, any alteration to which would require complicated restructuring of buildings, equipment, staff and children.

Within the Board of Education the initiative for a firm ruling came first from Secretary Bruce, who wanted authorisation to order separate accommodation and headteachers for the elementary and secondary parts of Brighton Higher Grade School and 'others in a like predicament'. Mackail was 'very glad you are doing this, as it is much needed', and stressed the particular importance of a separate head, to emphasise the 'fundamental distinction' between the two. Bluntly he stated that 'the conception of a secondary school as a sort of top storey to an elementary school will I hope become obsolete'. Morant agreed, so did Anson, and a major change in direction was thereby effected early in 1905. But all three civil servants agreed that it was to be put into effect discreetly. Bruce favoured it appearing in a prefatory memorandum rather than a specific regulation; Mackail thought 'we shall have to feel our way'; and Morant condoned that advice by 'we should gradually apply pressure ... It must be done cautiously and not upon one uniform rule'.[117] Such diffidence indicates that the top officials were aware of how unpopular this policy would be, and the difficulty in presenting a convincing rationale did not help, especially when preparatory departments to 'proper' secondary schools were entirely acceptable.

Through its own ineptitude, the Board of Education was forced to give up the battle to separate the elementary and secondary departments of Merrywood School in Bristol, but in almost every other instance, it bludgeoned reluctant schools and local authorities into effecting a change that few of them could see the point of. Dr Forsyth, head of the Leeds Central Higher Grade School, was one of those who fought to maintain his school intact, from the conviction that elementary scholars did not benefit from continuing education as much if they transferred to secondary schools with their different curriculum and methods. The HMIs, however, wanted an end to those customs – such as the marching of pupils between lessons, the absence of sixth-form prefects, and the dependence on terminal examinations – which gave all the school's work an elementary quality, and suggested abolishing the elementary school altogether. Leeds tried to make its elementary school more like a preparatory department, by requiring parents to commit their children to a minimum of two years in the secondary school and a fee of half a guinea per term, measures which led to 'a great falling off in attendance of the pupils of preparatory school age'. But, in 1909, the inspectors were cross to find that the so-called 'preparatory' school was still officially an elementary school and was organised as such, and the local education authority was told to remove the anomaly at once. It took until 1911 to sort out the formalities, including the complicated business of legally appropriating the land for purposes other than that for which it was originally bought.[118]

Nottingham was another authority which attempted to exploit the Board's equivocal stance on preparatory departments. Having lost the battle to get all three higher grade schools recognised as secondary schools, its secretary, Mr Abel, proposed that three schools (two higher grade and one ordinary elementary) be designated to provide for the 'special preparation' of children for entrance to secondary schools. The local elementary HMI thought this was a good idea: it would 'facilitate the preparation of children for Secondary Schools', would be much like preparatory sections of secondary schools, and would comprise a 'select body of scholars drawn chiefly from the middle and lower-middle class'. They would, for legal and grant purposes, be ordinary public elementary schools, although it would be necessary to distinguish them by means of a small fee (£1 per year), extra subjects in the curriculum, and the admission of pupils from all over the city and beyond. Morant was suspicious: 'Mr Abel is very fond of presenting the Board with a *fait accompli* and then saying it *must* be recognised to prevent hardship or injustice to the children.' The local elementary and secondary HMIs, who, significantly, did not normally work together and claimed to know little of each other's job, were told to visit the Nottingham schools together, 'to see everything' and satisfy themselves that their respective areas were alright 'without trenching on the other's'. Their detailed report showed that the proposed preparatory schools were to be independent under separate headteachers but in consultation with the secondary school, information which seemed to satisfy the Board.[119]

It is not a simple matter to identify precisely the effects of the Board's success in severing the organic connection between public elementary and secondary education. There is no need to repeat the feelings expressed by a number of early twentieth-century elementary school children[120] who were aware of the enormous gulf that lay between them and the next stage of education, a feeling that never existed when the next stage was located upstairs or in the next classroom. The Board had little sympathy for the unease of such children, and seemed to be preoccupied with preventing them from contaminating secondary education. It was not that they were not clever enough, for once they had swotted up a bit of Latin they more than held their own. Mark Grossek was bitterly disappointed by the lessons he received during his first year at an endowed secondary school, because he had been doing much of the work for months at his elementary board school. But the social atmosphere, the tone, the corporate ethos of the secondary school were vitally precious, and too many children straight from elementary schools might spoil that. Secondary schools which lacked those qualities were constantly urged to do better and leave their elementary origins behind them, while those that managed to safeguard their 'tone' and 'assimilate' a proportion of scholarship children were congratulated. Either way, the message was clear that the products of the public elementary system, however clever, deserving or anxious to succeed, had no automatic right to be in a secondary school.

POSTSCRIPT: THE HIGHER ELEMENTARY SCHOOLS

The higher schools which *were* organically connected to the elementary system are difficult to fit into any coherent pattern or tradition of English education. The higher elementary schools, invented almost out of thin air in 1900, remain one of the curiosities of English educational history. They never grew sufficiently in numbers or prestige to make much impact on the system, and are as under-researched as the higher grade schools, although perhaps more deservedly so. They were subject to more specific regulations than any other set of institutions in the country, yet there was enormous uncertainty, in all quarters, about what they were actually for. Heralded as the long-awaited legitimisation of the higher grade schools, it quickly became apparent that the higher elementary schools were no such thing, and education committees which had not rejected them out of hand were left puzzling over how to fit them into their education provision.

The local authorities did not have the benefit of Morant's detailed explanation contained in a memorandum to Balfour, which was peppered with phrases like 'limit their scope', 'on restricted lines', 'safeguards are necessary' and 'kept within proper limits'. It was hardly the language with which to launch an exciting innovation, the intended new summit of the burgeoning elementary school system. Higher elementary schools, Morant continued, would replace organised schools of science, with the loss of their more advanced courses, and would 'just suffice to permit the scholars to have a sound education' by the time they were 15, when they would be compelled to leave. They were to be 'definitely stamped' as elementary schools, to ensure that they would 'not compete in any real sense with ... the education offered in Secondary Schools', and to put a stop to 'the practice by which children stay on in a school ... thus ... gradually raising the level of the work done in the school'. Furthermore, there were not to be plenty of these schools, to serve the needs of the majority of the population; the avowed aim was 'to restrict the multiplication of these Schools', to guarantee which Morant insisted that the Board held an 'absolute power to veto' any plans.[121]

It came as something of a shock to many people – in Parliament, at local level, and even within the Board of Education itself – to realise just how limited were the plans for the higher elementary schools. The Minute had been introduced to the Commons in a thoroughly positive speech by Professor Jebb of Cambridge University, and was greeted in the same spirit by many supporters of the public education service: 'a new model and a new hope' said NUT Member of Parliament Yoxall; at long last establishing the higher grade schools' 'official position for the future' echoed his colleague, Gray.[122] However, within a matter of weeks, the Board had turned down London's application for recognition under the Minute of 79 higher grade departments, a decision which *The Schoolmaster* heard 'with amazement certainly, and little short of dismay'.[123] In March 1901, by which time only two out of 190 applications had been approved, a Commons debate of censure centred on the feeling that the government had been deliberately misleading, even duplicitous, in its original presentation of the Minute. There was talk of 'fraud', 'fatuous rulings' and 'inconsistencies',[124] and Bradford's leading higher grade school head added the accusation that the Minute was becoming 'an educational "Index Expurgatorius" in which shall be inscribed a list of subjects which must not be taught to children'.[125]

There was no way that a restricted number of small, closely supervised schools could mop up the higher aspirations of the whole elementary system. School boards which made a genuine attempt to apply the Minute found the Board of Education intractable on just about every issue, from the general role and purpose of the schools, to the minutely practical, even down to the mandatory shelves in the science preparation room and the two-feet wide gangways between the regulation-sized desks.[126] Most local authorities soon decided to ignore the Minute altogether, and so higher elementary schools remained small in number: 30 in 1906; 52, the maximum, in 1910; and 45 in 1917 just before they were abolished. They were highly localised in their distribution (mostly London and Lancashire). Furthermore, institutions which had spells as higher elementary schools never portray it as one of the prouder parts of their history, and local authorities which maintained them tended to spend much of their time trying to turn them into something else. Hence, the former Albert Road Higher Grade School in Aston, on the edge of Birmingham, had a quiet time as two higher elementary schools (boys and girls), having reduced its numbers by a third, curtailed its curriculum and limited its aspirations.[127] Birmingham itself thought that ten of its more · successful ordinary elementary schools would make good higher elementary schools but, having learned that the Board wanted 'such well equipped laboratories and other necessary appliances in practical scientific work as are now required in the existing Schools of Science', changed its mind. In Manchester five higher grade schools were converted into higher elementary schools but by 1910 the Education Committee was so disillusioned with the whole idea that it turned them into central schools, without the blessing of the Board of Education.

Nottingham School Board really wrestled with the Higher Elementary School Minute, believing that it had possibilities, but Morant suspected their motives and the lengthy negotiations which ensued became increasingly acrimonious. The whole business makes for an extraordinary story, which is worth telling for the illumination it sheds on several aspects of the Board of Education's attitude to post-elementary education in general.[128] The School Board moved fast when the Higher Elementary Minute was announced, and in June 1900 submitted applications for the conversion of its three higher grade schools, detailing facilities, staffing arrangements and curriculum. The Board objected to shared use of some facilities, otherwise 'high grants would be obtained for very little expense', and so, with rather less enthusiasm, the Nottingham School Board revised and resubmitted its applications the next year, this time successfully. The schools were duly reorganised from August 1901 in a way that the School Board thought complied with the Minute, although the High Pavement School continued to call itself 'the High Pavement Higher Grade School and School of Science and Higher Elementary School'. There was a hectic start at Mundella School, where 470 pupils turned up to occupy the 300 places the Board had designated there; the headmaster recorded that 'numerous visits have been made by parents seeking for information and guidance', and 'many objections' to the increased fee had been raised. And at the People's College, the headmaster clashed with the supervising HMIs: 'I expressed the opinion that Government had no right to limit our numbers to 340 when 580 children were willing to enter the Higher School and to pay its fees, and that the right of the taxpayer to this better education was higher than Government departments.' He was also extremely irritated that 'desks and rooms considered quite good enough to earn a £6 grant from the Secondary Branch of the Education Department, are now neither good enough nor adequate to earn a £2 10s 0d grant under the Elementary Branch of the Education Department!!'

Once in office, the new Education Committee was as keen as had been the School Board to turn all three higher grade/higher elementary schools into secondary schools. Sensing that he had a real battle on his hands, Morant despatched HMI Dale on a confidential mission to check if Nottingham was doing as it had been told in limiting the size and scope of the three schools. The latter reported back that he had 'tried to check as far as possible by the Registers. I do not think they imagine that the information was obtained for the Office', and hoped that his accompanying statement 'may be something like what you want'. That statement revealed, as Morant had no doubt suspected, that the three Nottingham higher elementary schools were not turning out their 15 year olds, but had been teaching 52 of them alongside other pupils, while listing them on a separate register and deducting their attendances from the grant submission. Morant was furious with the Education Committee and its secretary Mr Abel, at one point declaring privately (and untruthfully) that the schools 'were failures before and will probably be failures again'. He notified the Nottingham Committee that if it wanted secondary schools, it could have only two, and he suggested that High Pavement School, despite its 'old and honoured' history, was the 'weak spot'.

In its desperation, the Committee overstepped the mark. Arguing that its 'means for establishing the exact nature and extent of the educational requirements are not less complete than those possessed by the Board of Education', it told the Board that it 'feels so strongly upon the subject that even failing the consent of the Board of Education … they will be compelled to retain the scholars beyond the age of 15 ... even though such retention may involve forfeiture of recognition and grant'. Morant's terse response to this defiance was that 'if they try this in a Higher Elementary School we shall stop the grant for the whole of the School'. In fact, this obsessive determination to turn 15 year olds out of school had not been fully appreciated even by the Board's own senior officials; Secretary Bruce had advised Yoxall that there was nothing to prevent higher elementary schools keeping their 15 year olds provided no grant was claimed. Morant was quick to respond: 'No, this is incorrect. Article 40(ii) specifically prohibits this, in order to prevent competition with Secondary Schools', and in the event of Yoxall taking the matter further, he carefully briefed Sir William Anson, who promised to say that if the higher elementary schools broke the age rule, 'they will suffer materially'.

A further fruitless interview between Mr Abel and the Board meant that nothing was settled by the start of the 1904 school year, with the result that 'the whole of the work of the three Schools in question is seriously and increasingly disorganised'. Morant, apparently believing that only dishonourable motives could account for such resistance from a local authority, then sent to Nottingham another of his personal 'confidants', who hoped 'to get wind of any fresh move', and promised to let Morant know 'if anything of importance should reach my ears'. His confidential report strengthened Morant's inclination to hold Mr Abel personally responsible for what went on in Nottingham education. The latter, meanwhile, had to cope with the predicted hostile reaction when it was announced that High Pavement and Mundella would become secondary schools and the People's College an ordinary elementary school. 'Great opposition was aroused' among parents of the 224 High Pavement children told to move to the People's College, and only six consented to be transferred. Public meetings were held, and at the start of the school year in 1905, parents of 150 of the debarred children turned up 'in a body' and insisted upon them being admitted. Mr Abel, it was alleged by the Board, arranged for a superficial re-examination of the children, rejecting only those who were 'palpably unfit', thereby producing six first-year classes of more than 40 pupils each, and a secondary school of 634 instead of the 480 approved. He then challenged the Board to turn the children out and prove his re-examination at fault, adding, correctly, that there were no regulations about the size of classes in secondary schools or the manner in which pupils should be admitted.

Eventually the reorganisation in Nottingham reached a resolution: its three higher grades, after unhappy spells as higher elementary schools, became two secondary schools and one ordinary elementary (which was soon closed down). It had been an extraordinarily messy business, full of deceit, bitterness and personal invective, all very different from the friendly discussions with Nottingham High School in its time of need. The Education Committee's fall from favour exactly coincided in time with an appeal from the High School to the Board of Education for support in a dispute with the local authority. The School wanted to keep its government grants without sacrificing any of its independence, and was also trying to appropriate £7,000 from a local charity for a new cricket ground. The powerful intervention of James Gow, a governor and former headmaster of the school, ensured 'constant contact' between the school and the Board, as well as HMI Leach, who had begun to take a warm personal interest in the school, promising 'we will see you through'. The Board's help in 'frustrating the Nottingham Corporation's efforts' was thereby secured, and the High School not only got the money it wanted, but a further sum in 1908 for building improvements, even though it was not on the 'aided' list. It continued to enjoy favoured treatment from the Board of Education for many years, illustrating vividly the value to a school of friends in high places.[129]

Among a number of points which emerge from Nottingham's experience of implementing the Higher Elementary School Minute, three are of particular interest. Firstly, Morant was closely involved throughout, directing the Board's strategy, stiffening the resolve of colleagues, and setting the tone of their responses to the Nottingham Education Committee. The unpleasantness and wasted time and effort which Nottingham had to endure go a long way towards explaining why other less resolute authorities failed to protect, let alone advance the claims of, their municipal schools. Secondly, as Bristol had found, Nottingham was given no justification by the Board as to why two municipal secondary schools were just the right number for the city. Nottingham has been cited by a later writer as an example of the Board's very necessary policy of keeping a close eye on the amount of municipal secondary school provision in order to ensure its quality,[130] but there is not the slightest hint in the Nottingham records that the Board was guided by that principle. Rather, it was determined to protect the limited number of schools of which it did approve and thereby make secondary education a scarce commodity. Thirdly, it is clear from Nottingham's experience that Morant cared as little about the higher elementary schools as he did about local preferences. He had no belief in the value of the kind of education they embodied and no real interest in promoting it or them. They were a convenience, to get the higher grade schools out of the way, and so hedge them with confining restrictions that they could not break out and challenge the secondary schools. From the evidence assembled here, the suggestion that 'having got rid of the higher grade schools, Morant did not wish to find himself saddled with a substitute for them'[131] is entirely convincing.

The 1906 Consultative Committee Report on Higher Elementary Schools[132] adds weight to this interpretation. Riddled with class prejudice, it lamented the decline in moral qualities among the working classes, especially habits of discipline, ready obedience, self-help and pride in good work. It portrayed the homes of higher elementary school pupils as ones which 'at best, do little to favour the ends of School education, and at worst are antagonistic', an insult certainly belied by the concern and interest shown by higher grade school parents. According to the report, the whole point of higher elementary school education was to offer to pupils their only glimpse of humanitarian training, and to produce handy and willing unskilled workers. Shorthand, machine drawing, book-keeping, industrial chemistry and typewriting were ruled out as 'trade instruction', and modern languages had to go because they represented 'an approximation towards "secondary" education ... that we shall have occasion to deprecate'. In general, the big danger was that 'under the influence of an ambitious headmaster and staff', a higher elementary school may 'gradually tend to develop into a pseudo-secondary school', and for the same reason, external examinations were ruled out.

Even by the standards of the Board at that time, this was a reactionary perception not only of education, but of society in general; or perhaps it was more that the report tactlessly blurted out in public views that were normally confined within the walls of the Board of Education. It certainly confirmed the dismal future of the higher elementary schools, which were consistently undersubscribed,[133] and although a 'new type' was invented with slightly different rules and only a three-year course, all higher elementary schools were abolished in 1918. Until then, those that had not managed to pull themselves up to be secondary or central schools, either dragged on as higher elementary schools, or reverted to ordinary elementary school status, although it seems the majority never gave up hope of re-emerging when the climate was more favourable.

END OF A VISION

At the end of Chapter 2, an attempt was made to recreate the impact on the lower-middle and working classes of the opening up of possibilities which the higher grade school movement represented, and to register the perceptions of the schools held by their own headmasters. The question of what happened to the spirit of optimism and excitement that accompanied their early history is one·of the most important to consider in evaluating the post-1902 changes.

The Board of Education stated firmly in its 1906 report that when it came to the provision of secondary school places, 'supply must in the main follow ... demand', a principle whose apparent rationality has not infrequently been used to justify the parsimonious provision of services and benefits by those who have easy access to them. For it presupposes that 'demand' can come into existence out of thin air, that it is possible to want something of which one has no knowledge or experience. The higher grade schools came about not so much for the opposite reason, that demand followed supply, but because the two progressed hand in hand. As parents and children came to appreciate the value of elementary education, so some of them – without knowing precisely what more they wanted – felt reluctant to accept that it should end at the age of 12 or 13. The higher grade school movement was born out of that imprecise but growing yearning. It offered to those parents an upgraded version, in manageable quantities, of the sort of education with which they were familiar and in which their children had so far been successful. And it worked well: the parents and children wanted more, the schools found ways of providing more, and so the movement flourished. The short-lived higher grade school era stands out as being the most important time in our educational history, when a democratic surge can be identified and described: when ordinary people demanded more schooling, shaped the schools to suit them, and felt that the schools belonged to them.

There are no others with which to compare the higher grade schools, and so it is difficult to predict what would have happened had they not been superseded. A safe guess is that they would have gone on growing, both in quantity and scope, and that the happy coactivity between parental demand and local authority supply would have continued. There were effectively no barriers to entrance into the higher grade school system, and there would seem to be no identifiable reason why the 'demand' which had so far come mainly from the lower middle and upper working classes, should not have percolated further through the various social class strata, in time drawing in children and parents who in 1900 would not have considered voluntarily prolonging their formal education.

The Board of Education in the first decade of this century halted any possibility of that development. It placed the privileges of secondary education more firmly in middle-class hands than ever before, relying on the shared understandings of a minority class to justify its policy and smooth its path, and on the carefully controlled admittance to those privileges of a tiny, mouldable minority of the majority classes. In so doing, it gave an emphatic and lasting stamp of approval to a particular style of education, and thereby delivered a major blow to the development of any alternatives. With them went such progress as those alternatives had made in formulating a more varied and useful curriculum, in which there was a place for specialisation, scientific excellence, technical competence and vocational training. The higher aspirations and talents of the majority of the population were diverted into the pursuit of the few spaces accorded to them in the middle-class educational world with its liberal curriculum, which was the only way to achieve occupational and social advancement. The opportunities offered to the rest were dismal, and the fact that many of them chose that, rather than compete for one of the few places for social advancement,[134] is a remarkable comment on how estranged they felt from the newly shaped secondary education system.

NOTES

1. H.C. Richards and H. Lynn, *The Local Authorities' and Managers' and Teachers' Guide to The Education Acts* (London: Jordan & Sons, 1903), p. 32. Both authors were barristers, Lynn acting as counsel to the NUT, and Richards an MP.

2. Described as 'that uncommon personage ... a reasonable and Radical clergyman', McCarthy was the Anglican head of one of the King Edward endowed schools. He believed that 'the Church had not, and ought not to have, any jurisdiction over the intellect of the nation', and was 'wholly committed to doing the best for the children of the people during the limited time they were at school'. *School Government Chronicle*, 18 April 1903, 2 May 1903, 16 May 1903.

3. Jenkins, *'Magnificent Pile'*, pp. 81–2. Cockburn was a Liberal nonconformist who had devoted himself to education in Leeds, especially the higher grade school. Following the dramatic by-election success in North Leeds in July 1902 of a Baptist Liberal fighting solely on the Education Bill, Cockburn challenged Gerald Balfour, brother of the Prime Minister, to resign his Leeds seat and fight it on the education question.

4. *The Times*, 2 November 1904.

5. Michael Sadler resigned from the Office of Special Inquiries and Reports in May 1903 following a clash with Morant. After a spell at Manchester University, during which he was commissioned by six urban and three rural authorities to report on their provision for secondary education, he became Vice-Chancellor of Leeds University (1911–23) and then Master of University College, Oxford (1923–34).

6. By V.C. Greenhalgh, 'Local Educational Administrators, 1870–1914' (University of Leeds PhD thesis, 1974).

7. *School Government Chronicle*, 14 March 1903, 2 May 1903.

8. PRO Ed.35/2584 and 35/2554. Birmingham did not introduce governing bodies for its schools until 1982.

9. L. Connell, 'Administration of Secondary Schools: Leeds v. Board of Education', *Journal of Educational Administration and History*, 5, 2 (1973).

10. A.W. Thomas, *A History of Nottingham High School 1513–1953* (Nottingham: J. and H. Bell, 1957), pp. 225–8. Percival (first head of Clifton College) was speaking as chairman of the governors of Nottingham High School, in support of the headmaster against a serious challenge from a committee of parents which wanted less classics, more modern subjects and for teachers to be trained. The antagonism between the school and the Nottingham Education Committee after 1902 is returned to later in this chapter.

11. Bremner, *Education of Girls*, pp. 93–4.

12. S.A. Burstall, *English High Schools for Girls: Their Aims, Organisation and Management* (London: Longmans Green, 1907), pp. 13, 53, 193, 207.
13. PRO Ed 35/2579, 35/2554 and 35/2584.
14. Wilson, *Development of Secondary Education*, Appendices D and H.
15. Local authorities did, however, manage to avoid some of the more foolish suggestions that emanated from the Board of Education. The inspectors' concern at the absence of a fives court at St George School has already been mentioned; the Consultative Committee of 1906 thought that rifle-shooting was just the thing for higher elementary schools.
16. M. Grossek, *First Movement* (London: G. Bles, 1937), p. 140.
17. Distinctive clothing was originally the invention of charity and reformatory schools, to proclaim the poverty or delinquency of its wearers, often by the selection of unusually old-fashioned garments. Some charity schools, especially the hospital foundations, turned their 'uniform' into a symbol of status on becoming fee-paying middle-class institutions.
18. In girls' schools, 'tunics' and 'gym slips' were originally introduced, against strong resistance, to enable girls to exercise properly; thus they 'escaped the confines of stays and skirts, only to encounter institutional control' as 'young ladies' were transformed into 'schoolgirls'. P. Atkinson, 'Fitness, Feminism and Schooling' in S. Delamont and L. Duffin (eds), *The Nineteenth-Century Woman: Her Cultural and Physical World* (London: Croom Helm, 1978), pp. 117–20.
19. B. Bishop, *Secondary Education in Bournemouth from 1902 to Present Day* (Bournemouth: Bournemouth Press, 1966), p. 40.
20. Grossek, *First Movement*, pp. 10–11, 89–90.
21. Southgate, *That's the Way*, pp. 45, 90. This was when he left school to look for a job (wearing his first pair of long trousers plus bowler hat). His family was too poor for him to go to secondary school, but he continued his education at evening classes.
22. Campbell, *Eleven-Plus*, p. 146; Wilson, *Development of Secondary Education*, p. 296. Thornton Grammar School was an endowed school, which by 1905 was run mainly by the local authority as a small, low-fee co-educational school.
23. J. Honey, 'The sinews of society: the public schools as a "system"', in Muller, Ringer and Simon, *Rise of the Modern Educational System*, pp. 156–7. As J. Gathorne-Hardy put it in *The Public School Phenomenon, 597–1977* (London: Hodder & Stoughton, 1977), p. 127, 'in England accent has been to class what colour is to race'.
24. From oral sources, for example Bristolians Ellen Hallett (Fairfield Road) and George Creech (St George School).
25. M. Muggeridge, 'Forgotten in Tranquillity', in B. Inglis (ed.), *John Bull's Schooldays* (London: Hutchinson, 1961), p. 108. In *Through the Microphone* (London: BBC, 1967), pp. 28–9, Malcolm Muggeridge said: 'If Waterloo was won on the playing field of Eton, the class war was assuredly lost on the asphalt playgrounds of secondary schools like mine [Selhurst Grammar] ... Our South London cockney grated on the ear. Despite prefects' colours and other trappings reminiscent of Tom Brown's Schooldays we were irretrievably urchins of the suburbs.'
26. For example, 'the increasing tendency in Secondary Schools to drop Greek altogether' justified a special pamphlet (*1904–5 Report*); 'Latin is the necessary basis of a thorough linguistic and literary training' (*1905 Regulations*); municipal schools were 'too predominantly scientific' (*1905–6 Report*); 'the Board attach so much importance to the inclusion of Latin' (*1906–7 Report*).
27. PRO Ed.12/119.
28. PRO Ed.35/2554 and 35/2579; and Leamington Education Committee, Minutes, 14 December 1903.
29. St George School, Log Book, 29 April 1904, 27 April 1906.
30. The school's historian noted that 'quite a lot was achieved, but the modest equipment necessarily restricted the range of experimental work'! E. Freeth (ed.), *The Jubilee Book of Clapham County School 1909–1959* (London: Clapham County School, 1959), p. 12.
31. Board of Education, *Regulations for Secondary Schools* (various years), and PRO Ed.12/119. It was assumed that girls' schools did not normally do Greek, which retained its prestige in boys' schools as a required element in the examinations for Oxbridge awards.
32. Burstall, *English High Schools*, pp. 110, 132.
33. Burstall, *English High Schools*, pp. 198–9; Dyhouse, *Girls Growing Up*, p. 164.

34. PRO Ed.35/2579 and 35/860. The influence of the London Institute for the Advancement of Plain Needlework may be detected in these comments.
35. Board of Education, *Suggestions for the Teaching of Needlework* (1909).
36. The interpretation advanced by A.M. Kazamias in *Politics, Society and Secondary Education in England* (Philadelphia, PA: University of Pennsylvania Press, 1966), Ch. 8, that vocational and practical courses did not flourish because parents, LEAs and teachers were slower to change than the Board of Education really does stand the facts on their head.
37. PRO Ed.35/2554; Wilson, *Development of Secondary Education*, p. 296; PRO Ed.35/2579.
38. As characterised by T.W. Bamford, 'Public School Masters', in T.G. Cook (ed.), *Education and the Professions* (London: Methuen, 1973), p. 41: the public school headmaster 'was a potentate and there was no other job quite like it'. He suggested that it was only the great power and status of the job that attracted men to 'the battlefield' from the 'quiet contemplation' of Oxbridge colleges.
39. For example, during the bitter dispute with Nottingham Education Committee, Morant enlisted a 'spy' who sent back very unflattering descriptions of the local headmasters.
40. PRO Ed.35/2579.
41. PRO Ed.35/2584. It brings to mind Gathorne-Hardy's opinion that 'nuances of class can only be felt, they cannot be explained' in *Public School*, p. 133; and also the criticism levelled by Gordon and White in *Philosophers as Educational Reformers*, p. 175, at the influential group of late nineteenth-century English philosophers who did little to convert their idealist theories into guidance for the greatly enlarged teaching profession.
42. Board of Education, *Report for 1905–6* (1906), pp. 52–9.
43. Tropp, *School Teachers*, p. 189 and *passim*. Three-quarters of the total workforce were female.
44. Bourne and MacArthur, *Struggle*, p. 57; Simon, *Education and the Labour Movement*, pp. 244–6, 254.
45. Board of Education, *Regulations for the Instruction and Training of Pupil-Teachers* (1904), pp. 30–3.
46. For older teacher-trainees enrolling at colleges and universities, grants were explicitly conditional on the signing of a 'pledge' promising to teach after qualifying, as explained by H. Patrick, 'From Cross to CATE: The Universities and Teacher Education Over the Past Century', *Oxford Review of Education*, 12, 3 (1986), p. 245.
47. Tropp, *School Teachers*, pp. 186–7.
48. Burstall, *English High Schools*, p. 57. She also thought it 'important to ascertain at what college or university an applicant has studied, and at what school she was educated; these are often much more important than the actual degree'.
49. Bremner, *Education of Girls*, p. 175.
50. *Royal Commission on Secondary Education (Bryce Commission)*, VII, pp. 145–6. Laurie was the son of Scotland's leading educationist and teacher-trainer.
51. Reported in *The Schoolmaster*, 7 December 1895. This was, of course, a time of great progress in teacher education, especially with the establishment after 1902 of municipal training colleges, often linked to university colleges.
52. *The Times*, 22 September 1897.
53. Ch. 11 in Tropp, *School Teachers*, details how passionately keen was the Board, and Morant in particular, to resist the growing rapprochement between the 'elementary' and 'secondary' parts of the teaching profession. The shameful behaviour of the Board on the issue of a teachers' register certainly fuelled the onslaught on Morant over the Holmes–Morant Circular: 'only violent personal hostility can explain the venom with which the NUT officials attacked Morant' (p. 198).
54. Bourne and MacArthur, *Struggle*, p. 47.
55. Sneyd-Kinnersley, *H.M.I.*, p. 330.
56. Bridge Street School, Log Book, 11 September 1901; Wyggeston School, Governors' Meetings, Minutes, 11 November 1905, quoting from the Board of Education's Inspection Report.
57. PRO Ed.35/2584.
58. M. Seaborne and R. Lowe, *The English School: Its Architecture and Organization Vol II 1870–1970* (London: Routledge & Kegan Paul, 1977), pp. 96–104.
59. PRO Ed.35/2579 and 35/2554.
60. The Board's *Statistics* for 1910–11 show that of 128 boys' secondary schools with fewer than 100

pupils, only 12 were council schools; there was less discrepancy with girls' and mixed schools, although non-council schools were much more likely to have elementary/preparatory age pupils to include in their totals. The largest category then was 'over 500': just 19 schools in the whole country were in this category.

61. Seaborne and Lowe, *English School*, p. 96.
62. PRO Ed.35/2584. Playing fields could be as much as three miles – or a train journey – away.
63. PRO Ed.12/119; Board of Education, *Report for 1905–6*, p. 62.
64. Quoted in P. Gordon, *Selection for Secondary Education* (London: Woburn Press, 1980), p. 168.
65. Leicester Education Committee, Secondary Schools Sub-Committee, Minute Book, 5, 13 and 27 September 1904; Wyggeston Schools, Governors' Minute Book, 9 March 1904.
66. Board of Education, *Report for 1905–6*, p. 62.
67. Leamington Education Committee, Minutes, 10 July 1905; PRO Ed.35/2554.
68. Board of Education, *Statistics 1910–11*, (1912).
69. Compiled from various HMI Reports in the PRO files, and Wilson, *Development of Secondary Education*, Appendices E and H.
70. Campbell, *Eleven-Plus*, p. 74.
71. P.H.J.H. Gosden and P.R. Sharp, *The Development of an Education Service: The West Riding 1889–1974* (Oxford: Blackwell, 1978), pp. 86–9.
72. Adamson, *English Education*, p. 471.
73. Birchenough, *History of Elementary Education*, p. 160.
74. Birchenough, *History of Elementary Education*, p. 435, suggested that even by the 1930s there was an 'utter unwillingness' to face the true cost of educational opportunity for all children, as demonstrated by the mixed feelings about central schools, the local authorities' 'cheap' solution to the problem.
75. Quoted in Banks, *Parity and Prestige*, p. 67.
76. Quoted in Griggs, *Trades Union Congress*, p. 117.
77. People's College, Nottingham, Log Book, 31 January 1900, 16 February 1900, 21 February 1900, 3 July 1905.
78. R. Macleod, 'Science and Examinations in Victorian England', in Macleod, *Days of Judgment*, p. 11.
79. W.J. Reader, *Professional Men: The Rise of the Professional Classes in Nineteenth-Century England* (London: Weidenfeld & Nicolson, 1966), pp. 115–16
80. Southgate, *That's the Way*, *passim*.
81. Calculated from the admissions registers of four schools, two in Bristol and two in Birmingham 1902–7. By far the most popular occupations were clerk/typist (217, boys as well as girls) and teacher/pupil teacher (180, mostly girls), followed by accountant/bank clerk/civil servant/librarian (56), engineers of various kinds (50), chemist/laboratory assistant (23), designer/draughtsman (11) and an assortment of skilled trades. Records show 58 as having later attended university or training college.
82. See, for example, M.J. Price, 'Mathematics in English Education 1860–1914: Some Questions and Explanations in Curriculum History', *History of Education*, 12, 4 (1983), in which he described the battle between the non-establishment reformers who favoured a more practical syllabus and the 'markedly conservative' mathematicians of the public schools, Cambridge University and the Mathematical Association. G.R. Batho in 'Sources for the History of History Teaching in Elementary Schools 1833–1914', in T.G. Cook (ed.), *Local Studies and the History of Education* (London: Methuen, 1972) referred to a similar 'lively debate' over history as a school subject; and the establishment of English in the secondary school curriculum (initially as a linguistic and literary rival to the classics) has been outlined by M. Mathieson, *The Preachers of Culture: A Study of English and Its Teachers* (London: Allen & Unwin, 1975).
83. Grossek, *First Movement*, pp. 74, 85–6, 103. He was left 'with a discomfited feeling that an inferior substitute for what I really wanted was being foisted off on me'.
84. The average leaving age rose from 15.5 for boys and 15.11 for girls in 1906 to 15.7 and 16.0 in 1914. But the 30 per cent who left early (and therefore did not complete the secondary school course) persisted well into the 1920s and 1930s.
85. This attitude was expressed with stark tactlessness by the *Report of the Consultative Committee on Higher Elementary Schools* (1906), quoted in the section on those schools which follows.
86. PRO Ed.35/2554 and 35/2576.

87. Campbell, *Eleven-Plus*, p. 43. Grossek, *First Movement*, pp. 87–8, 248.
88. Gordon, *Selection*, p. 174 ff. J.A. Graham and B.A. Phythian (eds), *The Manchester Grammar School 1515–1965* (Manchester: Manchester University Press, 1965), p. 95.
89. Grossek, *First Movement*, p. 83.
90. The 'numbers' question is discussed in the next chapter.
91. The Schools Inquiry Commission has been called a 'landmark' (*Report of the Committee on Public Schools (Fleming Report)* (1944), p. 83); the Endowed Schools Act 'the Magna Carta of girls' education' (A. Zimmern, *The Renaissance of Girls' Education in England* (London: A.D. Innes, 1898)); and the Girls' Public Day School Company has been credited with 'outstanding progress' in the establishment of 'excellent schools for girls' (Kamm, *Hope Deferred*, p. 213).
92. The Endowed Schools Commissioners managed to create 94 girls' and seven mixed secondary schools, sometimes in the face of ferocious resistance, before running out of steam by the end of the century. The rate of expansion under the Girls' Public Day School Company also tailed off after a good start; by 1896 it had 36 schools and 7,200 pupils.
93. Zimmern, *Renaissance*, p. 167.
94. Duffin discussed the polarisation in medical attitudes towards women of different social classes: middle-class women did little and were 'pure but sick', while working-class women, suffering 'a life of back-breaking toil … were able-bodied but contaminated and sickening'. L. Duffin, 'The Conspicuous Consumptive: Woman as an Invalid', in Delamont and Duffin, *Nineteenth-Century Woman*, pp. 29–31.
95. Quoted in Dyhouse, *Girls Growing Up*, pp. 130, 134.
96. Board of Education, *Report of the Consultative Committee on the Differentiation of the Curriculum for Boys and Girls respectively in Secondary Schools* (1923). This report explained that 'girls' blood was lower in specific gravity, carrying less haemoglobin than did boys' blood after puberty'.
97. On these grounds, the GPSDC schools rejected Dr Elizabeth Garrett Anderson's advice that a midday break and afternoon school would be less stressful and more healthy. P. Atkinson, 'Fitness, Feminism and Schooling', in Delamont and Duffin, *Nineteenth-Century Woman*, p. 114.
98. Drawn from the writings of Sara Burstall, *English High Schools*, and *The Story of the Manchester High School for Girls 1871–1911* (Manchester: Manchester University Press, 1911), the school of which she was headmistress.
99. Bremner, *Education of Girls*, p. 169.
100. Burstall, *English High Schools*, pp. 13, 110; and *Manchester High School*, p. 43.
101. Duffin, 'Conspicuous Consumptive', argues that the useless life assigned to Victorian ladies may have adversely affected their health, that 'sickness filled the gap of inactivity so effectively that it came to pervade middle-class female culture'. The grim treatment they were likely to receive from their male doctors did not help, especially after about 1870 when crude gynaecological surgery became a popular remedy for a whole range of complaints. The fact that secondary education coincided with puberty made it especially vulnerable to criticism.
102. Zimmern, *Renaissance*, pp. 76–7.
103. John Rae, 75 years later, assessed his fellow public school headmasters as a group who 'are peculiarly susceptible to feminine charms' (in this case, those of Shirley Williams), in *The Public School Revolution* (London: Faber, 1981), p. 57.
104. PRO Ed.35/2554.
105. Gathorne-Hardy, *Public School*, pp. 126–7, amusingly depicted this kind of attitude: 'The upper classes inherited qualities just as their horses inherited fine fetlocks … you could almost catch lower classness like a disease.'
106. Burstall, *English High Schools*, p. 33.
107. PRO Ed.35/844.
108. *Bryce Commission*, VIII, pp. 24, 128. The first witness was Miss Woods, Principal of the Maria Grey Training College, and the second Revd Sharpe, Senior Chief Inspector of Schools.
109. PRO Ed.35/2584. Once the girls' lavatories had been suitably screened, co-education seems not to have been one of the (many) causes of complaint about this school, although the headmaster's inexperience with girl pupils was commented upon.
110. People's College, Log Book, 29 September 1901; PRO Ed.20/116.
111. Burstall, *English High Schools*, p. 77.
112. Seaborne and Lowe, *English School*, p. 99.

113. For example, R. Davis in *The Grammar School* (Harmondsworth: Penguin, 1967) alleged that co-education was only ever an administrative convenience, by which two schools were 'lumped together for half the cost'; and B. Wilson (ed.), *Education, Equality and Society* (London: Allen & Unwin, 1975), p. 32, thought that 'co-education may itself be another way in which human relationships are coarsened'.

114. In 1966, only 2 out of 179 direct grant schools were co-educational. E. Allsopp and D. Grugeon, *Direct Grant Grammar Schools* (London: The Fabian Society, 1966), pp. 2, 5.

115. Adverse changes to women's participation in education, particularly the school boards, has been linked to the founding of the Women's Social and Political Union (1903) and of the National Union of Women Teachers (1909) by R. Betts, '"Tried as in a Furnace": The NUT and the Abolition of the School Boards, 1896–1903', *History of Education*, 25, 1 (1996).

116. For example, 'it was only by continuing to glorify the Victorian domestic ideal ... that any educational progress could be made'. (Delamont and Duffin, *Nineteenth-Century Woman*, p. 184). One has to disagree with their statement that 'when the educational pioneers began it was inconceivable that mass secondary education would take less than a century to establish, or that all middle-class girls would soon be at school'.

117. PRO Ed.12/119. Mackail's choice of analogy is interesting in the light of a speech given by Morant in 1898, which contained a 'brilliant metaphorical description' of the education system as a basement (elementary), a first-floor (secondary) and upper-floor (university). Cited in Graves, *Policy and Progress*, p. 10.

118. Jenkins, *'Magnificent Pile'*, pp. 93–5.

119. PRO Ed.20/116. The interpretation advanced by Gordon, *Selection*, p. 99, that Nottingham was elitist in bringing a form of streaming into its elementary school system is a little unfair; it was primarily interested in finding a legitimate way of maintaining the educational opportunities which had existed before 1902.

120. Orally, and also in J. Burnett (ed.), *Useful Toil: Autobiographies of Working People from the 1820s to the 1920s* (London: Allen Lane, 1974). H.C. Dent, who went to an elementary school in 1900, wrote of the 'widespread suspicion (not altogether unjustified) of secondary schools, as middle-class institutions, not for working people', in *Century of Growth*, p. 64.

121. Reproduced in Eaglesham, *From School Board*, Appendix B.

122. Quoted in *The Schoolmaster*, 5 May 1900, whose editor added that the Minute 'marks an important stage in the progress of popular education'.

123. *The Schoolmaster*, 30 June 1900.

124. *The Schoolmaster*, 9 March 1901.

125. Richard Lishman, quoted in Jackson, *Belle Vue Boys' School*, p. 20.

126. Regulations reproduced in Davies, *Barnsley School Board*, Appendix IX.

127. D.L. Cattell, 'The Development of Albert Road Higher Grade School and the Education Department 1881–1900' (University of Birmingham MEd thesis, 1981); Birmingham School Board, School Management Committee, Minute Book, 21 June, 12 July, 20 September 1900.

128. The ensuing version of the saga (much abbreviated) is drawn from PRO Ed.20/114 and 20/116; Nottingham School Board, Minutes; Log Books of High Pavement and Mundella Schools and the People's College.

129. Thomas, *Nottingham High School*, pp. 241–51. James Gow was then head of Westminster School, and an active member of the Headmasters' Conference and the Board's Consultative Committee. It was he who as head of Nottingham High School had received Percival's support in frustrating an attempt to increase parental influence over the school.

130. Banks, *Parity and Prestige*, p. 62.

131. Curtis, *Education in Britain*, p. 46.

132. This report can be found, among other places, in PRO Ed.12/139.

133. In 1907 accommodation was 17,744 and 14,213 were on roll.

134. George Creech of Bristol recalled that 12 out of his 60 classmates took the scholarship examination in 1920 (two passed); in Cambridge in the 1920s and 1930s anything up to 60 boys a year turned down the places they had won at the Grammar School (A.B. Evans, *The Cambridge Grammar School for Boys 1871–1971* (Cambridge: Cambridge Grammar School, 1971), pp. 49–50); and in London in 1926 only 46,000 out of an eligible 75,000 sat the preliminary examination for secondary school selection (Campbell, *Eleven-Plus*, p. 97). No part of the country seems to have been able to solve this problem.

6

EDUCATION AFTER 1902: TENSIONS RESOLVED, POTENTIAL STUNTED

This book has depicted the last decade of the nineteenth century as a period of gathering tensions in several parts of the educational world in England. During the 1890s technical and scientific education had witnessed its greatest ever boom, the success of which was provoking increasingly anxious reactions at high levels. Partly as a result of this success the older institutions of secondary education were feeling so threatened that they were actively campaigning for their survival. Publicly provided elementary education, on the other hand, had become a powerful force with, by the 1890s, second-generation users of the system realising how much it could offer them and making ever greater demands of it. Underlying these developments, the idiosyncrasies of English educational administration were increasingly exposed, highlighting in the process the conflicts in attitudes between the 'metropolitan' elite who traditionally expected to provide education for the rest of the population, and those who were intimately involved at provincial level in the 'new' educational movements.

The fate of the higher grade schools, as a focus for all these tensions, can tell us a great deal about how the English education system responded as it entered the twentieth century. It has become clear that the higher grade school was not just a historical oddity, a failed and obsolete example of one generation's attempt to solve its own particular problems, but a powerful alternative model to the English grammar school. The reaction of the 'establishment' elite to this challenge provides an opportunity to analyse the underlying cultural and social climate at the beginning of this century, and to identify vestiges of it which still influence English values.

For they, like many of the basic tensions in English education and society, although modified in form over the years, have proved to be remarkably persistent. The problems of giving scientific and industrial activity real status in English society, of meeting the expectations of different socio-economic groups, of finding a style of schooling appropriate for all adolescents while also satisfying the desire for 'excellence', or of balancing power between the various levels of administration, are still high on the educational agenda.

RESOLUTION OF TENSIONS IN TECHNICAL EDUCATION

By the beginning of the twentieth century, the study of science and technical subjects had gained a foothold in England's educational system. Its strength resided almost exclusively in the publicly provided part of the system where, from tentative beginnings, it had mustered the resources to construct a complete vertical network of institutions. From the public elementary schools, where science 'showed a remarkable increase in popularity', being 'more real, more practical, and less bookish',[1] to the civic universities, which were doing 'incalculable service to the cause of Science in offering stimulating teaching and opportunities of research',[2] a new style of education could be pursued by any child of ability and determination. Propagandists who looked admiringly at the education systems of Germany or France, or even Scotland, at last felt that English education was starting to look more appropriate for a modern, democratic, industrial nation.

However, the fact that scientific education had found its place outside the prestigious mainstream of Victorian education only added to the stock of prejudices against it in some quarters. The vast majority of Oxbridge dons, politicians, churchmen, HMIs and Board of Education officials of the 1890s had themselves been taught so little science that it was perhaps comforting for them to believe that expertise in it should continue to rest largely with people not of their background or social milieu: nonconformists, foreigners, Scotsmen, artisans, school boards, technical and elementary school teachers, even their colleagues in the Science and Art Department.[3] In their own public schools, the science or modern 'side' was never accorded much prestige or money, and there was a general denial among the headmasters that 'anything could replace the classics as the best training for a first-class mind, or that anyone with a first-class mind could fail to be good at classical studies'.[4] As the Thompson Report later complained, 'there has in the Public Schools as a whole been no general recognition of the principle that Science should form an essential part of secondary education'.[5]

When the Board of Education turned its attention to the support of secondary schooling, 'classical' education became transmogrified into 'general' education. General education was, and is, an imprecise term which means nothing without knowing the intellectual and ideological context. As used by the Board at the beginning of this century, it meant education which had relatively little to do with the imparting of knowledge, particularly of the real world – scientific, economic or political – and even less interest in the passing on of skills other than certain cerebral ones. It was modelled on the system which was believed to have perfected the production of the empire's future rulers, without telling them much about the world they were to rule, or, as one critic has suggested, a system which 'did not see education as a preparation for the world, but as an inoculation against it'.[6] Such attitudes informed the crucial decision in 1899 to form three separate branches within the new Board of Education, so that the Technical Branch – and the influence of the Science and Art Department – was distanced from the Secondary Branch and rendered vulnerable to subsequent downgrading in status.[7]

The affection for general education was also a reaction to specialisation, which was perceived as characteristic of scientific education in publicly provided institutions and antipathetic to the principles of 'true' education. True education was not supposed to convey useful information and facts; if it did, it was merely instruction, of use only to the lower classes and available through part-time, low-status institutions. It was possible to 'specialise' only in science, technical and commercial subjects; a heavy bias towards classical or literary studies was not specialisation, but education. And so, just as the Bryce Report had done, the Board's 1904 Regulations asserted that literary, scientific and technical education were all important, yet made it clear that only the first could develop 'higher powers of thought and expression' and 'appreciation of what is best in the thought and art of the world ... which forms the basis of all human culture'. The distaste for specialisation expressed by the Board of Education in fact meant the banishment from secondary schools of all the 'specialisations' – scientific, vocational, commercial, technical – of most use to the majority of children.

General education did not lend itself to objective testing by external bodies, which strengthened the growing prejudice against written examinations. These were an intrinsic part of the Science and Art Department's nationwide sponsorship of scientific instruction – 'to "establish" science it was necessary to embrace the examination octopus as well'[8] – and it was convenient for opponents to dislike both. The early twentieth-century grammar school therefore displayed what to a later generation looks like a thoroughly casual approach to the levels of attainment of many of its pupils. It was shaped around a version of excellence standardised and accepted among those who regarded themselves as well-educated, which was still assumed to be classical, or at least literary, scholarship. Rothblatt has argued that at the highest level the classical scholars of Oxford and Cambridge successfully assimilated to their own discipline what might otherwise have been the challenge of the new 'scientific' or 'research' ethos which swept through western European intellectual life at the end of the nineteenth century.[9] This legitimated the assiduous promotion in aided secondary schools of the classical/literary curriculum, success in which could be achieved by only a minority of pupils.

The rejection of meritocratic mechanisms represented a fundamental change from the ideology of the higher grade schools. The fact that a few of their pupils got to university was maybe a source of pride and pleasure, but had no bearing on the way the rest of the school population was taught, or the goals held out to it. By default, the schools had been given a huge space to fill in the educational market, but it was less a case of offering a particular type of education to a select few, than of accepting a wide range of children and attempting to give each one of them something worthwhile, including the skills to earn their living at a relatively young age. The ability to care as much about the average or slower child as the high achiever was a marked attribute of higher grade school heads, who put on record their commitment to 'the feeling that the dull boys must be as carefully taught as the clever boys'. One of their number reacted typically to pressure to make his school more academically and socially prestigious after 1902 by declaring that his school was primarily for 'the average boy … it is not intended to be a preparatory school for the University'.[10] The higher grade schools' record in successfully accommodating a wide variety of pupils, with all the attendant teaching and organisational skills, was certainly one of their most noteworthy achievements, and one of the greater losses in the new system. *The Times'* advice that grammar schools should 'adopt the wholesome tradition that every boy in the school, dull or intelligent, is entitled to an equal share of attention'[11] was not heeded, and, after 1902, pupils were made to fit the education, rather than education fit the pupils.

Assumptions about the Board of Education's definition of general education in the secondary schools it aided – and especially the 1904 Regulations with their 'hours per subject' prescription for the curriculum

– therefore need to be treated with scepticism. It quickly became apparent that 'Division A' scientific secondary schools were regarded as abnormal, to be phased out as soon as decently possible, and in 1905 the Board guaranteed their future isolation by stating that 'it is not the intention of the Board to sanction the adoption of this special course in any fresh school'.[12] Indeed, the friendly reception accorded in 1904 to a delegation from the Incorporated Association of Head Masters suggests that some of the Board's senior officials would very much like to have swung the balance even further the other way. The delegates drew attention to the impossibility of complying with the Board's Regulations when three languages (Latin, Greek, French or German), each requiring six hours a week, were taught, and asked that the requirement for either English or science should be reduced. An even better solution, they suggested, would be that schools like theirs, which could 'satisfy certain tests of a higher liberal education', should be given 'comparative freedom' to design their own curriculum. In drawing up the next year's Regulations, the Board of Education toyed with the idea of giving higher grants to such schools; Morant was keen to 'fight the main issue of better grants for the non-science curriculum', and Mackail wished to counter 'a certain preference' given by the existing grant system to 'a particular class of school giving a rather highly specialised kind of instruction in physical science'.[13] With attitudes like that emanating from the highest Board officials, it is questionable whether the curricula of most older secondary schools changed at all. Those that had built science facilities to qualify for grants generally continued to teach science subjects, not least because they were popular with the pupils, but the schools were not encouraged to develop further in that direction. At the same time the former higher grade schools were being positively discouraged from maintaining their specialism, and any school with an explicitly technical orientation – or even the word 'technical' in its name – was a sure target for the Board's hostility.[14]

By 1918 the Thompson Committee was deeply unhappy about the weakness of science in the English school system. Opening with the comment that 'not for the first time our educational conscience has been stung by the thought that we are as a nation neglecting science', the report proposed a comprehensive set of measures in an attempt to ensure that the current wartime enthusiasm for science did not lapse in peacetime.[15] One of its special concerns was the 'dearth' of science and technical teachers and urgent remedies were called for, including more financial support for students, better salaries for teachers and 'a considerable raising of status'. It is ironic that the Science and Art Department had faced and overcome the same problem some 50 years earlier; indeed, the creation from nothing of a body of qualified science teachers was one of the greater achievements of that Department.[16] While the pupil teacher system operated in close relationship with the elementary and higher grade schools, at least a reasonable degree of competency in science among most new teachers had been guaranteed. And the early work of the civic universities, both in scientific research and in training teachers, enabled a fruitful liaison between the two activities, of which Thompson felt: 'that so much was done under such conditions only intensifies our regret that so much was lost'.[17] By moving all intending teachers into schools where science was not particularly highly regarded, and, in the case of girls, was an optional subject, the Board of Education profoundly affected the supply of science teachers.

Even allowing for changes in attitudes over the years, it is hard to accept the interpretation that the curriculum recommended by the early-century Board of Education was wisely balanced, the essence of a 'general' education. It was, of course, a happy convenience for the Board that the schools it most wished to get rid of were also those which were identified with the subjects it least valued. The classics, already so well ensconced in the more expensive echelons of the education system, were force-fed to schoolchildren who had no obvious use for them, while the areas of knowledge in which their schools were developing excellence were disdained and downgraded. The Board's determination to drive anything too useful or vocational out of the secondary schools reflected a particular approach to learning which was already under threat, and which represented a serious mismatch with the needs of the larger part of the population. In the Board of Education as structured and staffed by Morant, there was nobody at the higher levels trumpeting the calls of science and technical education. At no point in the education system did science and technical subjects even hold their ground under Morant's Board of Education; far less were they extended or encouraged in the nation's new secondary schools.

RESOLUTION OF TENSIONS IN SECONDARY EDUCATION

The growth of a style of secondary education which valued science and technical subjects had been contemporaneous with a period of increasing difficulties for the endowed schools. The work of reform which followed the Schools Inquiry Commission had produced a proportion of 'successful' schools, although even that is a relative term; of Manchester Grammar School, for instance, it has been said that 'the 1902 Act marks the point at which the School can be said to emerge from its vicissitudes'.[18] Many more endowed schools were conspicuously struggling. It is not surprising that they should have seen the flourishing higher grade schools as unfair competitors in the battle for pupils because they were cheaper to the parents, even when there is no clear evidence that this was in fact the case. A.P. Laurie was convinced that higher grade school parents in Yorkshire did not want what the more traditional schools were offering, and struggling endowed schools were not confined to areas where there were higher grade school rivals. In Southport, for example, the Boys' Grammar and Girls' High Schools were in difficulties, while the Modern School founded in 1892 – fee-paying but emphasising English, mathematics and modern languages 'for business and professional life' – thrived.[19]

The endowed schools were, however, highly successful in conducting the campaign for their own survival. That was done quite consciously during the 1890s under the auspices of the Incorporated Association of Head Masters (IAHM), which came to be seen by opponents as 'the real villain of the piece'.[20] It was jointly led by Dr Scott of Parmiter's School in London, where the large-scale provision of Technical Education Board scholarships 'brought into the open the antagonism of the grammar school headmasters', and the Reverend Keeling of Bradford Grammar School, a school which had violently resisted the Endowed Schools Commissioners' attempts to broaden its curriculum, but by the 1890s was feeling increasingly threatened by England's leading 'higher grade' school board.[21] These two men 'for several years have been moving heaven and earth to limit and cripple the Board Schools of science', according to Richard Lishman, head of Belle Vue Higher Grade School in Bradford.[22] The Bradford connection in all this was significant; with two leading and nationally known headmasters on opposing sides, 'verbal missiles continued to fly' in the city and the local newspaper became the 'forum for a national discussion' of education.[23]

The IAHM's strategy of seeking collusion with the more secure public schools encouraged the latter to extend a protective wing towards schools with which they had previously had little contact or sympathy. From there it was possible to present a powerful case for remedial action to politicians and Whitehall officials, who were, as Beatrice Webb pointed out, of the 'same social class ... they had easy access to them in unofficial and informal ways'.[24] With their shared conviction that in the public schools Britain had perfected the training of its leaders, and thereby arrived at the true purpose of education, there was a ready-made blueprint for the extension of state interest into the realm of secondary education. The officials of Morant's Board of Education formulated their prototype without much difficulty; as documents circulated around the Board of Education's offices, they were annotated not with fresh insights or alternative interpretations but endorsements, extra justifications and useful precedents. One of the main assets of the emerging model was that it did not require too many significant changes in most endowed schools, especially when rulings were introduced in a spirit of compromise.

What is more puzzling is the determination of the Board to make the public school the prototype for every secondary school it aided, regardless of local wishes to the contrary. Morant's natural liking for order and detail, reinforced by the Fabian equation of 'efficiency' with systemisation, would seem to be the guiding force behind this drive towards the standardisation of England's secondary schools, and of its higher elementary schools, pupil teacher training, evening classes and even ordinary elementary schools. Several writers have since looked favourably on this aspect of Morant's work, seeing it as a successful exercise in bringing order out of chaos,[25] but it can be argued that sameness is not a particularly useful or desirable quality in education. Countries like Germany, France and Switzerland – and Scotland and Wales nearer to home – had produced orderly 'systems' of post-elementary education which accommodated different kinds of schools, each with their own status and function, and linked to institutions below and above. Enthusiasts for the higher grade schools had never anticipated that they would be the model for all secondary schools, but rather that they had an undisputed place within the network of institutions which should comprise secondary education. There had been a strong expectation, confirmed by Bryce, that the public secondary school system would consist of higher grade and endowed schools operating under similar conditions of funding and management.

However, under Morant's Board of Education, variety was not an option and there was effectively no choice to be made. Considering their widely assorted pupils, higher grade schools must have been extraordinarily efficient and orderly places, but to critics – as to a number of educational historians since – they looked messy and rootless, floundering around in a sea of makeshift curricula, inappropriate examinations, under-qualified teachers and premature leavers. They would have to fall into line if they wanted to become maintained secondary schools. Private institutions could, of course, be as varied and unsystematic as they liked, provided they could support themselves, and the difference between the two sectors was thus emphasised in what has proved to be a remarkably enduring fashion. There is still support for the claim that, whatever its faults, the private sector of education is essential because that is where innovation and experimentation flourish, free from the rigid, stultifying uniformity of the state system. Morant's approach certainly encouraged the idea – all too familiar to teachers in the 1990s – that in order to guarantee standards and ensure value for taxpayers' money, maintained schools need to be told how to conduct themselves according to a set of rules imposed from above.

The practical ways in which such guidance manifested itself were clearly expressions of a deeper philosophical understanding of the purpose of education, which has left its imprint to this day. The desire to make secondary schools self-contained units providing for all their own needs (but nobody else's) established fundamental principles of selectivity and elitism in England's maintained secondary school system. For while one may applaud the early Board of Education for trying to make schools as spacious and stylish as possible, it has been proved at various times since that school buildings are remarkably elastic in their capacity when the need arises. The difference then was that the Board perceived no such need. It got very annoyed with local educationists who were misguided enough to want to extend opportunities to more children. It had no interest in continuing the higher grade school tradition of packing in as many children as were willing and suited to be there, nor would it allow the building or conversion of extra, less crowded schools to increase the overall secondary accommodation. Throughout the early part of the century, what seemed to be the infinite growth of secondary education surprised and alarmed the Board, as well as senior politicians: Balfour's remark that he did not realise the 1902 Act would lead to more bureaucracy and more expense is well known (see Chapter 1).

Many of the characteristics of the early century secondary school created by the Board of Education – its physical appearance, the corporate life, the organised games – add up to a powerful version of what in modern times would be called the hidden curriculum. There is scarcely a single aspect of it which would have been a normal part of working-class life; indeed, some of it would not necessarily have been familiar to members of the commercial middle class. Even if it was not deliberately intended to make the working-class entrant feel unsure and ill at ease, the fact that it did so was not seen as a drawback. There is evidence that scholarship children struggled to settle into grammar schools, and the schools made few concessions to them. Mark Grossek described it as 'a sense of being in somebody else's house', while historian S.J. Curtis, who won a scholarship to an endowed school in 1904, recalled that both staff and pupils 'constantly reminded' him that 'they regarded scholarship pupils as belonging to an inferior category'.[26] The same prejudices which in the nineteenth century had forced poor children out of their local endowed schools and segregated foundationers from fee-payers in the public schools, and which in 1907 produced widespread resistance to the free place regulations,[27] guaranteed that a major part of the learning which working-class children undertook at secondary schools was the absorption of middle-class mores, rather than the cultivation of their brains.

One feature deemed by the Board of Education to be essential to secondary schooling – organised games – illustrates graphically the class-based cultural divisions so carefully nurtured in the schools.[28] The school boards, mindful of the poor physical condition of many of their pupils, had done pioneering work in the development of 'physical education', using a basic programme of Swedish drill, perhaps with some swimming, gymnastics and occasional games in a nearby park.[29] Its replacement by certain outdoor team games was primarily because it was believed they imbued valuable qualities of character – determination, loyalty, competitiveness tempered by a sense of fair play, team spirit – which amounted to the importation of a version of 'muscular Christianity' into the state education system. Sir John Gorst thought it was hard for underfed children to enjoy the sort of physical training the governing classes 'highly approved' for them,[30] and team games, with their heavy demands on space, equipment and levels of expertise, have never been the best way of promoting fitness and habits of exercise in schoolchildren. The local authorities were not averse in principle to the acquisition of playing fields, but it was impossible to find for each secondary school around six acres of suitable empty ground, especially when much of it would, by urban standards, be seriously underused. It forced authorities to look to the outskirts of cities for sites, thereby adding to the tendency for schools to be no longer 'an intimate part of the fabric of local life'; instead, they were 'surrounded by a *cordon sanitaire* of playing fields which effectively insulated them from their immediate community'.[31]

The campaign for survival mounted by the endowed schools in the 1890s had therefore produced enormous rewards. The new system of secondary education was built around them and they entered the state system virtually on their own terms. Schools which favoured the public school style of education were given every assistance, while others were encouraged to abandon the features which had been bringing them closer to the local authority model. As intended, status very quickly attached to them, and their rescue was complete. As well as sympathetic treatment of deficiencies in buildings, facilities, curriculum and teaching skills, they were allowed to retain much of their independence from public control, and exercise sole rights of selection of their pupils. And, most precious, with the clearing away of any possible rivals, they were given a monopolistic position, which meant that they did not have to change much, or even be very good at what they did. In effect, the question posed by the NUT in 1900 – 'can the small Grammar Schools be really benefited by choking off competition and surrounding them with a ring fence?'[32] – was answered with an emphatic 'yes'.

The early-century Board of Education thereby formulated what became arguably the most uniformly recognisable and widely understood of any educational institution, the twentieth-century grammar school. As favoured schools which were not completely closed to less financially favoured children, the grammar schools attracted passionate devotees: 'one of the glorious successes of English education' or 'the finest secondary schools in the world'.[33] They became the pivot of our whole education system, so perfect that they did not need criticism or improvement, even from official reports supposedly reviewing the whole spectrum. Hence, Hadow in 1927 asserted that secondary (that is, grammar) schools were 'not within our purview ... we think it important that care should be taken ... to avoid any action which might undermine their efficiency or expose them to undesirable competition';[34] 20 years later Ellen Wilkinson, herself the product of a Manchester higher grade/central school, explained that in England's new tripartite system, the grammar schools' 'long history and the standards they have already achieved help to give them a sense of direction, and there is comparatively little that need be said about them in this pamphlet'.[35] As an educational model, the grammar school has certainly exercised a powerful hold (and continues to do so in some quarters) which has been only partially loosened by the recognition of how severely parallel institutions suffer in its shadow, and of how impossible it is to categorise 11-year-old schoolchildren. The ethos and style of education which the grammar school was able to develop by virtue of its special circumstances have infused our whole secondary school system. They became widely accepted as the highest goals for all secondary schools, which are still implicitly applied as a measure against schools operating in very different circumstances. Having been given from the outset a privileged and monopolistic position from which it would have been very difficult to fail, the grammar school succeeded handsomely, accumulating prestige and making it impossible for any alternative style of secondary education to resurface in a viable form.

RESOLUTION OF TENSIONS IN ELEMENTARY EDUCATION

No one in England in 1900 could have been unaware of the great progress in 'elementary' education which had been made during the previous 30 years. Despite the fairly limited obligations imposed on school boards by the 1870 Education Act, most of the larger ones had of their own volition taken on a range of additional responsibilities with the blessing of their local electors and people like Mundella, Acland and Kekewich in the central administration. The care of handicapped and hungry children, the preparation of intending teachers, the raising of the elementary school-leaving age were logical and desirable goals pioneered by the urban school boards. So too was the provision of an integral summit for the system; it could not just be sealed off as a self-contained entity fulfilling its own limited needs, bringing on its most successful children to a certain point but no further. To the higher grade school heads, their schools were 'the resultant apex of the broad-based pyramid of the Elementary Education Act – the only schools that continued the work of the elementary schools'.[36] The rapid growth of the higher grade movement and the way in which it was spreading all over the country proved that there was considerable enthusiasm for the new opportunities and, for the first time, real potential for change through the public education system.

The success of the movement was precisely what was seen as a threat by those who had a vested interest in curtailing opportunities and resisting change. Elementary education was bound to be profoundly affected by the adoption of a standardised model of secondary schooling drawn from another part of the social and educational world. The crucial change was that the chosen model was firmly based on social-class distinctions. This has been denied by a number of historians: it 'placed advanced instruction within the reach of the major part of the people of England' said one, and produced 'an adequate supply of schools which, though wonderfully varied, appear to meet all needs', according to another.[37] Such claims are contradicted by the Board of Education's insistence that all secondary schools charge fees, thereby reflecting a powerful middle-class view of which the Bryce Commission had heard much, that parents ought to pay fees for secondary education and if they could not, they were self-evidently not of the right type to participate in it.

The Board's own statistics suggest that although secondary schools were dominated by the middle class, about 20 per cent of their pupils came from working-class homes. Recalling the figures known about the late 1890s, 20 per cent was an improvement on the 9 per cent of working-class children admitted to endowed schools, but represented a significant worsening of access compared with the higher grade schools, which were 40 per cent working class. Lower-middle-class parents – white-collar workers and shopkeepers – remained at a remarkably constant 45 to 50 per cent in both types of school before 1902, and in many aided secondary schools after that date. But professional families, which constituted 1 per cent of the total population and were almost negligible among higher grade parents, comprised nearly 20 per cent of those recorded at post-1902 secondary schools.[38] It is certain that access to secondary education was in fact narrowed after 1902, with the abolition of the higher grade schools and pupil teacher centres representing a serious reduction in opportunities for the 75 per cent of the population categorised as manual workers.

Intimately tied up with the class-based nature of the new secondary school system was its deliberately engineered separation from the public elementary system. Reference has been made to the numerous practical ways in which the Board of Education sought to distance the one from the other, and to the emotional intensity with which some HMIs executed this aspect of Board policy. That it was discriminatory on the basis of social class alone is beyond dispute. For, while the Board had no objection to preparatory departments in 'proper' secondary schools, it strongly condemned a similar close relationship between elementary departments and the higher classes in local authority schools. Both would seem to have been fulfilling the same function – the supply and smooth transition of a solid core of pupils on to the next stage – but the second was as consistently deplored as the first was wholly to be encouraged. Trevelyan confirmed in 1911 that it was the policy of the Board to encourage preparatory schools in connection with existing secondary schools: at this time no less than 699 out of 862 aided secondary schools had pupils under 10 years of age, amounting to 6.5 per cent of the total 'secondary' school population.[39] In the competition for secondary school places, preparatory departments gave an unfair advantage to children who could afford to use them, but they remained in favour at the Board even when scholarship winners were being turned away from secondary schools for lack of room. By 1920 there were 11,134 such children, and the West Riding of Yorkshire, for example, witnessed a bitter controversy as Labour councillors on the Education Committee battled to force grammar schools to reduce their under-10s to make room for more children who had won secondary school places on merit.[40]

This was one clear indication of the inadequacy of the free place system in bridging the gap between the public elementary and secondary school systems. As well as being unfair in principle and susceptible to non-educational pressures, it relied on methods of selection which were then an infant science.[41] The Board of Education's Report for 1911–12 claimed that 'the "free-place" regulations were not framed with the intention of instituting a scholarship system for the intellectual elite of the elementary schools', but they instantly became exactly that, and it can only be inferred that the Board expected qualities other than intellectual ones to qualify children for secondary school places. While local education authorities grappled with the problem of selecting their free-place pupils, the Board seemed to be more interested in pushing secondary school fees up and reducing the 25 per cent free-place requirement in schools of which it approved. Fees continued to be presented almost as a moral issue – although they were also a very convenient way of safeguarding the social exclusivity of secondary schools – and free places were thus a form of state benevolence to a 'deserving' minority from among those who could not pay. This ending of automatic access to any further education for public elementary schoolchildren constituted an absolutely fundamental ideological change in England's education system. It had been an intrinsic feature of the higher grade school system, whose headmasters could not believe there was any way of constructing a national system of secondary education other than on the basis of the national system of elementary education. Even judged by the standards of its own time, the Board of Education's deliberate construction of barriers between ordinary elementary and secondary education to protect its elitist model was unnecessary and retrogressive.

It also challenged working-class traditions in education, which can be characterised as optimistic but wholly realistic: education is a 'good thing', but it must also produce useful results. Richard Church, for example, described as typical his schoolteacher mother's submergence of her own cultural tastes as she 'talked frequently of careers' and the 'advantage of a good education'.[42] There is now a substantial body of evidence[43] for a striking and consistent appetite for education among the working classes long before it was provided for them, which contradicts the earlier assumption of working-class apathy and/or antipathy to education. It has been suggested that the much-maligned 'dame schools' of history textbooks were in fact highly efficient at ensuring the speedy acquisition of basic skills (which did not include religion), usually from a familiar local figure who, with minimal resources, became adept at 'child-centred' techniques to cope with all ages of children attending at various times of the day and for differing lengths of time. And, since small fees were paid, the customers could ensure that the 'school' functioned according to their requirements.

However, middle-class propaganda made much of the unsuitable premises, the unqualified teachers and the absence of religious instruction, and a number of critical reports succeeded in putting the schools out of business by a clause in the 1876 Elementary Education Act. Communities then had to adjust to a new style of schooling: on a mass scale, with professionally qualified and publicly employed teachers in formal buildings, and new pressures on the pupils to attend regularly and punctually and submit themselves to examinations. The rise of the higher grade school movement strongly suggests that they were successfully making that adjustment. At a time of changing employment patterns, the well-resourced higher grade schools offered far more scope for occupational and social mobility than the 'dame schools' could ever have done. There were thus growing expectations of the publicly provided education service, based on a simple adaptation of the older traditions. In a number of respects, the school boards and their schools represented a compromise on the issues previously intrinsic to working-class schooling, rather than being wholly antagonistic to it. Schools were not in neighbours' homes, but they were nearby and maintained open access. John Braine said of his board school days, it was 'an extension of home; fear did not exist there'.[44] Teachers were of similar social backgrounds and theoretically, any working-class child could join their ranks. The education on offer enabled pupils to work hard and gain quick, tangible results. And the school boards were directly answerable to public opinion.

The Board of Education's separation of secondary from elementary education had major implications for these expectations. The transformation of higher grade schools into municipal secondary schools gave them a fresh identity, which made almost no concessions to working-class traditions in education. Parents and children who had previously regarded the higher grade school as their own felt alienated and distanced from the typical secondary school. The schools were further removed from pupils' normal lives, often geographically and always in ethos. The teachers were from different social and educational backgrounds and it became increasingly difficult for working-class children to enter the profession. The education offered was leisurely both in terms of the aspects of knowledge it favoured and the length of time it took, so that tangible rewards came only after several years, requiring advance planning of a kind which poorer families were simply not in a position to make.[45] And, far from being responsive to working-class interests, the schools tended to be antagonistic, and the bodies which controlled them far removed from any susceptibility to working-class pressure.

If it was the case that the Board of Education's new model of secondary schooling – class-based, fee-paying and distanced from both the public elementary system and the traditions it embodied – excluded the vast majority of ordinary children, what happened to them? They are a rather shadowy entity. No doubt the prominence of educational issues in municipal and parliamentary by-elections, the recurring criticisms from the labour movement, parental campaigns and pupil strikes at some individual schools were expressions of opposition. But, on the whole, people made remarkably little fuss. Some parents were prepared to fight and make sacrifices all the more to gain entrance to the new secondary school system, but they were moving onto increasingly unfamiliar territory and risking becoming virtual isolates within their own communities. Quite apart from material considerations, it must have been a huge psychological decision for most working-class families to take. It is not in the least surprising that many of them turned their backs on secondary education, their children not even bothering to sit the examinations for scholarships and free places. It has been proved that among children who did sit the examinations, more children rejected the places they had won than accepted them, even in 'favourable' areas, and in the West Riding in the 1930s there was 'still a significant number of children who, although recommended to sit for examination, failed to obtain their parents' consent to do so'.[46] This premature rejection of the style of secondary schooling on offer was a nationwide phenomenon, which by the 1920s and 1930s had become so disturbingly persistent as to merit top-level investigation. It stands as a remarkable indictment of the work of the early Board of Education in formulating a 'national' system of education.

So, the vast majority of children, deterred or barred from entering secondary schools, spent their whole school career in ordinary elementary schools. This meant until the age of 14 in most cases, since in the very same year (1900) that the abolition of higher grade opportunities got under way, school boards were permitted to raise the school-leaving age. Many 'elementary' schools thus had more older pupils on their hands, with rather less obvious purpose to offer them. Morant, with his firm commitment to the differentiation, and therefore containment, of each part of the educational system was more interested in curtailing the elementary curriculum than expanding it. Hence, 'it is intended to exclude higher science teaching from the curriculum of the ordinary Public Elementary School';[47] he was not at all happy about modern languages; and Walter Southgate, a talented artist, never had an art lesson at his elementary school.

The early part of the century has been acclaimed by some as 'the dawn of a new era' for elementary education,[48] in which the liberalisation that followed the end of payment by results and new educational theories, particularly with regard to infant schooling, played a part. Such enthusiasts have expressed great admiration for Morant's 1904 Regulations; the introduction, 'remarkable for its fineness of conception and its dignity of expression',[49] stressed the importance of inculcating habits of industry, self-control, truthfulness and loyalty into children, and encouraged practical and physical activities as well as intellectual and character-forming ones. Nineteenth-century attitudes to the education of the lower classes were thus interwoven into the apparently lofty ideals held out to twentieth-century elementary schools, which, it has been suggested, were 'essentially designed to ensure discipline and to act as agents of social control'.[50] The contradiction built into elementary education – and the impossible task expected of its teachers – was to rebound on Morant when the 'leaked' Holmes–Morant Circular provoked a major NUT campaign which brought about his undignified removal from the world of education in 1911.[51]

One new function which elementary schools did have to embrace was the preparation of their pupils for whatever secondary school places were available. Despite the fact that many of them did not even want to try, and the vast majority would not succeed, the various examining mechanisms used to identify the chosen few instantly became a highly competitive business, instead of a means of establishing suitability. Indeed, it is hard to imagine that anyone was so naive as to expect it to do otherwise; although heads of grant-maintained schools and specialist schools in the 1990s are still trying. It should be remembered that at the beginning of the century this kind of selective examination was a real novelty for elementary schools; indeed it was another symptom of the distance between elementary and secondary schooling that a different test was believed necessary to establish 'suitability', rather than accepting the elementary schools' own measure of success, the Standards, as the higher grade schools did. Inevitably it had a disruptive effect. In many schools there was a concentration of effort, including the best teachers, on children of ten to 11 years of age, which one 'successful' pupil recalled as being 'rigidly purposeful'.[52] The more progressive members of the Board of Education's 1920 *Committee on Scholarships and Free Places* (who emphatically dissented from the majority report in favour of testing all but subnormal 11 year olds) were emphatic that the scholarship examination had 'devastating effects' on elementary schools, cramping the curriculum, encouraging streaming, cramming and mechanical testing, and giving children a lifelong distaste for learning.[53] In time, the whole of elementary education became permeated by the demands of secondary education, and as Simon has suggested, it was essentially a process of 'selection by elimination', masquerading as the more acceptable and positive-sounding 'selection by ability'.[54] The skills and energies of top educationists were thus directed for much of this century at divining the perfect method of selection, rather than working to expand and variegate post-elementary education so that selection was less significant.

In the absence of that kind of expansion, for the vast majority of children – 399 out of every 400 Walter Southgate estimated at his school, nine out of ten nationwide – schooling lost any overt goal. Some schools and local authorities did their best to encourage effort and a sense of purpose by organising internal school competitions, awarding certificates, prizes and gold medals, and stressing the importance of obtaining a good character reference. Walter Southgate was pleased to have accumulated quite a collection of these awards, although he was ashamed of the 'pinchpenny piece of cardboard' which the London County Council gave to school leavers and critical of the 'parsimonious' and 'reactionary' decision to abolish these incentives soon after.[55] But for many, many children, it was just a question of carrying on with Standards work until they could leave. It emerges clearly from oral research that to many youngsters in the early part of this century, school was at best an irrelevance, and at worst a sworn enemy to be evaded or resisted. Yet many of them also recollect that a wholly 'elementary' education was nevertheless considered preferable to the new style of secondary schooling, which not only contained a number of insuperable practical barriers, but also forcefully conveyed the message that that kind of education was not for the likes of them.

This was a specifically English problem and in 1911 a number of local authorities sent representatives to Scotland to investigate the provision for older pupils there. They were very impressed with what they saw, and urged the Board of Education to give grants for more varied advanced courses, but the answer was 'no'. So, thousands of children were left in the depressing situation described by the West Riding Education Committee in 1908:

> In many schools all pupils in the top two or three Standards had to be taught simultaneously by the same teacher. This led to wasteful repetition of work for the older scholars and gave them the impression that they had already learnt all that school could offer them and were just marking time.[56]

At one 'elementary' school all the older pupils were put in three classrooms where 'no more serious attempts were made to educate them' for their last three years. And, as late as the 1940s, Brian Simon came across an 'unreorganised' elementary school which still worked children through the Standards to the age of 14 by 'a system of mass instruction with strictly limited objectives ... often by rote learning and offering little or nothing outside it'.[57]

There was a brighter side to the story, thanks to the efforts of progressive teachers and 'the rise of humaner and more liberal Authorities',[58] but overall the dismal picture amounts to a very half-hearted national investment in several younger generations. Whatever was achieved in the creation of a secondary education system, other parts of the educational world were obliged to pay a heavy price to ensure the safe progress of the favoured one. Given the advantages with which he endowed the secondary schools, Morant's anxiety seems excessive, but, as Eaglesham suggested, Morant had long believed that too much of the national effort was devoted to elementary education. He concluded that in attacking it with 'headlong vigour', Morant 'helped to contain, to repel, and in some respects to destroy the upward striving of the elementary schools ... elementary education was put into a strait-jacket'.[59] This is a long way from the ideals which accompanied the late-nineteenth-century expansion of the elementary system, and it was undoubtedly backward rather than forward in direction. Unless it can be believed that the Board of Education simply misjudged the demand for education from the lower-middle and working classes, it has to be concluded that the Board consciously ruled against the satisfaction of that demand and attempted to turn back the clock.

RESOLUTION OF TENSIONS IN EDUCATIONAL ADMINISTRATION

Much of the reformist talk of the 1890s was of the urgent need for the better organisation and administration of education, especially at secondary level. Even the most fervent school board supporters conceded the necessity of rationalising the situation by which several bodies had an interest in secondary education but none had overall responsibility. In all the discussions the desirability of local authority involvement in education was scarcely challenged but, as became clear after the 1902 Education Act, that could mean different things to different people. For, while the Act clearly defined a new set of administrative bodies, it was imprecise about their powers and duties. The gusto with which many of

the newly created local authorities set about the job they thought they had
been given shows that they fully expected to play a decisive role in
shaping the educational provision of their own areas. But the central
authority was concerned above all to use the Act to salvage the voluntary
and endowed schools, which had never been subject to local authority
control. Their rescue could best be achieved by direct intervention from
the centre, and the local authorities would be needed only as agents to
carry out the instructions. The balance of power in the central/local
relationship was therefore crucial to the manner in which the Act was
implemented and, in establishing where the balance should lie, the underlying tensions between the 'metropolitan' and the 'provincial' outlooks
came explosively to the surface.

In a number of ways, the sheer size and diversity of the new local
authorities[60] represented the biggest challenge to the Board of Education's
direction of a uniform national strategy. By and large, as had been the case
in the school board days, the urban authorities were dynamic and self-
confident, and prepared to confront the Board of Education if necessary,
while the rural counties were more cautious, both about the spending of
public money and about how to proceed in general. But it is interesting
that various kinds of local authorities found themselves in dispute with the
Board of Education over educational policy; disaffection was not confined
to a few notably radical or assertive cities. The more left-wing elements
of some of the later school boards were normally missing from the
education committees, and the new bodies were less directly answerable
to public opinion, but they did have an awareness of and commitment to
the interests of local people, including those of a lower socio-economic
class than the Board of Education thought were likely to be involved in
secondary education. They were also much better informed than the
Board or its inspectors about alternative models of secondary schooling,
learned from the higher grade school experience. Most of all, they liked
neither being told how to run the schools they maintained, nor the Board's
idea that they should abdicate control of them to governing bodies
comprised of the sort of people who knew instinctively what a 'proper'
secondary school was like.[61]

While it was felt in many areas that relations between the education
committee and the schools were never quite as intimate as in the school
board days, links were nevertheless strong and sometimes, when a
particular local councillor became identified with a school over a long
period, very strong. The Board of Education always disliked this kind of
collaboration and mutual support; it seems to have assumed that the close
links between the school boards and their higher grade schools were an

aberration assigned to the past by the abolition of both. When the key local authority figure was one of the new breed of directors of education, the Board – and especially Morant – reacted even more strongly. The twentieth century's widespread adoption of full-time salaried officials in charge of important areas of local administration was a development which he could not fail to understand, but which he resisted at every opportunity. The adversarial nature of the relations between Morant and the men who are often regarded as the founding-fathers of education in their various areas, is extremely revealing both of his attitudes and of the general tensions between the centre and the localities. A cynic might suggest that it was his personal knowledge of how powerful an efficient administrator could be that made Morant so determined to keep at arm's length his local equivalents!

The Association of Directors and Secretaries for Education (ADSE) evolved smoothly out of the Conference of School Board Clerks, which had by 1902 become a coherent and important body. It was accustomed to meeting quarterly in London, printing its minutes and resolutions, and forwarding them to the Board for discussion at a regular conference. But, when the secretary of ADSE followed this procedure in late 1903, he received from Morant a reply that was bristling with hostility: 'I am afraid I do not understand from your letter what it is you desire from me in the nature of a reply. You ask no questions in your letter, and merely send, apparently, a printed copy of the minutes.' Morant obviously felt the need to establish his relationship with the secretaries (he never called them directors) on a different footing from his predecessor. He did so in the most convoluted way imaginable,[62] constructing a plot designed to frustrate and undermine the members of ADSE, and he continued to treat the organisation in an extremely distant manner. Replies were deliberately delayed, the Association asked to repeat the main points of perfectly explicit letters, and the Board's real reasons disguised under 'very carefully worded' explanations.

In particular, Morant's insistence on the Board's right to recognise and aid schools whatever the local education authorities' views seriously compromised their work. Requests and protests from ADSE over this issue brought forth the ruling from Morant that the Board will 'deal directly with the Managers of Schools without requiring the correspondence and Forms to pass through the County Office', which 'rescinded the rule which made "acting in unison with" the County or County Borough Authority a condition precedent to the eligibility of a new School to receive Government Grants'. This really was a nonsense of a policy, and the antagonistic atmosphere which surrounded it was to linger for many years after Morant's departure.[63] Nearly 100 years later, it has a striking resonance with the difficulties introduced into the education system by the invention of grant maintained status.

Examinations of disputes between the central and local authorities repeatedly reveal one of Morant's less statesmanlike qualities, his habit of personalising opposition. A senior colleague, Sir John Craig, wrote of Morant that he believed that 'beasts beset his every step', and a later assessment concluded that he 'was too prone to treat opposition as something personal and unreasonable, something he must hammer into submission'.[64] He is known to have browbeaten the most senior politicians in the land so can hardly have been fearful of the local directors of education, yet he was always reluctant to accept that their opinions were almost certainly shared by their education committees, and possibly by local popular support as well. Not surprisingly, individuals who had the most decided opinions on the secondary education in their areas, and who put up the sternest resistance to the Board, came in for the harshest treatment. Some of the more unfriendly exchanges with Bristol have already been mentioned and the long-running disputes with Bradford and Leeds have been documented elsewhere.[65] Reference to the two lesser-known examples of Worcestershire and Nottingham, which follow, illustrates some of the common points of contention and suggests strongly that they were more than just an unlucky personality clash.

As a predominantly rural county, Worcestershire might well have been expected to display the cautious conservatism and respect for central direction which would have made life easy for the Board of Education. In fact, the appointment as Director of Education of Dr Rawson, formerly of the Technical Institute in Huddersfield, heralded the start of a belated struggle to make up the deficit of secondary school places in suburbs around the fringes of Birmingham and the Black Country for which the county was responsible.[66] Worcestershire speedily became characterised by the Board as an authority 'in which delay seems to alternate with rushing things through at the eleventh hour', and where 'want of preparation and of attention to details ... made efficiency impossible'. Its major fault was that 'nothing was left to local initiative' (presumably the same local initiative which had so far failed to provide the much-needed schools), and the Board made much of 'how disastrous were the effects of the extreme centralisation at Worcestershire'. No doubt one of the more disastrous effects was that too much control remained in the hands of Dr Rawson, with whom 'the chief responsibility for the unsatisfactory state seems to lie'. His chief sin was his failure to 'realise the nature and object of a Secondary School', because he 'assumes that every child has a right to such an education, at the expense of other people, with little regard to his fitness to profit by it'. As other authorities and directors found, the desire significantly to extend opportunities was not acceptable at the Board of Education.

Mr Abel, in charge of education in Nottingham, was even more villified than Dr Rawson. The Board of Education had real problems with Nottingham Education Committee which, as we have seen, was wholly committed to preserving its three higher grade schools. Morant's tactics were aggressively uncooperative.[67] When, after several delays, he eventually agreed to meet an urgent Nottingham deputation in May 1904, the internal summary of the discussion was annotated by Morant: 'this is a queer reason – and shows the rotten basis of the whole affair'. He reported to Anson that Nottingham's argument was 'absurd', its reasons 'sentimental and hollow', and its plans 'a malversation of public funds'. Mr Abel persevered. He wrote repeatedly and in uncompromising terms, turned up at the House of Commons to talk directly to Anson, and arrived to see Bruce 'without notice' – all to no avail. Following further specially commissioned reports from a personal friend of Morant about what Nottingham was up to, Morant delivered his most swingeing condemnation to date:

> I have long known Mr Abel, Clerk of the Nottingham School Board [this was more than two years after the School Board ceased to exist], to be a person whose dealings are tortuous. He has to be very carefully watched and his proposals closely investigated ... We cannot be too careful in probing Mr Abel's presentation of things.

Morant's low opinion of these individuals was not just a question of personalities; it is evidence of the scant respect he showed for genuine local initiative, and of the autocratic manner in which the new secondary school system was delivered to different parts of the country. He showed no concern for Nottingham Education Committee's problems with its angry parents, and was thoroughly annoyed to find that Dr Rawson enjoyed 'very good relations' with the Worcestershire committee. Life cannot have been easy for the men in the middle, the secretaries and directors, many of whom – like Brockington in Leicestershire, Bolton King in Warwickshire, Balfour in Staffordshire, Graham in Leeds, and Spurley Hey in Rotherham, Newcastle and Manchester – became distinguished and revered figures at local level. As the first holders of the now familiar post, they had to design their own functions and responsibilities to a considerable extent, often in what turned out to be an extremely hostile climate, bowing to unwanted Board rulings while maintaining a show of competence and control at home. It produced among them a sense of camaraderie which prompted them to rally round any of their number in dispute with the Board, and thereby served to intensify the differences between the centre and the provinces.

The Board's irritation with its local 'partners' strongly flavoured the 1906 Report, which castigated the local authorities for a whole catalogue of faults, including 'many errors, many false starts, much wasted labour and misapplication of machinery'. It characterised the fruits of their work over the preceding very difficult three to four years as 'too often little less than disastrous ... as soon as we pass beyond the sphere of Elementary Education proper ... we plunge into chaos'. It also criticised their hesitancy in establishing new secondary schools, which it attributed to their 'great reluctance' to incur higher rates.[68] To those authorities which did try to get secondary schools recognised, the rates must have seemed a minor problem compared with the hindrances offered by the Board of Education, and it is no wonder that many of them hesitated to launch into programmes of school foundation.

Essentially the local authorities were assigned a role in the wings while the Board of Education and the endowed schools occupied centre-stage; they would be called upon only to support the main protagonists and possibly step in if they faltered. It underlines the value to Morant of having constructed a piece of legislation which was imprecise and permissive, and which gave the local authorities no clear rights in the field of secondary education. He had created a void in which to operate, and did not intend to share it with the local authorities; their role was to rubber-stamp the changes effected by the Board working in concert with the nation's endowed schools. However, the victory of the centre was not total, and it was gained at the cost of stimulating the provinces (or at least parts of them) into a new confidence both in their ability to control their own educational affairs and in the rectitude of so doing.[69] Once Morant had gone from the Board of Education in 1911 'the existence of strong and alert local authorities ... contributed materially in raising the general level of national education'.[70] This formed the basis of the central-local partnership which endured in education for the next three-quarters of a century, until in the 1980s Margaret Thatcher's government upset the balance by circumscribing local control with a combination of financial emasculation, statutory direction and central regulation.

THE SCALE OF ENGLAND'S NEW EDUCATIONAL MODEL

This chapter has so far concentrated on evaluating how the leading contentious issues in the field of publicly provided education were resolved as England entered the twentieth century. Having expressed a number of serious reservations about the quality of the system which was shaped at that time, we must   consider the question of quantity. Superficially, the statistics of secondary school growth after 1902 make impressive reading. Halevy was certainly taken with the figures he quoted – 'With what zeal ... the statute was applied! ... It was a social revolution of the first magnitude' – and Ensor deduced that 'the board under Morant made great exertions to increase and improve the facilities for secondary and technical education throughout the country'.[71] More recently, Rogers wrote of the 'torrent of secondary education which it undammed', Hewitson paid tribute to a 'vast expansion in the secondary field', Dent referred to growth of 'spectacular rapidity', and Mann said that by 1910 there were 980 new secondary schools.[72]

Knowing from the earlier chapters of this study that, in every area investigated, there was either no growth or a reduction in publicly aided secondary school provision, a more thorough examination of the national statistics is clearly worthwhile.[73] Two years have been taken as samples for analysis: 1907, when 'free place' schools were about to come onto the official list for the first time; and 1911, by which time the new secondary school system as shaped by Robert Morant had had nearly a decade to settle down and he himself lost control of it. Secondary schools recognised for 1907 totalled 674, compared with 576 two years earlier and 341 two years before that. Those 674 comprised 168 provided and maintained by the local authority, 377 endowed schools and another 31 in which the local authority had some say, 33 belonging to the Girls' Public Day School Trust, 47 run by the Roman Catholics, and 18 by other bodies such as the Wesleyans or Masons. It can be assumed that none of the endowed schools or the Girls' Public Day School Trust schools was a new foundation, and the Roman Catholic ones mostly grew out of existing small schools, so that the Catholics could educate their own intending teachers when the shift was made from pupil teacher centres to secondary schools.

The 168 schools provided by local authorities are therefore of the most interest as possible 'new' schools, and as evidence of the growth of the secondary education system. Of these, 66 can be positively identified as continuations of higher grade or central schools. A further 78 were located in places where a local authority (a school board or occasionally a technical instruction committee) was already involved in providing post-elementary education before 1902, most commonly as substantial institutions attached to technical colleges or in pupil teacher centres. A significant number (38) of those 78 were apparently 'new' schools for girls, but in fact were in towns where girls had previously attended co-educational establishments, about which the HMIs were rarely happy. So, for instance, Leeds Central Higher Grade School and Leeds Pupil Teachers' College became Leeds Central High School for Boys and Thoresby High School for Girls; and in Battersea the Polytechnic School and the pupil teachers' school together produced Clapham County School for Girls and Henry Thornton School for Boys.

In other places an older boys' endowed school earned Board recognition, and so the local authority in the area concentrated on rearranging its provision to meet the deficit of girls' secondary places, particularly for scholarship holders and pupil teachers. Several of London's 'new' girls' schools came into being in this way: for example, Fulham Secondary School for Girls was the only recognised secondary school in an area in which the school board had previously catered for 275 pupil teachers and 281 higher board school children to at least Science and Art Department examination standard; and Peckham Secondary School for Girls was the only 'provided' school alongside three endowed schools in Camberwell, where before 1902[74] there was a pupil teacher school for over 300 and five board schools entering nearly 600 day pupils for Science and Art examinations. It seems likely that areas such as these had no more provision for post-elementary education after 1902 than before, and almost certainly had less. The London County Council took full advantage of the generous supply of endowed and other independently provided schools in the capital, as well as adopting a policy of locating its secondary schools only in middle-class areas and thereby requiring 'inner-city' pupils to travel long distances. The extremely low success rate (under 1 per cent) in the scholarship examination among elementary schoolchildren in the poorer London boroughs[75] was one of the consequences. Overall, the LCC's record of secondary school provision was a surprisingly modest one (11 out of 78 in 1907 and 17 out of 86 in 1911), although neighbouring Middlesex was one of the most active authorities, increasing its provision from three out of 14 in 1907 to 13 (with eight others partly municipalised) out of 26 in 1911, while Surrey and Kent were responsible for about half the secondary schools in their respective counties by the latter date.

Overall, then, 144 of the 168 'provided' schools, and 650 of the total of 674 state-aided schools in 1907, existed in some form before the legislation of 1902. A mere 24 (eight for girls, two for boys and 14 co-educational) have no traceable antecedents through official sources, although close perusal of the relevant local archives might well reveal some. In other words, this 'landmark' of an Act had generated, at most, just 24 secondary schools in four years. Unquestionably, higher grade schools were multiplying at a faster rate than that by the late 1890s, and so it is not unreasonable to suggest that the early administration of the 1902 Act brought about a reduction in secondary school accommodation rather than a growth. In many parts of the country, this actually meant the ending of opportunities previously available to ordinary children. It is difficult to see, for example, how the 1902 Act benefited the children of Clay Cross in Derbyshire (nearly 200 Science and Art examination candidates in the higher grade school in 1901, but no secondary school after 1902); Burton-on-Trent in Staffordshire (300 candidates, mostly in the higher grade school, in 1901, two endowed grammar schools recognised after 1902); or Oxfordshire (250 candidates in four institutions in Oxford, Banbury and Witney in 1901, but by 1911 no fully maintained school among its six aided secondary schools, the cheapest of which charged fees of £6 15s 0d per annum).

Moving on to 1911, 198 schools had been added to the grant list since 1907. Of them, 28 were endowed schools which decided to come into the system, and 43 others were older foundations which opted to hand over control or share responsibility with the local authority, and thereby become 'municipalised' in the Board's language. So again, the 'new' LEA-provided schools – a total of 115 added between 1907 and 1911 – are of the most interest. Just over half of them were in places where some form of publicly provided post-elementary education was available before the 1902 Act; most of the 'new' Cornish schools, for example, were in towns where daytime Science and Art Department classes had earlier existed in public institutes or schools of science and art. Only 54 schools (22 for girls, 4 for boys and 28 co-educational) out of the apparent increase of 198 between 1907 and 1911 can be categorised as possible 'new' schools resulting from the Act, and, again, further local research would be more likely to diminish than increase that number.

If this analysis of the statistics is correct, what did the 1902 Act do to stimulate the growth of secondary education? Firstly, it did give education committees potentially more power than the most dynamic school boards had ever had. As before, the bigger urban authorities tended to be the most active, and the somewhat unexpected continuity of approach from school board to education committee meant that the interests of local elementary schoolchildren were safeguarded to a certain extent. The preceding chapters have shown that the Board under Morant did its utmost to minimise the direct involvement of local authorities in secondary education, forcibly preventing them from expanding their own provision and from exercising any influence over other institutions. However, local commitment to developing secondary education was an irresistible force. Some early victories were gained despite the Board's opposition, notably the hard-won recognition of most higher grade schools as secondary schools, and in due course most of the innovations in post-elementary education – central schools, junior technical schools, free secondary schooling – came from the larger urban authorities. The 1902 Act in itself did nothing to create that more progressive climate and the early administration of it was positively antagonistic; progress had to wait until later, by which time more than a generation of children had been deprived of their educational opportunities.

Secondly, the Act did make it possible for county areas where secondary school provision was haphazard to get organised, simply because they now had the administrative machinery to do so. Worcestershire's early enthusiasm has already been mentioned; other predominantly rural counties were a little slower, but by 1911 Cornwall County Council was responsible for 12 out of the 17 recognised secondary schools in the county, Cumberland for seven out of 12, and Hampshire for nine out of 24. They must be balanced by counties in which the education authority was apparently doing very little. Like Oxfordshire, Westmoreland continued to rely wholly on endowed schools (five in 1907, eight in 1911), the local authority bearing none of the responsibility – or cost – of secondary school provision; and by 1911 Hertfordshire was maintaining just one out of a county total of 14, Dorset one out of 11, Buckinghamshire one out of seven, Somerset two out of 17 and Lincolnshire three out of 22. It seems, then, that while some counties seized the new opportunities with enthusiasm, others moved very slowly, relying on endowed school provision coupled with the free-place system to cater for the demand for secondary school places.

The picture of rural secondary education is therefore patchy. Until the advent of modern motor transport it was always problematic, but England was very slow to evolve a solution. Both Scotland and Wales, with rather worse geographical conditions, had found ways of placing post-elementary education within the reach of nearly all children, regarding it as one of the fundamental principles on which their education systems were based. Scotland had its long-established parish schools, where, having developed a system of support for isolated teachers and rejected the 1861 Revised Code, any child could learn Latin, higher mathematics and science and gain direct access to the universities. Wales had taken the vital decision in 1889 to create a large number (95 by 1902) of small 'intermediate' day schools rather than a few big boarding schools. In England it was not until the 1930s that the Board of Education 'finally abandoned the principle that the main object of country schools was to prepare children for agricultural work and life in the countryside'.[76] The take-up of free places won at secondary schools was particularly poor in rural areas, and there was no longer access to the examination system of the Science and Art Department, which, as one perceptive contemporary had pointed out, deserved great praise for raising educational standards in rural areas, being the only way by which 'work in the remotest village may be recognised'.[77] By outlawing the merging of elementary/ secondary/pupil teacher functions which was the only realistic way of operating in small rural schools – and, significantly, the supply of intending teachers from rural authorities dropped from 2,141 in 1904–5 to just 29 in 1911–12 – the Board of Education actually set back such progress as had been made in rural post-elementary education.

Thirdly, the 1902 Act did encourage some bad secondary schools to get better and to get bigger. The analysis outlined in this book proves that higher grade schools were already much more efficient and purposeful places than endowed schools, yet it was the former which were subjected to rigorous school improvement campaigns by the Board of Education. The latter did, however, find that their new financial security enabled them to extend their curriculum, facilities and staffing, and to accommodate more children. There is some truth in the suggestion that the growth in the size of aided secondary schools was a more significant feature than the growth in the number of schools, although three qualifications need to be made. Firstly, the average school size actually dropped in the first decade of the century, to 150 pupils in 1911, but then rose rapidly during the First World War when demand was growing but major new building was impossible. It was 250 in 1919 and climbed more steadily to around 300 in the 1930s, and it was only then that the proportion of secondary school pupils per 1,000 population reached 10 per cent, compared with 7 per cent of the pre-War period.[78] It is therefore debatable how much effect the 1902 Act had on the total size of the secondary school population, and rather likely that in different hands, many schools could have grown more rapidly.

A second qualification is that a fair number of endowed schools had been very small indeed, too small to offer a full spread of subjects or to divide their very wide age-range of children into appropriate classes. Sara Burstall explained at some length that from her experience of girls' high schools, 300 was the minimum size for efficiency, to produce ten classes

of 30 pupils each between the ages of 9 and 18.[79] That was much larger
than most endowed schools – in 1911 there were 49 recognised secondary
schools with fewer than 50 children – and it may reasonably be deduced
that rather than giving secondary education to more children, such schools
were offering education of a secondary nature for the first time. And
thirdly, in marked contrast, most higher grade schools were forced to
reduce drastically their nominal capacity on becoming municipal
secondary schools, mainly as a device to exclude elementary children and
generate the desired spaciousness of a secondary school. After a while,
their numbers crept up again, but can hardly be regarded as a growth in
size since they were still smaller than the schools had once been.
Bradford's Belle Vue School, for instance, dropped from 616 in 1904 to
207 in 1905/06, before climbing back up to 456 in 1907/08.[80] It seems
then, that the biggest effect which the 1902 Act had on the total size of
secondary school provision was, by the injection of grants and scholarship
pupils, to prevent the extinction of a number of struggling endowed
schools, so that they were able to increase in size later in the century. In
London, for instance, it has been claimed that for the first half of this
century 'the overwhelming majority of grammar schools' could not have
existed without state-aided pupils.[81]

A further interesting aspect of this statistical investigation concerns the
assumption which is usually twinned with the 'rapid growth' argument,
that more secondary school pupils meant different secondary school
pupils. If it is the case that the increase in secondary places after 1902 has
been much exaggerated, and also that access to lower social classes was
narrowed, the 'growth' in the secondary school population can only have
been the result of a shift to fee-paying aided schools from fee-paying
unaided schools. The hypothesis is not easy to explore, because nobody
knew how many pupils were receiving secondary education in non-
recognised schools, and the charting of private schools is a notoriously
difficult business. But it is clear that, with aided secondary schools made
relatively more efficient and more socially acceptable, private schools had
less to offer. This was particularly true in the case of girls, who had been
the main patrons of private secondary schools of variable quality, but for
whom state provision was considerably expanded after 1902. It was able
to appeal to parents who would not have dreamt of sending their daughters
to a co-educational higher grade school, and it consequently became a
priority in the new secondary schools to exclude too many of the lower
classes in order to attract that kind of parent.

Testing this theory in the case of Bristol, Kelly's Directory[82] shows that
the number of private schools in the city dropped from 110 in 1902 to 84

in 1914; 30 schools clearly survived the 12-year period, 80 disappeared
and 54 new ones were founded. In both years the number of kindergartens
and boys' and junior preparatory schools was fairly constant, but there
seems to have been a major shift in girls' education. Of the 30 schools
which survived the 12-year period, 12 changed their status from girls'
schools to preparatory ones and 40 out of the 80 that disappeared were
girls' schools, to be replaced by just 17 new ones, with a greater
concentration than previously around wealthy Clifton, where social
exclusiveness was still highly valued.[83] In other words, there were 35
fewer girls' private schools in 1914 than in 1902, and the only sensible
explanation is that the class of girls which had previously patronised them
– and possibly some of the teachers too – were to be found occupying
places in the aided secondary schools. Everything that was discovered
about the changes urged upon Bristol's three municipal schools by the
HMIs – the fees, the school uniform, the banishment from the premises of
elementary school children, the attention to 'tone' and 'corporate spirit' –
confirms the impression that their priority was to make the schools more
attractive to wealthier families than to poorer ones. And there are signs
that they were succeeding, particularly at Fairfield Road where a small but
significant number of entrants after 1907 were coming from professional
or semi-professional homes (accountants, bankers, a veterinary surgeon,
the cricket coach at Clifton College, the subsacristan at Bristol Cathedral)
or had previously attended private schools, or left to take further private
tuition (in violin or art) or to be 'at home'.

What can be concluded about the main effects of the 1902 Act on the
scale of secondary school provision? The only early beneficiaries were the
children in a handful of county towns and city suburbs where county
councils speedily provided secondary schools, and the small proportion in
larger towns and cities who gained access to schools previously closed to
them. It could well be argued that the second of these would have
happened anyway, and quite likely on a more generous scale, if the
endowed schools which could not pay their own way had been brought
onto the same footing as the higher grade schools. To achieve the first
might have required some central direction, such as reconstituting or
better coordinating the school board system; this could have been coupled
with greater statutory responsibilities so that reluctant authorities would
have been obliged to do more, and with a more imaginative policy
towards secondary education in rural areas.

One therefore arrives at the conclusion that the reorganisation of 1902
and after could have been much more fruitful than it was. Many towns
would have been better off without any legislation at all; those not quite

qualifying for county borough (Part II) status had their hopes of developing education beyond the elementary definitely handicapped by the legislation. Darlington, for example, a Part III authority until 1915, could offer only a daytime course at the technical college for 14-year-old leavers and a higher elementary school, although the local boys' grammar school charged fees of £11 per annum and refused to liaise with the local authority and the public elementary school system.[84] It seems too that the real growth in secondary school provision nationwide was delayed until the time of the First World War, and was then almost immediately engulfed in over two decades of financial stringency. That expansion owed almost nothing to the 1902 Act or the Board of Education under Morant; rather, its very promising progress in the 1890s was retarded by at least 20 years. It was inevitable that progress would resume, but it did so in a climate changed by the sanctification of an elitist model of secondary education and the devaluation of technical and elementary school alternatives and of local autonomy. It engendered a legacy of low expectations of what education can offer, and left little room for the flair and experimentation that had characterised the pre-1902 development of the public education service founded on inclusive, comprehensive principles.

NOTES

1. Birchenough, *History of Elementary Education*, pp. 309–10.
2. *Committee to Enquire into the Position of Natural Science in the Educational System of Great Britain (Thompson Committee)* (1918), p. 6.
3. Only one of the nine *Statesmen of Science* profiled by J.G. Crowther (London: Cresset Press, 1965) had a traditional English education, and he (the Duke of Devonshire) was a wealthy, aristocratic amateur, of the type which prompted Reader, *Professional Men*, pp. 6–7, to write: 'Science and technology might provide an agreeable means of spending money; hardly of earning it … The view of science as a fit hobby for well-bred amateurs, but nothing more, persisted long in England.'
4. Reader, *Professional Men*, p. 108. For the extremely tentative entry of natural sciences into the public schools and Oxbridge, see the contributions of R. Macleod and W.H. Brock to Macleod, *Days of Judgment*.
5. *Thompson Committee*, p.11.
6. C. Barnett, *The Collapse of British Power* (London: Eyre Methuen, 1972), p. 37.
7. Daglish, *Education Policy-Making*, pp. 93–101, has detailed the bitter debate surrounding this decision, which conveys that senior officials well understood what was at stake for the future form of secondary education.
8. Macleod, 'Science and Examinations', p. 9.
9. Rothblatt, *Tradition and Change*, pp. 164–73: 'Instead of being demoted by the ethic of new knowledge, classical learning at the universities took advantage of its enormous existing base of financial support and flourished.' The chief casualty was classical (and all other) literature, ejected in favour of philology and 'scientific' textual analysis.
10. *The Schoolmaster*, 11 November 1899; *Cambridgeshire High School for Boys: History of the School 1900–1950* (Cambridge: Cambridgeshire High School for Boys, 1950), p. 15.
11. *The Times*, 22 September 1897. HMI Theodosius's willingness to sacrifice the majority of Bristol

children to ensure high grammar school achievement by a few may be recalled.

12. Board of Education, *Report for 1904–5* (1905).

13. PRO Ed.12/119.

14. Several 'municipal day technical schools' in the industrial West Midlands were forced into closure, as described in M. Vlaeminke, 'The Subordination of Technical Education in Secondary Schooling, 1870–1914', in P. Summerfield and E.J. Evans (eds), *Technical Education and the State since 1850: Historical and Contemporary Perspectives* (Manchester: Manchester University Press, 1990). In the case of one Derbyshire school, an internal Board memo saying 'I should prefer to get rid of "technical" out of the name, but I do not like to do so if the Authority have deliberately used it' was met with the ruling that 'we'll call it "Heanor Secondary School" anyway'. PRO Ed. 35/426.

15. *Thompson Committee*, pp. 5–6.

16. F. Foden, 'The Technology Examinations of the City and Guilds', in Macleod, *Days of Judgment*, p. 68.

17. *Thompson Committee*, p. 6.

18. Graham and Phythian, *Manchester Grammar School*, p. 82.

19. H.J. Foster, 'Private, Proprietary and Public Elementary Schools in a Lancashire Residential Town: A Contest for the Patronage of the Lower Middle Classes', in Searby, *Educating the Victorian Middle Class*, p. 78.

20. Bradford Trades Council, cited in Wilson, *Development of Secondary Education*, p. 78.

21. Gordon, *Selection*, pp. 50, 148. R.P. Scott developed a close relationship with Morant and was rewarded with a Secondary Inspectorship in 1904; Daglish, *Education Policy-making*, pp. 231–2.

22. Jackson, *Belle Vue Boys' School*, p. 20. To Lishman, the higher grade schools 'meant more than a vested interest … [they] produced only good results, and when they were abolished in 1903 he felt it was a criminal act and it dealt him a powerful blow, one with which he could never come to terms' (p. 27).

23. Wilson, *Development of Secondary Education*, pp. 80, 83.

24. Tropp, *School Teachers*, pp. 173–9, attached considerable importance to these 'behind the scenes' activities.

25. Leese, *Personalities and Power*, p. 230, actually uses that phrase; other examples were quoted towards the end of Chapter 1.

26. Grossek, *First Movement*, p. 164; Curtis, *Education in Britain*, p. 62.

27. See Gordon, *Selection*, Chs 3, 6 and 8. He quoted the complaint of the headmaster of Bromsgrove Grammar School in 1889 that recent foundation scholars 'have everything to learn in diction, manners and many of the qualifications of gentlemen' (p. 197).

28. These proved to be remarkably long-lived. Rugby union illustrated until recently some of the sillier vestiges in its attitude towards amateurism. Rugby league came into being because southern rugby union clubs refused to compensate the more working-class teams from the North for loss of an afternoon's wages. In cricket, there was the gentleman/player divide, and in soccer, once the Old Etonians were beaten in the 1883 F.A. Cup Final by a team from Blackburn, 'the public schools withdrew from the competition, to devote their energies towards building up the amateur tradition of the privileged. Professional football was left to develop as a spectator sport for the urban masses'. Meller, *Leisure*, p. 234.

29. The dynamic pioneer of Swedish drill for the London School Board became thoroughly impatient with middle-class schools for resisting her methods simply because they were popular in public elementary schools, according to Atkinson, 'Fitness' in Delamont and Duffin, *Nineteenth-Century Woman*, pp. 95–9. Board school drill (often ridiculed in quaint old photographs) looks remarkably like the exercise routines which have recently became so popular.

30. J.E. Gorst, *The Children of the Nation* (London: Methuen, 1906), Ch. 12.

31. Mann, *Education*, p. 163.

32. NUT Circular 370 (April 1900).

33. Hewitson, *Grammar School Tradition*, pp. 4, 95; C.B. Cox and A.E. Dyson (eds), *Black Paper Two: The Crisis in Education* (London: Critical Quarterly Society, 1970), pp. 4, 26.

34. *Hadow Report* (1927), p. 48

35. Ministry of Education, *The New Secondary Education* (1947), p. 25.

36. *The Schoolmaster*, 14 January 1893.

37. Adamson, *English Education*, p. 471; Archer, *Secondary Education*, p. 323.

38. Compiled from Board of Education, *Statistics* (various years), and HM Inspection Reports in the PRO files.

39. PRO Ed.12/139.

40. Gosden and Sharp, *Development of an Education Service*, pp. 85–7.

41. K. Lindsay, *Social Progress and Educational Waste* (London: Routledge, 1926) investigated the wide variety – and almost universal injustice – of selection processes in a number of areas; and Gordon, *Selection*, Chs 6 and 7, describes the faltering efforts to refine methods of selection.

42. Church, *Over the Bridge*, p. 144.

43. See, for example, P. Gardner, *The Lost Elementary Schools of Victorian England* (London: Croom Helm, 1984), who found numerous small, cheap private 'schools' in Bristol before 1870; and J.F.C. Harrison, *The Common People* (London: Fontana, 1984), pp. 286, 292–3, who identified much higher pre-1870 rates of literacy than used to be assumed, as well as individuals who devoured classical literature, built up nature collections or wrote poetry, as evidence of working-class autodidactism.

44. In Inglis, *John Bull's Schooldays*, p. 22.

45. F.H. Spencer in *Inspector's Testament*, p. 68, pointed out that most working-class children were completing their education at the same age (13) as public-school boys began theirs.

46. Lindsay, *Social Progress*; Gosden and Sharp, *Development of an Education Service*, p. 88.

47. PRO Ed.20/114.

48. By Lowndes, *Silent Social Revolution*, p. 136.

49. Birchenough, *History of Elementary Education*, p. 330.

50. G. Bernbaum, *Social Change and the Schools 1918–1944* (London: Routledge & Kegan Paul, 1967), p. 10.

51. This has been detailed by various writers, including Daglish, *Education Policy-Making*, pp. 426–437. The role of Edmond Holmes, Chief Inspector of Schools, emerged as an interesting one after the publication of his *What Is and What Might Be* (London: Constable, 1911), in which he described himself as 'the victim of a vicious administrative system, perhaps the most vicious that has ever been devised', and went on to outline a thoroughly idealistic, progressive approach to elementary school teaching.

52. John Braine recalling Thackley Board School, Bradford, in Inglis, *John Bull's Schooldays*, p. 23.

53. Gordon, *Selection*, Chapters 6 and 8.

54. B. Simon, *The Politics of Educational Reform 1920–1940* (London: Lawrence & Wishart, 1974), p. 232.

55. Southgate, *That's the Way*, pp. 21, 53–4.

56. Gosden and Sharp, *Development of an Education Service*, pp. 56–7.

57. George Scott in Inglis, *John Bull's Schooldays*, p. 129; Simon, *Politics*, pp. 228–31. The Bristolian who could remember almost nothing of his last uninspiring 18 months at school may be recalled.

58. According to Bolton King, Warwickshire's first director of education, in *Schools of To-Day: Present Problems in English Education* (London: J.M. Dent, 1929), p. 7.

59. Eaglesham, *Foundations*, pp. 51–2, and 'Centenary', p. 5. This view has been echoed by S. Maclure who said that after 1902 the elementary curriculum was 'in retreat and a new and artificial rigidity introduced at just that point when it appeared the elementary school might have been about to develop extended education on an open-ended basis'. *One Hundred Years of London Education 1870–1970* (London: Allen Lane/Penguin Press, 1970), p. 50.

60. The Act is commonly held to have produced a much more logical administrative structure, but by taking education into the heart of local government and politics in a way that the *ad hoc* school boards had never been, (as well as complications like the Part II/Part III authorities), the new system was bound to display considerable variations in different parts of the country.

61. The radical Graham Wallas, passionate defender of the London School Board, found it hard to adjust to the new requirements after 1903: 'he will not budge from his principle of "starving out" the secondary schools under separate management. He will not agree to run both systems side by side', said Beatrice Webb who knew him well. Mackenzies, *Diary*, 2, p. 339.

62. Detailed in PRO Ed.10/3 from which these paragraphs about ADSE are drawn.

63. It has been suggested that 'the memories of local authorities and officers of their struggles to establish their identity while Morant was at the Board is a factor which goes a long way to explain the intensity of their opposition' to subsequent proposals from the Board. Greenhalgh, *Local*

Educational Administrators, pp. 179–87. She cited as evidence ADSE's somewhat unreasonable opposition to Fisher's Bill in 1917, and its long struggle for the recognition of its members' official status, which was eventually achieved in the 1944 Act.

64. Craig, *History of Red Tape*, p. 155; Eaglesham, 'Centenary', p.10.
65. For Bradford, see Jackson, *Belle Vue Boys' School* and Wilson, *Development of Secondary Education*; for Leeds, Greenhalgh, *Local Educational Administrators*, Jenkins, *'Magnificent Pile'*, and Connell, 'Administration of Secondary Schools'.
66. This paragraph is drawn from PRO Ed.35/2584.
67. This paragraph is drawn from PRO Ed.20/114 and 20/116.
68. Board of Education, *Report for 1905–6* (1906), pp. 45, 49.
69. Armytage in *Four Hundred Years*, p. 204, thought Morant's departure from the Board 'showed how strong local authorities were becoming, especially when led by imaginative and resourceful officers … From being virtually agents of the board they became partners'.
70. Birchenough, *History of Elementary Education*, p. 160.
71. Halevy, *Imperialism*, p. 205; Ensor, *England*, p. 536.
72. Rogers, 'Churches', p. 29; Davis, *Grammar School*, p. 36; Hewitson, *Grammar School Tradition*, p. 27; Dent, *Century of Growth*, p. 61; Mann, *Education*, p. 159.
73. It is based primarily on a comparison between the Board's *Statistics* for various years, together with cross-references from a wide variety of sources.
74. 1902 is used for the sake of consistency; London did not in fact get its Act until 1903.
75. Campbell, *Eleven-Plus*, pp. 13, 43, 87.
76. Gordon, *Selection*, pp. 176, 200.
77. Bremner, *Education of Girls*, p. 103.
78. Bristol's figure was 4 per cent, and in London it has been estimated that in 1901 and 1911, one child in 20 between the ages of 10 and 15 was getting 'a fairly satisfactory secondary education'. Campbell, *Eleven-Plus*, p. 10.
79. Burstall, *English High Schools*, p. 36.
80. Jackson, *Belle Vue Boys' School*, p. 22. It is appreciated that higher grade figures would not all have been children of secondary age, but then neither were those of endowed secondary schools; in 1911, 25 per cent of all 'secondary' school pupils were under 12, making the small schools even smaller as far as secondary tuition was concerned.
81. Campbell, *Eleven-Plus*, pp. 101–2.
82. As indicated above, the absence of any form of registration for private schools makes this kind of survey hazardous. But there is no reason to suppose that Kelly's Directory was any more or less reliable in 1914 than in 1902, and until census enumerators' books can be checked in 20 years' time, after the 100-year embargo, greater certainty about the extent of private schooling is impossible.
83. Some of these schools in Clifton and neighbouring Redland extended into next-door houses, and acquired names like Badminton House, Mortimer House and Hampton House School.
84. M.M. Cullen, *Education in Darlington (1900–1974)* (Darlington: Darlington Corporation, 1974), pp. 8–9, 14.

7

A LOST OPPORTUNITY

In conclusion, it is necessary to stand back from the evidence and place the higher grade school phenomenon in the broad context of English attitudes to intellectual and cultural priorities, industrialisation and questions of social class. The phenomenon will be considered within the general framework of the debate which argues that liberal-romantic attitudes in English culture have been remarkably persistent, despite their inappropriateness for modern economic, social, political and military conditions. Such attitudes, it may be recalled, include a devotion to literary studies, a disdain for science and technology, a wariness of intellectuals and professionals, a sense of high moral purpose supported by religious observance, a belief in character formation as a function of education, and an attachment to stability and conformity tinged with nostalgia.

Of particular relevance to the higher grade school movement, to which it has not previously been applied, is the theory that for most of its modern history England has accommodated a strong alternative cultural tradition. This, while not eschewing moral values or ancient learning, consciously attuned itself to the realities of life, finding popularity above all with people who, because of social or religious disadvantage, could significantly enhance the quality of their lives through the acquisition of knowledge and qualifications. In the educational context, it has been commonly identified with the dissenting academies of the eighteenth century and sometimes with certain twentieth-century institutions, but rarely with anything in between. This concluding chapter will argue that the higher grade school movement represented a successful re-emergence of England's alternative cultural/educational tradition in the latter part of the nineteenth century, which fell victim to the remarkable strength of the dominant liberal-romantic tradition in the hands of England's elite.

By way of orchestrating the conflicting traditions, it is salient to note the formidable weight of criticism directed at the performance of England's elite at critical moments in its history. Various writers have expounded upon the naive ineptitude of the nation's rulers when faced with the harsh reality of economic decline, imperial disintegration and foreign aggression, and have bemoaned the fact that the upper echelons of the education system have done so little to prepare them for the reality of modern life. Well over a century ago, Henry Sidgwick of Cambridge University was arguing that, as opposed to physical science, the study of language was 'so obviously inferior as a preparation for the business of life, that its present position in education seems ... absolutely untenable', while T.H. Huxley predicted that the time would come when Englishmen would cite his generation's neglect of science as 'the stock example of the solid stupidity of their ancestors in the nineteenth century'.[1] Seventy years later, in 1940, Worsley was in no doubt that their 'terrible failure in moral purpose' together with 'defective intelligence, defective imagination and a defective understanding of the world we live in, have landed us in our present mess'.[2] Gilmour believed that Britain 'has paid a heavy price to have the sons of its entrepreneurs educated alongside the traditional elite',[3] and Wilkinson argued that a concept of leadership which adopts a 'very high degree of educational elitism' and respects 'the guardian more than the innovator' is an anachronism in a modern democracy.[4] To Barnett, the romantic idealism transmitted to generations of governing-class Britons 'averted its gaze from the muddy topics of the contemporary world and real human nature, and neglected science in favour of the moral precepts, the chivalric code and the ideal humanity enshrined in religion and the classics'.[5]

Education has always been identified as the best means of modernising such attitudes. Towards the end of the nineteenth century, education at all levels was in a state of tension, with some of its older established parts struggling to maintain a role, and some of its newer additions succeeding so conspicuously that they demanded reassessment. The competing values embodied in those tensions presented real alternatives – perhaps more than at any time since – which could have guided Britain's cultural traditions in a different direction. The manner in which the old and the new were brought into juxtaposition could have been enormously fruitful, the foundation of a genuinely fresh approach to the purpose, content, style and availability of education.

THE CHALLENGE OF THE NEW

Despite the seemingly unassailable supremacy of the liberal-romantic tradition in English culture, it is possible to find a recurring and important preference for alternative priorities in education. Deriving from a different view of the world, this alternative cultural strand has concentrated on other areas of knowledge and styles of learning than those revered in the liberal-romantic tradition. It achieved its greatest sophistication among urban nonconformists, especially the Unitarians, in the eighteenth and early nineteenth centuries. It was a key factor in their drive to attain the high culture that was a necessary concomitant to the status which their economic importance and philanthropic instincts merited, but which was denied to them by the traditional English value system. The broad, forward-looking scientific culture which they devised performed important social functions, in strengthening a sense of community and providing opportunities for social mobility; as one writer has expressed it, 'a fertile scientific culture was generated among marginal men as a means of social legitimisation'.[6]

Translated into educational terms, this alternative cultural tradition, while stressing the need for relevance to the actual circumstances of living, was never purely utilitarian or vocational but what Fred Clarke called 'nothing less than a re-interpretation of the content of culture'. He identified links between the dissenting academies of the past and the technical high schools of his own time (in which he mistakenly saw great possibilities), which offered the opportunity for adapting 'the concept of culture to real life', something the grammar schools had signally failed to do. Tracing the dissenting academies back to the seventeenth century wave of 'modernism' in education, he saw them as prime examples of 'specialised' or 'realistic' education, in contrast to the classical-aristocratic 'education for culture'.[7] For much of the eighteenth century, they offered the 'best liberal education obtainable at the time', defined by one admirer as 'libertarian ... rational, scientific, humane and democratic'.[8] But then the dissenting academies 'forgot the breadth of view with which they had started'[9] and declined, although their spirit lived on in certain private academies of the nineteenth century, to which parents in search of a 'realistic' education increasingly lent their support.

Clarke's analysis neglected the proposition made here: that by the end of the nineteenth century, specialised or realistic education had found a new home in the network of publicly provided institutions which had developed since 1870. It was no accident that, based on their experience of their non-sectarian British and Foreign Society schools, dissenters brought higher expectations to the public provision of elementary education than did Anglicans, whose National Society (for Promoting the Education of the Poor in the Principles of the Established Church) schools still placed a higher priority on social control. Birmingham's knowledgeable Reverend McCarthy defined higher grade education in 1900 as a 'specialized advanced education combined with a wider intellectual training',[10] and Michael Sadler perceived in it 'the germs of a wider and more liberal conception of secondary education than this country had yet recognized'.[11] The higher grade schools were unmistakably of that same tradition of useful and cultural education which Clarke believed to be essential to England's survival in the modern world. His admirable characterisation of the dissenting academies can almost exactly be applied to the higher grade schools:

> A vigorous and sustained effort to think out a 'modern' curriculum and apply it in practice. While not departing from the dominant idea of education for culture, and while remaining thoroughly English in temper, they cut loose from the prevailing tradition of classical training, and aristocratic accomplishments, looked at their own actual world with open eyes, and worked out a curriculum which would prepare for effective living in such a world. In it, as it developed, classics and the customary linguistic studies had no great place; instead, we find English, history and modern languages with a good deal of mathematics and science.[12]

Like the dissenters, although for different reasons, the patrons of higher grade schools were excluded from the country's leading educational institutions. Relatively free of cumbersome traditions, they devised a style of education suited to their needs, 'not by copying the grammar schools and educating themselves as "arrivistes", aspiring imitators from afar of the governing-class tradition',[13] but by offering a real alternative. That the higher grade school movement became important in barely a quarter of a century of operating in fairly unfavourable circumstances is evidence of just how vigorous and effective its version of education was. Nothing can be identified within the movement which would have ended or even weakened it. It was exceptionally well tuned to the wishes of a large part of the population, and with ever-developing links upwards into teacher-training, technical colleges and provincial universities, showed every sign of becoming a complete system of education, containing a genuine 'reinterpretation of the content of culture'. It should have been an invaluable source of ideas at the very moment when England was deciding for the first time what kind of secondary school system it wanted, and which cultural tradition(s) it thereby wished to promote.

There are clear indications that an awareness of the significance of this 'reinterpretation' was developing among the participants in the alternative system. At first, the higher grade school heads saw themselves as merely filling a gap in the educational provision which no one else wanted to occupy and, puzzled by the hostility which this seemed to arouse in some quarters, argued that 'there is practically no antagonism between our schools and the grammar schools ... We are working an entirely different stratum'. But they became increasingly irritated by the apparent determination of the Incorporated Association of Head Masters to 'make everything conform to the antiquated monastic Grammar Schools which are altogether behind the times', and began to use phrases like 'this renascence of learning' and 'educating the whole powers of man' to validate their work. The higher grade schools were described as 'firstly places of education, and secondly utilitarian', introducing children to 'literary culture ... their own glorious inheritance of English literature', as well as giving them 'much-needed training in modern living languages' and preparing them for 'the practical needs of after life'.[14] Sir George Kekewich seems to have grasped the significance of what had been happening when he wrote that in ordinary secondary schools the study of Latin and Greek 'was generally time wasted ... it is the new knowledge, not the old knowledge, that is all-important in commercial and industrial competition'.[15] The supreme but misplaced confidence of the higher grade school heads, that the style of education they had pioneered would survive in any reorganisation that was to come, was therefore based on a conviction that it was not only modern but broad and liberal, in contrast to the old-fashioned, narrow grammar schools.

It is important to note that the emergence of a demand for 'specialised' or 'realistic' education was a characteristic of all industrialised countries. Some illuminating comparisons can be drawn between the responses to it of England's ruling elite and those of other countries, which show that the failure to accommodate alternative styles of secondary education within the national system was a peculiarly English phenomenon. In most other western European countries classical-liberal education had its influential adherents, but in none were they able to impose their values on the whole system. Ringer has shown how successfully European education, with the exception of England, adapted itself to modern conditions. From the early industrial days when 'traditional secondary education stood in antithetical relationship to the economy', Germany had by the late nineteenth century developed a style of secondary education which 'was really rather progressive for its time', and at the same time in France a practically oriented secondary curriculum was flourishing while the 'classical stream entered a period of stagnation and decline'. In both countries, the main beneficiaries were from the lower socio-economic classes.[16] In the United States, meanwhile, the period between 1890 and 1914 saw a dramatic increase in the number of public high schools, the virtual abandonment of both fee-paying and selection, and transformations in the curriculum, notably a successful 'blurring of the sharp lines that used to separate academic and vocational education'.[17]

England could also have learned much from its two nearest neighbours. Many of the same educational tensions were apparent in Wales and Scotland as in England, but both those countries managed to retain distinctive educational patterns, despite pressures to move closer to the English model. In Wales, the reforms which followed the Aberdare Committee and the Intermediate Education Act of 1889 had engendered 'tremendous enthusiasm' among the Welsh people, and initiated '45 glorious years of real achievement' in secondary and university education. The 16 joint education committees responsible for creating the new intermediate schools looked 'rather to the continent than to England for their model', and 'were determined that the new schools should not follow the old grammar school traditions. They hoped to bring secondary education to the door of every cottage, and cater, if possible, for every type of child, academic or otherwise'. Mundella, who had overseen this remarkable achievement during his tenure of office in Whitehall, hoped that the Welsh example would act as a 'leavening' for the 'larger and more inert mass of Englishmen. I always desired to see Wales become a model for our national system'.

After 1902, it is true, Welsh education became subject to the regulations and inspection of the English Board of Education, but it preserved some independence through the creation in 1907 of a separate Welsh Department. Its early Chief Inspector, O.M. Edwards, had risen from humble nonconformist origins to enjoy a 'glittering educational career', and then to become 'a maverick' at the Board of Education where his convictions ran counter to those of both the Welsh and English Permanent Secretaries, A.T. Davies and Robert Morant. He fought hard to retain the scientific–vocational character and the generous access of Welsh secondary schooling, and to resist the values of the English grammar school which he regarded as an 'entirely inappropriate model' for Wales.[18] Interestingly, Welsh divergence from the English model has resurfaced during the late-twentieth-century centralisation of education.

Scotland, to which English higher grade school supporters often looked with envious eyes, had even longer established educational traditions of its own. Green has outlined the special (and continuing) role of Scottish education in fostering cultural autonomy, stressing the importance of the universal system of parochial schools strongly rooted in the community, the generous university provision, and the respect for science, engineering and medicine.[19] In practical terms, this meant that Scotland had by the end of the nineteenth century already introduced such advances as inspection of secondary schools, a leaving certificate, special training for ordinary teachers, and county secondary education committees which received lump capitation grants, Scotland's share of the money which in England was used to make elementary education free.

At the turn of the century, many of the same tensions over curriculum and access were in evidence, but the campaign which favoured the English model and wished to make Scottish secondary schools 'organizationally and socially distinct, and based on a classical culture' foundered against the solid belief that secondary education should be 'available for all who desire to take advantage of it, modern in its outlook, and flexible in its social function'. With refreshing insight, Scottish teachers argued through their journal that 'the principle of merit was specious ... when the rich started with so many advantages', and that 'any subject could impart "culture" if it was properly taught'. Even the Scottish Education Department, which was moving towards the creation of a distinctive secondary school system at roughly the same time that the Board of Education was shaping England's, 'was prepared to deal heavy blows to the classics in order to insist on a proper teaching of science', and to give the higher grade schools a recognised place regulated by a progressive national certificate scheme. Scotland's continuing acknowledgment of the importance of 'specialised' education meant that Lyon Playfair's earlier jibes that while the Scottish universities taught a man how to make a thousand a year, the English universities merely taught him how to spend it, and that 'every Scotchman knows it to be his own fault if he is not educated' remained largely true; the same could certainly not be said of every Englishman after 1902.[20]

THE TRIUMPH OF THE OLD

If in other industrialised countries the upholders of the ancient classical style of education were obliged to come to terms with 'specialised' education, why was England – which had 'the greatest accumulation of unsolved educational problems'[21] – different? The answer lies in the unusually strong identification of classical education with a leadership ethos which was enormously powerful. By the end of the nineteenth century, a complete system of socialisation had been constructed to ensure a regular supply of recruits to the governing classes, which, to borrow two words usually applied to a later period of history, was not only totalitarian but monolithic. In other words, it required the full submergence of participants in its values and customs, and was both intolerant of alternative ways of qualifying 'experts' and indifferent to the frustrated needs of the excluded majority.

So, the enormous strength of the English liberal-romantic cultural tradition became inextricably bound up with overtly elitist attitudes to social class. Liberal humanistic education had become so closely identified with the gentlemanly ideal in Victorian England that it was impossible for anyone who admired the latter to contemplate major changes in the former. Gentlemanliness, it has been suggested, was 'a moral and not just a social category';[22] it had become a 'sub-Christian culture .... a second religion, one less demanding than Christianity'.[23] In a changing world, it was seen as a major responsibility of an 'educated' gentleman to preserve civilised values in order to combat the evils of industrialism and materialism. Only non-utilitarian studies could sufficiently free the mind to stand apart from the turbulence of the modern world, and it came to be assumed that 'the person who assumed the leadership in an industrial and democratic society had to be prepared to take a stand against the wishes of the majority. This was the meaning of the phrase "a man of character".'[24] The fundamental anti-industrialism which the liberal-romantic ideal had always contained was thus assuming a new guise, becoming a positive virtue with a moral justification based on an agreed perception of the best interests of a civilised nation. And it has persisted well into this century; the Hadow Report, for example, said that 'industrialism has its grave effects on national life ... it may, unless it is corrected, infect the minds of men with the genius of its own life. Education can correct industrialism.'[25]

The Victorian version of the liberal-romantic tradition, having decided that industrialism had no place within it, readily lent itself to looking back rather than forward, and to emphasising the seeming antiquity and unchanging continuity of the values it espoused. Educational institutions would play a key part in promoting this interpretation, and the temptation 'to concentrate on the successes rather than the apparent failures of history, success being measured usually by sheer survival'[26] has been with us ever since. Because many schools and Oxbridge colleges were endowed centuries ago, and are still in existence, there is a tendency to exaggerate the unwavering strength of the educational tradition they embody. This preoccupation with the past has, it is suggested, 'lowered the temperature of society' and in so doing, 'drained prestige from innovation to preservation, from novelty to antiquity, and from change to continuity'.[27] Certainly, school histories generally underplay periods when the masters were incompetent or absentee, the curriculum narrowed to the classics, the pupils down to a handful, and the governors dead, or as good as. In fact it has been only since 1902 that grammar schools as a whole have enjoyed the success which their admirers tend to present as a timeless characteristic, and their academic prestige came very much later.

Two further characteristics which were enlivened within the English liberal-romantic tradition towards the end of the nineteenth century were its attachment to established religion and its instinctive anti-democratic elitism. The first of these witnessed a powerful surge of High Church fervour which gave the Church of England a new missionary zeal against the alleged atheism of school board education. Well-organised and vociferous, it aimed at nothing less than the 'ultimate extension of the denominational school throughout the whole of England', and found extremely useful allies among the influential Cecil family and in Robert Morant.[28] To the latter, the religious issue was the ideal way to 'get up steam' against the school boards. It not only ensured Conservative support for their abolition, but also made it possible to extend into the higher grade schools a version of the religiosity of the public schools, with their 'strong emphasis on the episcopal nature of the headmaster and a quasi-religious emphasis in school assemblies and speech days'.[29] All historians of 'popular' education agree that most parents were indifferent to the religious and moral instruction their children received at school, provided neither was too intrusive; they 'were tolerated as necessary evils only to be accepted if the secular and vocational education accompanying them were considered worthwhile'.[30] The establishment elite therefore effected a reversal of the growing secularisation of public education, which, like many of their early twentieth-century changes, has proved to have a surprisingly enduring quality.

The second of these characteristics became a powerful force after 1895 in the hands of leading members of the government and administration who espoused an extremely old-fashioned, anti-democratic Conservative philosophy. Their sense of the righteousness of their cause was enhanced by the conviction that the rising new forces in education, coinciding as they did with extensions in the franchise, the growth of socialism and a period of turbulent labour relations, were dangerously out of control. The whole social order – even civilisation itself – was thought to be under threat, and the guardians of civilisation, the old boys of the traditional public school/Oxbridge education, began to feel that only firm action could avert the disaster. There was an obvious target, for an important part of education, in which the preservation of social order and of civilised values were entrusted, was in the hands of what have been described as 'the most democratic organs of local administration of the century'.[31]

A number of clues point to a fairly sophisticated understanding among ordinary people of the implications of abolishing the directly elected school boards. They were definitely seen as an important organ of democracy, not just as a political slogan, but in the popular involvement which they made possible. To cite just a few of many examples, the 'intensity ... of working men's attachment to the school boards' in the London context has been commented upon,[32] and Mundella believed that the enormous progress in education before 1902 was because the school boards 'had behind them the driving force of a compelling and approving democracy'.[33] The NUT Conference, in a farewell tribute to the school boards in April 1903, affirmed its belief that they had 'done more in a shorter time for a larger number of people than any other authority in the world',[34] and, looking back on that time some 25 years later, Selby-Bigge believed that it was the school boards which had 'created a local public spirit in education'.[35] Simon has depicted the widespread popular protest which greeted the 1902 legislation,[36] and there was an unusually strong anti-government vote in municipal and parliamentary by-elections, culminating in overwhelming defeat for the Conservatives in the next general election. That the nation's leaders should have chosen to curtail what had become accepted as popular rights in the field of education can only be construed as a wilful disregard of rising democratic sentiment.

The combination of aristocratic and 'county' Conservatives, High Church Anglicans and panicking endowed school headteachers which came into being in the latter part of the 1890s as a 'mutual protection society for certain privileged educational establishments'[37] was therefore guaranteed a sympathetic response from the people who could do most to help. The formidable weight of support for the liberal-romantic tradition in English education, to which the vast majority of 'educated' people subscribed, was brought to bear against the upstart institutions which harboured different intellectual and cultural values. That those institutions were patronised primarily by less well-off members of the community made it easier, both practically and emotionally, to halt their progress. The two aspects – culture and class – could be used to complement each other, and the segregation of secondary from elementary schooling reinforced divisions in both. As Bamford has said:

the schism was real and deep and unjust, if expedient ... The result was a
virtual obliteration of the promising expansion in science and applied
science that had been building up in some lower-class schools. The result
was a triumph for traditional thought.[38]

Attitudes of this kind were reinforced by the fact that the new style of
education was unmistakably an urban phenomenon. As discussed earlier,
the metropolitan elite had always felt the greatest unease about England's
industrial cities, but it seems they became really alarmed when the higher
grade school movement began to spread beyond its original locations in
the North and Midlands. From the very end of the 1880s, higher grade
schools were taking root in non-industrial cities such as Brighton, Bristol,
Plymouth, Norwich, and even London, Oxford and Cambridge. This
constituted a new challenge, no longer confined to areas which the
metropolitan elite customarily regarded as unfamiliar territory; the 'new'
education was not just a feature of industrial life but an expression of
modern democracy. And as things stood, there was very little the elite
could do to control the development; higher grade schools were simply
not susceptible to the influence of the liberal-romantic tradition. Financed
by the Science and Art Department and managed by local bodies which
showed scant regard for metropolitan values, they were setting their own
goals and fitting into place as part of a complete and self-contained
alternative system of education.

Proof of the divergence in attitudes between the centre and the
provinces was furnished by the very determined campaigns put up by a
number of local authorities against the metropolitan model of secondary
education. Somewhat unexpectedly a number of them – mostly but not
exclusively urban ones – proved to be firmly in the tradition of the school
boards, committed above all to that large part of the population unable to
pay for the privilege of secondary education. There can be no other
possible explanation for them struggling to keep their schools cheaper and
less 'prestigious' than the Board of Education wanted them to be. The
higher grade schools and associated institutions were providing an
important focus of urban aspirations, and not just for the working and
lower middle classes to whom they were of most direct benefit. They had
been created and nurtured by school boards composed of members of the
urban elite drawn from higher social classes than those who used the
schools, who had come to feel a strong protective pride in their work. It
became clear very soon after 1902 that, as a vehicle for the exercise of
local authority power, the endowed schools were not going to be
permitted in any way to replace the higher grade schools. By vesting

control in largely co-opted governing bodies answerable to the central authority, the non-local character of their loyalties and traditions was strengthened. All the local enthusiasm and experience which had been built up in the management of the higher grade schools had to be concentrated on the municipal secondary schools, which thus became the setting for the battle between a whole range of deep-seated conflicting attitudes.

But it was always an unequal struggle, for the governing elite had the ultimate weapon. Since the higher grade 'realistic' style of education, however flourishing, could never be financially self-supporting, it was ultimately at the mercy of those who controlled state expenditure on education. The seemingly obvious point that the nature of secondary education would be decided by whoever won control of its administration is of great significance. If more power had been left in the hands of the local authorities, either by statutory regulation or by a system of block grants from the centre, the future of the higher grade school movement – and of secondary education in general – would have been very different. The spending of money on education has never come easily to councils or governments, and at the beginning of the century both were under pressure, the former because of their customary accountability to the ratepayers and the latter because of the constant scrutiny of the Treasury.[39] However, one is tempted to think that, if Morant had happened to believe in policies which required larger government funding, he would have manipulated the Treasury just as effectively as he did the Chancellor of the Exchequer and other senior politicians.[40] He chose to concentrate on creating a relatively small number of well-endowed secondary institutions, and constantly complained about the parsimony of local authorities which were in fact trying to spread their resources more widely and more equitably. In any case, the assertion by the wartime President of the Board, Fisher, that if England 'really wants a good system of education, this country ... is perfectly rich enough to pay for it',[41] has the ring of truth; to believe otherwise is to accept the rationale not infrequently advanced by privileged groups when explaining why the rest of the population cannot share their advantages.

CONCLUSION: A LOST OPPORTUNITY

Differentiated educational provision has continued throughout the twentieth century to be a dominant feature of English education. As overt social class distinctions ceased to be acceptable, the invention of psychometric testing conveniently gave the educational establishment a means of sorting children, so that when secondary education was extended to the whole population the best version of it remained a limited resource. It is astonishing in retrospect that the term 'parity of esteem' could ever seriously have been applied to the tripartite system; secondary modern schools were grossly under-funded and expectations of them low. It is a tribute to the best of them that their achievements increasingly made a mockery of 11-plus selection, and one can detect in them something of the same spirit of aspiring optimism and determination which characterised the higher grade schools. But, as a school 'type', the twentieth-century comprehensive school is the most recognisable descendant of the nineteenth-century higher grade school. A number of features – its size, its community orientation, the accessibility to all, the broad and varied curriculum – distinguish it both from the grammar school and independent school traditions.

The fact that England has persisted in operating several styles of secondary education with contrasting levels of public prestige suggests that the 'system' created at the beginning of the century was powerful, if unjust. In destroying the valid and popular version of general education which existed in the higher grade schools, Morant and his colleagues ably helped the social class which they represented to retain both its privileged position and its most important means of self-perpetuation. This also served to deflect any chance of a social and cultural revolution from below through the medium of the education system, and to minimise the contribution of education to the modernisation of attitudes to science and technology. It can still be said that England has struggled to develop 'a philosophical attitude' towards science, that attitudes towards industry are equivocal, and that technological studies have tended to be 'tolerated, but not assimilated' in universities, reaching their highest standards only in less prestigious institutions.[42] Much the same can be said of studies with a fairly explicit vocational intention. Meanwhile, educationists continue to be perplexed by the number of teenagers who see education as an irrelevance or an enemy, even now that superficially equal opportunities are available to all. While there has been an understandable reluctance to build early vocational choices into compulsory schooling, a system which certificates children late in their school careers and affords status only to the minority who complete the whole extended process, is of dubious value to the majority.

At the beginning of the century, there was every likelihood that a fair proportion of endowed grammar schools would have moved closer to the higher grade style of education, especially when public funding became more widely available. Instead, they were 'rescued' from having to adapt and get up to date, and with relatively few changes to their curriculum, teaching style, ethos, clientele or independence, were elevated to a position of unprecedented status and influence. Essentially they were given a firm helping hand to put the recent bad times behind them, and return to former, if often imagined, glories. Henceforth they were to be evaluated primarily by people who were instinctively sympathetic to their continued existence, and the problem of persuading customers to come through the doors was solved by the removal of any competing forms of education. The more progressive tradition which gave status to 'modern' subjects and made them available to any member of the school population, was thereby subordinated to the tradition which still held the winning of an Oxbridge scholarship, preferably in classics, to be the ultimate intellectual and cultural achievement. It was a remarkable transformation and a remarkable victory for the liberal-romantic tradition.

The losers were the children whose education was curtailed in elementary school careers which were extended in length but not in quality. It is, of course, impossible to be precise about the transformation which the higher grade school movement could have effected had it been allowed to continue its development, but it had few weaknesses and many strengths. Tailor-made for the lower middle and working classes without being unsuitable for the better-off, it seems certain that increasing numbers of children would have been attracted to its possibilities. Clever ones like Walter Southgate, or his friend who had to forgo a scholarship at the Parmiter's Foundation School because his sister was already on a secondary school scholarship, could have learnt a wider variety of subjects, and gained some marketable qualifications. Others, like Mark Grossek, could have taken their education further without tackling a new hostile world, and alienating themselves from their friends and neighbourhoods. Higher grade schools emphasised by their very existence the notion that extending one's education was a normal thing for ordinary children – including girls – to do. As a result of their abolition, the school life of the majority of children was stunted in scope, in potential and in status, and a very clear message was thereby conveyed about the role that such children were expected to play in society. It was indeed a lost opportunity.

NOTES

1. H. Sidgwick, 'The Theory of Classical Education', in F.W. Farrar (ed.), *Essays on a Liberal Education* (Farnborough: Gregg International, 1867), p. 133; T.H. Huxley, 'A Liberal Education; and Where to Find it' (1868), in his collected essays, *Science and Education* (London: Macmillan, 1905; reprint of 1893 edition), p. 94.
2. T.C. Worsley, *Barbarians and Philistines: Democracy and the Public Schools* (London: n.d. [1940?]), pp. 172–3.
3. R. Gilmour, *The Idea of the Gentleman in the Victorian Novel* (London: Allen & Unwin, 1981), p. 96.
4. Wilkinson, *Prefects*, pp. 99, 108–9; and (ed.), *Governing Elites: Studies in Training and Selection* (London: Oxford University Press, 1969), p. 224.
5. Barnett, *Audit of War*, p. 14.
6. I. Inkster, 'Aspects of the History of Science and Science Culture in Britain, 1780–1850 and Beyond', pp. 17–19, 43, and M. Neve, 'Science in a Commercial City: Bristol 1820–60', p. 179, both in Inkster and J. Morrell (eds), *Metropolis and Province: Science in British Culture, 1780–1850* (London: Hutchinson, 1983). Inkster thought that general neglect of this lively scientific culture 'has without doubt led to both a false belief in the ascientific nature of the industrial revolution and to the thesis that Britain's lag in formalized scientific and technical training after 1870 was simply a continuation of a 100-year trend'.
7. Clarke, *Education and Social Change*, pp. 17, 20.
8. Worsley, *Barbarians*, p.121. Unlike Clarke, he predicted that the technical high schools of the 1930s were 'doomed to failure' by the class and status divisions in British society, which would be vigorously defended by the privileged (p. 243).
9. I. Parker, *Dissenting Academies in England* (Cambridge: Cambridge University Press, 1914), p. 122.
10. E.F.M. McCarthy, 'Thirty Years of Educational Work in Birmingham' (1900), *Journal of Sources in Educational History*, 1, 3 (1978) p. 35.
11. Curtis, *Education in Britain*, p. 33.
12. Clarke, *Education and Social Change*, p. 16.
13. Clarke, *Education and Social Change*, p .15.
14. From reports of the annual conferences of the Association of Headmasters of Higher Grade Schools, reported in *The Schoolmaster*.
15. Kekewich, *Education Department*, pp. 194–7.
16. Ringer, *Education and Society*, pp. 18, 74, 139, 232.
17. Lindsay, *Social Progress*, p. 27.
18. The paragraphs on Welsh education are based on L.W. Evans, *Studies in Welsh Education: Welsh Educational Structure and Administration 1880–1925* (Cardiff: University of Wales Press, 1974), and G.E. Jones, *Controls and Conflicts in Welsh Secondary Education 1889–1944* (Cardiff: University of Wales Press, 1982). The latter takes a more nationalistic line, arguing that, after its dazzling start, Welsh secondary education was subjected to 'inexorable anglicisation'.
19. A. Green, *Education, Globalization and the Nation State* (London: Macmillan, 1997), p. 96.
20. This paragraph is drawn from R.D. Anderson, *Education and Opportunity in Victorian Scotland* (Oxford: Clarendon Press, 1983); N.A. Wade, *Post-Primary Education in the Primary Schools of Scotland 1872–1936* (London: University of London Press, 1939); and J. Strong, *A History of Secondary Education in Scotland* (Oxford: Clarendon Press, 1909).
21. Green, *Education and State Formation*, p. 312.
22. Gilmour, *Idea of the Gentleman*, p. 3.
23. P. Mason, *The English Gentleman: The Rise and Fall of an Ideal* (London: Deutsch, 1982), pp. 12, 148.
24. Rothblatt, *Tradition and Change*, p. 135. In typically trenchant style, R.H. Tawney in *Equality* (London: Allen & Unwin, 1931), p. 37, said the gentlemanly ideal had England's leaders 'by the throat; they frisk politely into obsolescence on the playing-fields of Eton. It is all very characteristic, and traditional, and picturesque. But it is neither good business nor good manners. It is out of tune with the realities of today'.
25. *Hadow Report*, p. xxiv.
26. M. Bryant, 'Topographical Resources: Private and Secondary Education in Middlesex', in Cook,

Local Studies, p. 125.

27. M.J. Wiener, *English Culture and the Decline of the Industrial Spirit, 1850–1980* (Cambridge: Cambridge University Press, 1981), p. 44.

28. Rogers, 'Churches', pp. 34–8. Halevy, in *Imperialism*, pp. 183–9, presented a fascinating picture of the growth of ritualism and anglo-catholicism – in some very high places – at this time.

29. Taylor, 'The Cecils', p. 42.

30. Tropp, *School Teachers*, pp. 34–5.

31. Lawson and Silver, *Social History of Education*, p. 314. They also said that, as the 'most advanced model of democratic control available in British society', the school boards had unique potential for generating social change (p. 352).

32. By E.J.T. Brennan (ed.), *Education for National Efficiency: The Contribution of Sidney and Beatrice Webb* (London: Athlone Press, 1975), p. 48.

33. Written in 1902 and quoted by Lawson and Silver, *Social History of Education*, p. 370. This was the nephew of the more famous Mundella.

34. *School Government Chronicle*, 18 April 1903.

35. Selby-Bigge, *Board of Education*, p. 83.

36. Simon, *Education and the Labour Movement*, Chapter VII.

37. Bishop, *Rise of a Central Authority*, p. 273.

38. T.W. Bamford, *Rise of the Public Schools* (London: Nelson, 1967), p. 262.

39. Lowe, 'Robert Morant', presents evidence of the Treasury's pressure on the Board of Education, particularly in relation to grants to schools specialising in science.

40. Note Eaglesham's comment concerning 'the foremost statesmen of the day ... On educational issues not one of them could match Morant: Balfour, Hicks-Beach [Chancellor of the Exchequer] and Chamberlain had all to bow the knee to his ruthless tenacity in argument', in 'Centenary', p. 6. In the same article (pp. 10–11) he described Morant's victory over the Treasury in 1907 as a 'policy of beating up the Treasury representative in argument ... with a series of sledgehammer blows'.

41. Quoted in Simon, *Politics of Educational Reform*, p. 15.

42. As it was by E. Ashby, *Technology and the Academics: An Essay on Universities and the Scientific Revolution* (London: Macmillan, 1958), pp. 30, 66.

REFERENCES

DOCUMENTARY SOURCES: NATIONAL

Board of Education

Higher Elementary Schools Minute (1900)
Regulations for Elementary Schools (1904)
Regulations for Secondary Schools (1904)
Regulations for the Instruction and Training of Pupil Teachers (1904)
Report of the Consultative Committee on Higher Elementary Schools (1906)
Report of the Consultative Committee on the Differentiation of the Curriculum for Boys and Girls respectively in Secondary Schools (1923)
Report of the Consultative Committee on the Education of the Adolescent (Hadow Report) (1927)
Report of the Consultative Committee on Secondary Education with Special Reference to Grammar Schools and Technical High Schools (Spens Report) (1939)
Report of the Committee of the Secondary School Examinations Council on Curriculum and Examinations in Secondary Schools (Norwood Report) (1943)
Reports of the Board (various years)
Special Reports on Educational Subjects (various years)
Statistics of Public Education in England and Wales (various years)
Suggestions for the Teaching of Needlework (1909)

Committee of Council on Education

Minutes of the Committee (various years)

Department of Science and Art

> *Reports of the Department* (various years)

Ministry of Education

> *The New Secondary Education* (1947)
> *Education 1900–1950* (1951)

Official Reports

> *Royal Commission to Enquire into the State of Popular Education in England (Newcastle Commission)* (1861)
> *Royal Commission to Enquire into the Revenues and Management of Certain Colleges and Schools and the Studies Pursued and Instruction Given Therein (Clarendon Commission)* (1864)
> *Schools Inquiry Commission (Taunton Commission)* (1867–9)
> *Report from the Select Committee on Scientific Instruction (Samuelson Report)* (1868)
> *Royal Commission on Scientific Instruction (Devonshire Commission)* (1872)
> *Royal Commission on Technical Instruction (Samuelson Commission)* (1884)
> *Royal Commission to Enquire into the Elementary Education Acts, England and Wales (Cross Commission)* (1888)
> *Royal Commission on Secondary Education (Bryce Commission)* (1895)
> *Committee to Enquire into the Position of Natural Science in the Educational System of Great Britain (Thompson Committee)* (1918)
> *Record of the Science Research Scholars of the Royal Commission for the Exhibition of 1851, 1891–1950* (1951)
> *Report of the Committee on Public Schools (Fleming Report)* (1944)

Public Record Office (PRO)

General

> Ed.10/3 File of Association of Directors and Secretaries for Education
> Ed.12/40 Courses of Instruction (Commercial Subjects) 1903–11
> Ed.12/45 Courses of Instruction 1904–12
> Ed.12/50 Courses of Instruction (Manual Work/Handicraft) 1904–8
> Ed.12/113 Special File 72 1897–1902
> Ed.12/114 Complaints from Parents 1907–11
> Ed.12/119 File of Papers relating to Regulations for Secondary Schools 1905–6
> Ed.12/120 Regulations 1904–5 and 1905–6
> Ed.12/138 Government (or Management) of Secondary Schools 1910–11
> Ed.12/139 Grading of Secondary Schools 1907–11

Higher Elementary School Files

Ed.20/47 Barnsley – Higher Elementary School
Ed.20/62 Leicester – Melbourne Road (Proposed) Higher Elementary School
Ed.20/114 Nottingham – High Pavement School
Ed.20/116 Nottingham – The People's College
Ed.20/123 Burton on Trent - Proposed Higher Elementary School
Ed.20/137 Aston (Birmingham) – Albert Road Higher Grade Board School
Ed.20/140 Handsworth (Birmingham) – Proposed Higher Elementary School

Public Elementary School Files

Ed.21/2968 Clay Cross, Derbyshire – Iron Works School
Ed.21/6128 Bristol – Fairfield Road School
Ed.21/6142 Bristol – Merrywood School
Ed.21/6162 Bristol – St George School

Secondary Education Files

Ed.35/410 Derbyshire – Chesterfield Grammar School
Ed.35/426 Derbyshire – Heanor Secondary and Technical School
Ed.35/453 Derbyshire – Clay Cross School of Science
Ed.35/830 Bristol – Christian Brothers' College
Ed.35/844 Bristol – Colston's Girls' School
Ed.35/845 Bristol – Colston's Boys' School/Merchant Venturers' Technical College School
Ed.35/846 Bristol – Fairfield School
Ed.35/847 Bristol – Fairfield School
Ed.35/855 Bristol – Merrywood School
Ed.35/860 Bristol – St George School
Ed.35/2056a Nottingham – County High School for Girls
Ed.35/2060 Nottingham – The High School (Boys)
Ed.35/2158 Bath City – Science, Art and Technical Schools
Ed.35/2275 Hanley – Municipal Secondary School
Ed.35/2299 Walsall – Technical School
Ed.35/2300 West Bromwich – Municipal Day Technical School
Ed.35/2450 Wimbledon – Girls' Pupil Teacher Centre
Ed.35/2554 Birmingham – George Dixon School
Ed.35/2556 Birmingham – Handsworth Day Science School
Ed.35/2576 Birmingham – Municipal Technical Day School
Ed.35/2579 Birmingham – Waverley Road School
Ed.35/2584 Birmingham – Yardley School
Ed.35/2588 Coventry – Bablake School for Boys
Ed.35/2978 Leeds – Central High School
Ed 35/2980 Leeds – Girls' High School
Ed.35/2983 Leeds – Grammar School

Ed.35/3054 Sheffield – Pupil Teacher Centre

National Union of Teachers

Higher Grade Schools (file of miscellaneous documents)

DOCUMENTARY SOURCES: LOCAL

Birmingham School Board

Minutes (1870–1903)
School Management Committee Minutes (1881–1903)

Birmingham Education Committee

Minutes (1903–12)
Higher Education Sub-Committee Minutes (1903–11)

Birmingham: George Dixon (Bridge Street) School

Log Book (1884–1906)
Admission Registers (boys' school)
Staff Register (boys' school)
Admission Register (girls' school)
Staff Register (girls' school)
Miscellanea (box containing agreements with parents (1904–9), admission examination marks (1906), etc.)
The George Dixon Centenary (printed 1984)

Birmingham – Municipal Technical Day (Central) School

Register of Day Scholars (1897–1919)
Headmaster's Register of Day School (1897–1908)
Register of Scholarship Winners (1893–1902)
Staff Register

Bristol School Board

Minutes (1871–1903)
School Management Committee Minutes (1886–1906)
Special Committee Minutes (1887–1905)
Sub-Committee and Committee Minutes (1871–1902)

Bristol Technical Instruction Committee

Minutes (1891–1903)

Bristol Education Committee

Minutes (1903–12)
Higher Education Committee Minutes (1903–21)
Higher Education Sub-Committee Minutes (1903–53)
H.M.Inspectors' Reports

St George (near Bristol) School Board

Minutes (1890–3)
Higher Grade and Technical School (Prospectus 1894–5)

Bristol: St George School

Log Books (1894–1908)
Admission Registers
School Visitors' Report Book (1900–12)
Nellie Nott's homelesson book (1902)
Honours Book of Redfield Council School (1903–34)
Register of Moorfields School (1900–9)
'Historical Development of Barton Hill' (typescript)
The Georgian (school magazine from November 1905)
The Georgian Jubilee Number: St George Secondary School, Bristol 1894–1944 (1944)
Old Georgians' Society (two boxes of the records of the old boys' society collected by W.T. Sanigar 1894–1947)

Bristol: Fairfield Road School

Admission Register
Staff Register
Fairfield School Magazine (from Christmas 1905)

Bristol Grammar School

400th Anniversary, 1532–1932 (newspaper cuttings, and such like)
Colston's Boys' School/Merchant Venturers' Technical College School
Bristol Schools, 1874–1930 (volume of newspaper cuttings)

Leicester School Board

Minutes (1871–1903)

Official Correspondence
Education Act 1902 – Returns from Public Elementary Schools

Borough of Leicester Education Committee

Secondary Schools Sub-Committee Minutes (1903–12)
Leicester: Wyggeston Schools
Governors' Meetings – Minutes (1899–1909)
Applications for Admission (boys' school 1898–1915)
Applications for Admission (girls' school 1889–1901)
Leicester Education 1892–1900 (volume of newspaper cuttings)

Nottingham School Board

Minutes (1870–1902)
Managers' Meetings – Minutes (1896–1905)

Nottingham: High Pavement School

Log Books (1892–1912)
Staff Register
Collection of Miscellany (including W. Hugh (headmaster), 'Some Notes,
Historical and Educational, 1788–1904' (1904))
The Pavior (school magazine)

Nottingham: People's College

Log Books (1881–1907)

Nottingham: Queen's Walk/Mundella School

Log Book (1895–1918)
Staff Register

Warwickshire: Leamington School Board

Minutes (1881–1904)

Warwickshire Technical Education Committee

Minutes (1893–1901)

Leamington Borough Council Education Committee

Minutes (1903–17)
Higher Education Sub-Committee Minutes (1903–10)

Leamington: Municipal Technical School

Minutes (1901–10)

NEWSPAPERS/JOURNALS

Bristol Guardian
Bristol Mercury
Bristol Observer
Bristol Times and Mirror
Educational Times (Journal of the College of Preceptors)
Leamington Spa Courier
Leicester Chronicle and Leicestershire Mercury
Record of Technical and Secondary Education (Journal of the National Association for the Promotion of Technical and Secondary Education)
School Government Chronicle
Schoolmaster
Schoolmasters' Yearbook and Directory
The Times
Western Daily Press

BOOKS/ARTICLES/PAMPHLETS/THESES

Acland, A.H.D. and Llewellyn-Smith, H. (eds), *Studies in Secondary Education* (London: Percival, 1892).

Adamson, J.W., *English Education 1789–1902* (Cambridge: Cambridge University Press, 1930).

Allen, B.M., *Sir Robert Morant: A Great Public Servant* (London: Macmillan, 1934).

Allsobrook, D.I., 'An Investigation of Precedents for the Recommendations of the Schools Inquiry Commission 1864–1867' (University of Leicester PhD thesis, 1979).

Allsopp, E. and Grugeon, D., *Direct Grant Grammar Schools* (London: Fabian Society, 1966).

Anderson, R.D., *Education and Opportunity in Victorian Scotland* (Oxford: Clarendon Press, 1983).

Archer, R.L., *Secondary Education in the Nineteenth Century* (London: Cambridge University Press, 1921).

Armytage, W.H.G., *Four Hundred Years of English Education* (London: Cambridge University Press, 1964).

Ashby, E., *Technology and the Academics: An Essay on Universities and the Scientific Revolution* (London: Macmillan, 1958).

Bamford, T.W., *Rise of the Public Schools* (London: Nelson, 1967).

Banks, O.L., *Parity and Prestige in English Secondary Education* (London:

Routledge & Kegan Paul, 1955).

Barnard, H.C., *A History of English Education from 1760* (London: University of London Press, 1947).

Barnett, C., *The Collapse of British Power* (London: Eyre Methuen, 1972).

Barnett, C., *The Audit of War: The Illusion and Reality of Britain as a Great Nation* (London: Macmillan, 1986).

Bernbaum, G., *Social Change and the Schools 1918–1944* (London: Routledge & Kegan Paul, 1967).

Betts, R., 'Dr Macnamara and the Education Act of 1902', *Journal of Educational Administration and History*, 25, 2 (1993).

Betts, R., '"Tried as in a Furnace": The NUT and the Abolition of the School Boards, 1896–1903', *History of Education*, 25, 1 (1996).

Bingham, J.H., *The Sheffield School Board 1870–1903* (Sheffield: Northend, 1949).

Birchenough, C., *History of Elementary Education in England and Wales from 1800 to the Present Day* (London: University Tutorial Press, 1938).

Bishop, A.S., *The Rise of a Central Authority for English Education* (Cambridge: Cambridge University Press, 1971).

Bishop, B., *Secondary Education in Bournemouth from 1902 to Present Day* (Bournemouth: Bournemouth Press, 1966).

Bourne, R. and MacArthur, B., *The Struggle for Education 1870–1970: A Pictorial History of Popular Education and the National Union of Teachers* (London: Schoolmaster Publishing, 1970).

Bradford Corporation, *Education in Bradford since 1870* (Bradford: Bradford Corporation, 1970).

Bremner, C.S., *Education of Girls and Women in Great Britain* (London: Swan Sonnenschein, 1897).

Brennan, E.J.T. (ed.), *Education for National Efficiency: The Contribution of Sidney and Beatrice Webb* (London: Athlone Press, 1975).

Bristol Broadsides (Co-op) Ltd, *Bristol's Other History* (Bristol: Bristol Broadsides, 1983).

Bryher, S., *An Account of the Labour and Socialist Movement in Bristol* (Bristol: Bristol Labour Weekly, 1931).

Burnett, J., *Plenty and Want: A Social History of Diet in England from 1815 to the Present Day* (London: Nelson, 1966).

Burnett, J. (ed.), *Useful Toil: Autobiographies of Working People from the 1820s to the 1920s* (London: Allen Lane, 1974).

Burstall, S.A., *English High Schools for Girls: Their Aims, Organisation, and Management* (London: Longmans Green, 1907).

Burstall, S.A., *The Story of the Manchester High School for Girls 1871–1911* (Manchester: Manchester University Press, 1911).

Butterworth, H., 'The Department of Science and Art (1853–1900) and the Development of Secondary Education', *History of Education Society Bulletin*, 6 (1970).

Cadbury, E., Matheson, M.C. and Shann, G., *Women's Work and Wages: A Phase of Life in an Industrial City* (London: T. Fisher Unwin, 1906).

Cambridgeshire High School for Boys: History of the School 1900–1950 (Cambridge: Cambridgeshire High School for Boys, 1950).

Campbell, F., *Eleven-Plus and All That: The Grammar School in a Changing Society* (London: Watts, 1956).

Cattell, D.L., 'The Development of Albert Road Higher Grade School and the Education Department 1881–1900' (University of Birmingham MEd thesis, 1981).

Church, R., *Over the Bridge: An Essay in Autobiography* (London: Reprint Society/Heinemann, 1956).

Clare, L.H., 'Change and Conflict in Bristol Public Education 1895–1905' (University of Bristol MLitt thesis, 1975).

Clarke, F., *Education and Social Change: An English Interpretation* (London: Shaldon Press, 1940).

Connell, L., 'Administration of Secondary Schools: Leeds *v.* Board of Education', *Journal of Educational Administration and History*, 5, 2 (1973).

Cook, T.G. (ed.), *Local Studies and the History of Education* (London: Methuen, 1972).

Cook, T.G. (ed.), *Education and the Professions* (London: Methuen, 1973).

Cox, C.B. and Dyson, A.E. (eds), *Black Paper Two: The Crisis in Education* (London: Critical Quarterly Society, 1970).

Craig, J., *A History of Red Tape: An Account of the Origin and Development of the Civil Service* (London: Macdonald & Evans, 1955).

Crowther, J.G., *Statesmen of Science* (London: Cresset Press, 1965).

Cruickshank, M., 'A Defence of the 1902 Act', *History of Education Society Bulletin*, 19 (1977).

Cullen, M.M., *Education in Darlington (1900–1974)* (Darlington: Darlington Corporation, 1974).

Curtis, S.J., *Education in Britain since 1900* (London: Dakers, 1952).

Daglish, N., *Education Policy-Making in England and Wales: The Crucible Years, 1895–1911* (London: Woburn Press, 1996).

Davidoff, L., *The Best Circles: Social Etiquette and the Season* (London: Croom Helm, 1973).

Davies, A.M., *The Barnsley School Board 1871–1903* (Barnsley: Cheesman, 1965).

Davis, R., *The Grammar School* (Harmondsworth: Penguin, 1967).

Delamont, S. and Duffin, L. (eds), *The Nineteenth-Century Woman: Her Cultural and Physical World* (London: Croom Helm, 1978).

Dent, H.C., *1870–1970: Century of Growth in English Education* (Harlow: Longmans, 1970).

Dent, H.C., *Education in England and Wales* (London: Hodder & Stoughton, 1982).

Duckworth, J., 'The Board of Education and the Establishment of the Curriculum in the New Secondary Schools of the Twentieth Century', *History of Education Society Bulletin*, 16 (1975).

Dyhouse, C., *Girls Growing Up in Late Victorian and Edwardian England* (London: Routledge & Kegan Paul, 1981).

Eagar, W.M., *Making Men: The History of Boys' Clubs and Related Movements in Great Britain* (London: University of London Press, 1953).

Eaglesham, E.J.R., *From School Board to Local Authority* (London: Routledge & Kegan Paul, 1956).

Eaglesham, E.J.R., 'Implementing the Education Act of 1902', *British Journal of Educational Studies*, 10, 2 (1962).

Eaglesham, E.J.R., 'The Centenary of Sir Robert Morant', *British Journal of Educational Studies*, 12, 1 (1963).

Eaglesham, E.J.R., *The Foundations of Twentieth-Century Education in England* (London: Routledge & Kegan Paul, 1967).

Ensor, R.C.K., *England 1870–1914* (Oxford: Clarendon Press, 1936).

Evans, A.B., *The Cambridge Grammar School for Boys 1871–1971* (Cambridge: Cambridge Grammar School, 1971).

Evans, L.W., *Studies in Welsh Education: Welsh Educational Structure and Administration 1880–1925* (Cardiff: University of Wales Press, 1974).

Farrar, F.W. (ed.), *Essays on a Liberal Education* (Farnborough: Gregg International, 1867).

Fletcher, S., *Feminists and Bureaucrats: A Study in the Development of Girls' Education in the Nineteenth Century* (Cambridge: Cambridge University Press, 1980).

Fox, A., *A History of the National Union of Boot and Shoe Operatives 1874–1957* (Oxford: Blackwell, 1958).

Freeth, E. (ed.), *The Jubilee Book of Clapham County School 1909–1959* (London: Clapham County School, 1959).

Gardner, P., *The Lost Elementary Schools of Victorian England: The People's Education* (London: Croom Helm, 1984).

Gathorne-Hardy, J., *The Public School Phenomenon, 597–1977* (London: Hodder & Stoughton, 1977).

Gilmour, R., *The Idea of the Gentleman in the Victorian Novel* (London: Allen & Unwin, 1981).

Gittins, D., *Fair Sex: Family Size and Structure, 1900–1939* (London: Hutchinson, 1982).

Glass, D.V. and Eversley, D.E.C. (eds), *Population in History: Essays in Historical Demography* (London: Edward Arnold, 1965).

Gordon, P., *Selection for Secondary Education* (London: Woburn Press, 1980).

Gordon, P. and White, J., *Philosophers as Educational Reformers: The Influence of Idealism on British Educational Thought and Practice* (London: Routledge & Kegan Paul, 1979).

Gorst, J.E., *The Children of the Nation* (London: Methuen, 1906).

Gosden, P.H.J.H. and Sharp, P.R., *The Development of an Education Service: The West Riding 1889–1974* (Oxford: Blackwell, 1978).

Graham, J.A. and Phythian, B.A. (eds), *The Manchester Grammar School 1515–1965* (Manchester: Manchester University Press, 1965).

Graves, J., *Policy and Progress in Secondary Education 1902–1942* (London: Thomas Nelson, 1943).

Green, A., *Education and State Formation* (London: Macmillan, 1990).

Green, A., *Education, Globalization and the Nation State* (London: Macmillan, 1997).

Greenhalgh, V.C., 'Local Educational Administrators, 1870–1974' (University of Leeds PhD thesis, 1974).

Grier, L., *Achievement in Education: The Work of Michael Ernest Sadler* (London: Constable, 1952).

Griggs, C., *The Trades Union Congress and the Struggle for Education 1868–1925* (Lewes: Falmer Press, 1983).

Grossek, M., *First Movement* (London: G. Bles, 1937).

Halevy, E., *Imperialism and the Rise of Labour* (London: Benn, 1951 edn).

Halsey, A.H., *Trends in British Society since 1900* (London: Macmillan, 1972).

Hammond, N.G.L. (ed.), *Centenary Essays on Clifton College* (Bristol: J.W. Arrowsmith, 1962).

Harrison, D. (ed.), *Bristol between the Wars: The City and its People 1919–1939* (Bristol: Redcliffe Press, 1984).

Harrison, J.F.C., *The Common People* (London: Fontana, 1984).

Hennock, E.P., *Fit and Proper Persons: Ideal and Reality in Nineteenth-Century Urban Government* (London: Edward Arnold, 1973).

Hewitson, J.N., *The Grammar School Tradition in a Comprehensive World* (London: Routledge & Kegan Paul, 1969).

Hill, C.P., *The History of Bristol Grammar School* (London: Pitman, 1951).

Holcombe, L., *Victorian Ladies at Work: Middle-Class Working Women in England and Wales, 1850–1914* (Newton Abbot: David & Charles, 1973).

Holmes, E., *What Is and What Might Be* (London: Constable, 1911).

Hughes, K.M., 'A Political Party and Education. Reflections on the Liberal Party's Educational Policy, 1867–1902', *British Journal of Educational Studies*, 8, 2 (1960).

Humphries, S., *Hooligans or Rebels? An Oral History of Working-Class Childhood and Youth 1889–1939* (Oxford: Blackwell, 1981).

Hurt, J.S., *Elementary Schooling and the Working Classes 1860–1918* (London: Routledge & Kegan Paul, 1979).

Hutchins, B.L., *Women in Modern Industry* (Wakefield: EP Publishing, 1980; reprint of 1915 edn).

Huxley, T.H., *Science and Education* (London: Macmillan, 1905; reprint of 1893 edn).

Hyndman, M., *Schools and Schooling in England and Wales* (London: Harper & Row, 1978).

Inglis, B. (ed.), *John Bull's Schooldays* (London: Hutchinson, 1961).

Inkster, I. and Morrell, J., *Metropolis and Province: Science in British Culture, 1780–1850* (London: Hutchinson, 1983).

Jackson, J.C., *Belle Vue Boys' School* (Bradford: typescript, 1976).

Jenkins, E.W., *'A Magnificent Pile': A Centenary History of the Leeds Central High School* (Leeds: City of Leeds School, 1985).

Jones, G.E., *Controls and Conflicts in Welsh Secondary Education 1889–1944* (Cardiff: University of Wales Press, 1982).

Judges, A.V., 'The Educational Influence of the Webbs', *British Journal of*

Educational Studies, 10, 1 (1961).

Kamm, J., *Hope Deferred: Girls' Education in English History* (London: Methuen, 1965).

Kazamias, A.M., *Politics, Society and Secondary Education in England* (Philadelphia, PA: University of Pennsylvania Press, 1966).

Kekewich, G.W., *The Education Department and After* (London: Constable, 1920).

Kelly's, *Bristol Directory* (Bristol: Kelly's, various years).

King, B., *Schools of To-Day: Present Problems in English Education* (London: J.M. Dent, 1929).

Latimer, J., *The Annals of Bristol in the Nineteenth Century* (Bristol: W. and F. Morgan, 1887).

Latimer, J., *The Annals of Bristol in the Nineteenth Century (concluded) 1887–1900* (Bristol: William George, 1902).

Lawson, J. and Silver, H., *A Social History of Education in England* (London: Methuen, 1973).

Leese, J., *Personalities and Power in English Education* (Leeds: E.J. Arnold, 1950).

Lester Smith, W.O., *Education in Great Britain* (London: Oxford University Press, 1958).

Lindsay, K., *Social Progress and Educational Waste* (London: Routledge, 1926)

Little, B., *The City and County of Bristol* (London: Werner Laurie, 1954).

Lowe, R., 'Robert Morant and the Secondary School Regulations of 1904', *Journal of Educational Administration and History*, 16, 1 (1984).

Lowndes, G.A.N., *The Silent Social Revolution: An Account of the Expansion of Public Education in England and Wales 1895–1935* (London: Oxford University Press, 1937).

McCann, P. (ed.), *Popular Education and Socialization in the Nineteenth Century* (London: Methuen, 1977).

McCarthy, E.F.M., 'Thirty Years of Educational Work in Birmingham' (1900), *Journal of Sources in Educational History*, 1, 3 (1978).

McCulloch, G., 'Science Education and the Historiography of National Decline', *History of Education Society Bulletin*, 30 (1982).

Mackenzie, N. (ed.), *The Letters of Sidney and Beatrice Webb* (Cambridge: Cambridge University Press, 1978).

Mackenzie, N. and J. (eds), *The Diary of Beatrice Webb* (London: Virago, 1983).

Macleod, R. (ed.), *Days of Judgment: Science, Examinations and the Organization of Knowledge in Late Victorian England* (Driffield: Nafferton Books, 1982).

Maclure, S., *One Hundred Years of London Education 1870–1970* (London: Allen Lane/Penguin Press, 1970).

Mann, J.F., *Education* (London: Pitman, 1979).

Martin, C., *A Short History of English Schools 1750–1965* (Hove: Wayland, 1979).

Mason, P., *The English Gentleman: The Rise and Fall of an Ideal* (London: Deutsch, 1982).

Mathieson, M., *The Preachers of Culture: A Study of English and Its Teachers* (London: Allen & Unwin, 1975).

Meller, H.E., *Leisure and the Changing City, 1870–1914* (London: Routledge & Kegan Paul, 1976).

Midwinter, E., *Schools in Society: The Evolution of English Education* (London: Batsford Academic, 1980).

Morgan, E.T., *A History of the Bristol Cathedral School* (Bristol: J.W. Arrowsmith, 1913).

Muggeridge, M., *Through the Microphone* (London: BBC, 1967).

Muirhead, J.H. (ed.), *Birmingham Institutions* (Birmingham: Cornish Bros, 1911)

Muller, D.K., Ringer, F. and Simon, B., *The Rise of the Modern Educational System: Structural Change and Social Reproduction 1870–1920* (Cambridge: Cambridge University Press, 1987).

Parker, I., *Dissenting Academies in England* (Cambridge: Cambridge University Press, 1914).

Patrick, H., 'From Cross to CATE: The Universities and Teacher Education over the Past Century', *Oxford Review of Education*, 12, 3 (1986).

Pike, W.T., *Bristol in 1898–99: Contemporary Biographies* (Brighton: W.T. Pike, 1899).

Price, M.J., 'Mathematics in English Education 1860–1914: Some Questions and Explanations in Curriculum History', *History of Education*, 12, 4 (1983).

Pugsley, A.J., *The Economic Development of Bristol* (Bristol: Bristol Times and Mirror, 1922).

Pugsley, A.J., *The Door of Opportunity: Being an Account of Higher Education in East Bristol and Especially St George Secondary School* (Bristol: Pugsley, 1944).

Rae, J., *The Public School Revolution* (London: Faber, 1981).

Reader, W.J., *Professional Men: The Rise of the Professional Classes in Nineteenth-Century England* (London: Weidenfeld & Nicolson, 1966).

Richards, H.C. and Lynn, H., *The Local Authorities' and Managers' and Teachers' Guide to the Education Acts* (London: Jordan & Sons, 1903).

Richards, P.G., *Patronage in British Government* (London: Allen & Unwin, 1963).

Ringer, F.K., *Education and Society in Modern Europe* (Bloomington and London: Indiana University Press, 1979).

Roach, J., *Secondary Education in England 1870–1902* (London: Routledge, 1991).

Robinson, W., 'Pupil Teachers: The Achilles Heel of Higher Grade Girls' Schools 1882–1904?', *History of Education*, 22, 3 (1993).

Rogers, A., 'Churches and Children: A Study in the Controversy over the 1902 Education Act', *British Journal of Educational Studies*, 8, 1 (1959).

Rose, K., *The Later Cecils* (London: Weidenfeld & Nicolson, 1975).

Rothblatt, S., *Tradition and Change in English Liberal Education: An Essay in History and Culture* (London: Faber, 1976).

Scudamore, C.N.J., 'The Social Background of Pupils at the Bridge Street Higher Grade School, Birmingham' (University of Birmingham MEd thesis, 1976).

Seaborne, M. and Lowe, R., *The English School: Its Architecture and Organization Vol II 1870–1970* (London: Routledge & Kegan Paul, 1977).

Searby, P. (ed.), *Educating the Victorian Middle Class* (Leicester: History of Education Society, 1982).

Selby-Bigge, L.A., *The Board of Education* (London: G.P. Putnam's Sons, 1927).

Shaw, M.G., *Redland High School* (Bristol: J.W. Arrowsmith, 1932).

Simon, B., *Education and the Labour Movement 1870–1920* (London: Lawrence & Wishart, 1965).

Simon, B., *The Politics of Educational Reform 1920–1940* (London: Lawrence & Wishart, 1974).

Simon, B., 'The 1902 Education Act: A Wrong Turning', *History of Education Society Bulletin*, 19 (1977).

Smith, D., *Conflict and Compromise – Class Formation in English Society 1830–1914: A Comparative Study of Birmingham and Sheffield* (London: Routledge & Kegan Paul, 1982).

Sneyd-Kinnersley, E.M., *H.M.I. Some Passages in the Life of One of H.M. Inspectors of Schools* (London: Macmillan, 1908).

Southgate, W., *That's the Way it Was. A Working Class Autobiography 1890–1950* (Oxted: New Clarion Press, 1982).

Spencer, F.H., *An Inspector's Testament* (Edinburgh: Edinburgh University Press, 1938).

Strong, J., *A History of Secondary Education in Scotland* (Oxford: Clarendon Press, 1909).

Summerfield, P. and Evans, E.J. (eds), *Technical Education and the State Since 1850: Historical and Contemporary Perspectives* (Manchester: Manchester University Press, 1990).

Sutherland, G., *Policy-Making in Elementary Education 1870–1895* (London: Oxford University Press, 1973).

Tawney, R.H., *Equality* (London: Allen & Unwin, 1931).

Taylor, T., 'Lord Salisbury and the Politics of Education', *Journal of Educational Administration and History,* 16, 2 (1984).

Taylor, T., '"An Early Arrival of the Fascist Mentality": Robert Morant's Rise to Power', *Journal of Educational Administration and History*, 17, 2 (1985).

Taylor, T., 'The Cecils and the Cockerton Case: High Politics and Low Intentions', *History of Education Society Bulletin*, 37 (1986).

Taylor, T., 'Lord Cranborne, the Church Party and Anglican Education 1893–1902: From Politics to Pressure', *History of Education*, 22, 2 (1993).

Thomas, A.W., *A History of Nottingham High School 1513–1953* (Nottingham: J. and H. Bell, 1957).

Tropp, A., *The School Teachers: The Growth of the Teaching Profession in England and Wales from 1800 to the Present Day* (London: Heinemann, 1957).

Wade, N.A., *Post-Primary Education in the Primary Schools of Scotland 1872–1936* (London: University of London Press, 1939).

Wardle, D., *Education and Society in Nineteenth-Century Nottingham* (London: Cambridge University Press, 1971).

Widdowson, F., *Going Up Into the Next Class. Women and Elementary Teacher Training, 1840–1914* (London: Hutchinson, 1980).

Wiener, M.J., *English Culture and the Decline of the Industrial Spirit, 1850-1980* (Cambridge: Cambridge University Press, 1981).

Wilkinson, R., *The Prefects: British Leadership and the Public School Tradition* (London: Oxford University Press, 1964).

Wilkinson, R. (ed.), *Governing Elites: Studies in Training and Selection* (London: Oxford University Press, 1969).

Wilson, B. (ed.), *Education, Equality and Society* (London: Allen & Unwin, 1975).

Wilson, E., 'The Development of Secondary Education in Bradford from 1895 to 1928' (University of Leeds MEd thesis, 1968).

Wood, F.K.D., 'The Beginnings of Municipal Secondary Education in the City and County of Bristol (1895–1919)' (University of Bristol MEd thesis, 1968).

Worsley, T.C., *Barbarians and Philistines: Democracy and the Public Schools* (London: Robert Hale, n.d. [1940?]).

Wright, J. and Co., *Bristol and Clifton Directory* (Bristol: J. Wright, various years).

Zebel, S.H., *Balfour: A Political Biography* (London: Cambridge University Press, 1973).

Zimmern, A., *The Renaissance of Girls' Education in England* (London: A.D. Innes, 1898).

FURTHER READING

Allsobrook, D.I., *Schools for the Shires: The Reform of Middle-Class Education in Mid-Victorian England* (Manchester: Manchester University Press, 1986).

Anderson, G., *Victorian Clerks* (Manchester: Manchester University Press, 1976).

Argles, M., *South Kensington to Robbins: An Account of English Technical and Scientific Education since 1851* (London: Longmans, 1964).

Armytage, W.H.G., *A.J. Mundella 1825–1897: The Liberal Background to the Labour Movement* (London: Ernest Benn, 1951).

Arnold, M., *Higher Schools and Universities in Germany* (London: Macmillan, 1882).

Arrowsmith's Dictionary of Bristol (Bristol: J.W. Arrowsmith, 1906).

Banks, O.L., 'Morant and the Secondary School Regulations of 1904', *British Journal of Educational Studies*, 3, 1 (1954).

Barnsby, G., *A History of Education in Wolverhampton 1800 to 1972* (Wolverhampton: Wolverhampton Communist Party, 1972).

Bernbaum, G. (ed.), *Schooling in Decline* (London: Macmillan, 1979).

Betts, R., 'Robert Morant and the Purging of H.M. Inspectorate, 1903', *Journal of Educational Administration and History*, 20, 1 (1988).

Bloomfield, P., *Uncommon People: A Study of England's Elite* (London: Hamish Hamilton, 1955).

Bottomore, T.B., *Elites and Society* (Harmondsworth: Penguin, 1966)

Browne, J.D., 'The Formation of an Educational Administrator', *History of Education*, 10, 3 (1981).

Cane, B.S., 'Scientific and Technical Subjects in the Curriculum of English Secondary Schools at the Turn of the Century', *British Journal of Educational Studies*, 8, 1 (1959).

Cardwell, D.S.L., *The Organisation of Science in England* (London: Heinemann, 1957).

Chapman, J.V., *Professional Roots: The College of Preceptors in British Society* (Epping: Theydon Bois, 1985).

Church, R.A., *Economic and Social Change in a Midland Town: Victorian Nottingham 1815–1900* (London: Cass, 1966).

Clements, R.V., *Local Notables and the City Council* (London: Macmillan, 1969)

Connolly, C., *Enemies of Promise* (London: Routledge, 1949).

Corbett, J., *The Birmingham Trades Council 1866–1966* (London: Lawrence & Wishart, 1966).

Cotgrove, S.F., *Technical Education and Social Change* (London: Allen & Unwin, 1958).

Crossick, G. (ed.), *The Lower Middle Class in Britain 1870–1914* (London: Croom Helm, 1977).

Daglish, N., 'The Politics of Educational Change: The Case of the English Higher Grade Schools', *Journal of Educational Administration and History*, 19, 2 (1987).

Elliott, A., 'The Bradford School Board and the Department of Education, 1870–1902: Areas of Conflict', *Journal of Educational Administration and History*, 13, 2 (1981).

Evans, K., *The Development and Structure of the English Educational System* (London: Hodder & Stoughton, 1975).

Firth, G.C., *Coventry. 75 Years of Service to Education* (Coventry: Coventry Education Committee, 1977).

Fletcher, S., 'Co-education and the Victorian Grammar School', *History of Education*, 11, 2 (1982).

Floud, J.E., Halsey, A.H. and Martin, F.M. (eds), *Social Class and Educational Opportunity* (London: Heinemann, 1956).

Fraser, D., *Urban Politics in Victorian England* (Leicester: Leicester University Press, 1976).

Goodson, I.F. (ed.), *Social Histories of the Secondary Curriculum: Subjects for Study* (Lewes: Falmer Press, 1985).

Gordon, P., *The Victorian School Manager: A Study in the Management of Education 1800–1902* (London: Woburn Press, 1974).

Gordon, P., 'Commitments and Developments in the Elementary School Curriculum 1870–1907', *History of Education*, 6, 1 (1977).

Gordon, P., 'The Writings of Edmond Holmes: A Reassessment and Bibliography', *History of Education*, 12, 1 (1983).

Gosden, P.H.J.H., 'The Board of Education Act, 1899', *British Journal of Educational Studies*, 11, 1 (1962).

Green, A., 'Technical Education and State Formation in Nineteenth-Century England and France', *History of Education*, 24, 2 (1995)

Guttsman, W.L., *The British Political Elite* (London: MacGibbon & Kee, 1963).

Haines, G., *Essays on German Influence upon English Education and Science, 1850–1919* (Connecticut: Connecticut College/Archon Books, 1969).

Harrison, J.F.C. *Learning and Living, 1760–1960* (London: Routledge & Kegan Paul, 1961).

Hawkes, G.I., *The Development of Public Education in Nelson* (Nelson: Nelson

Corporation, 1966).

Heyck, T.W., *The Transformation of Intellectual Life in Victorian England* (London: Croom Helm, 1982).

Honan, P., *Matthew Arnold: A Life* (London: Weidenfeld & Nicolson, 1981).

Honey, J.R. de S., *Tom Brown's Universe: The Development of the Victorian Public School* (London: Millington, 1977).

Howarth, T.E.B., *Culture, Anarchy and the Public Schools* (London: Cassell, 1969).

Howson, A.G., *A History of Mathematics Education in England* (Cambridge: Cambridge University Press, 1982).

Hunt, F. (ed.), *Lessons for Life: The Schooling of Girls and Women, 1850–1950* (Oxford: Blackwell, 1987).

Hutton, T.W., *King Edward's School Birmingham, 1552–1952* (Oxford: Blackwell, 1952).

Jenkins, E.W., 'Science Education and the Secondary School Regulations, 1902–1909', *Journal of Educational Administration and History*, 10, 2 (1978).

Jones, J.M., 'George Dixon. The Man and The Schools' (Birmingham: typescript, 1980).

Kang, H.-C., 'Equality of Educational Opportunity: Ideas and Politics, 1900–1918', *British Journal of Educational Studies*, 32, 1 (1984).

King, R.B., Browne, J.D. and Ibbotson, E.M.H., *Bolton King. Practical Idealist* (Warwickshire: Warwickshire Local History Society, 1978).

Kitson Clark, G.S.R., *An Expanding Society. Britain 1830–1900* (Cambridge: Cambridge University Press, 1967).

Layton, D., *Science for the People* (London: Allen & Unwin, 1973).

Lewis, C., 'The Bristol Trade School 1856–1885' (University of Wales MEd thesis, 1977).

Lilley, R.C., 'Attempts to Implement the Bryce Commission's Recommendations', *History of Education*, 11, 2 (1982).

Lockwood, D., *The Blackcoated Worker: A Study in Class Consciousness* (Oxford: Clarendon Press, 1958).

Lowe, R. (ed.), *New Approaches to the Study of Popular Education 1851–1902* (Leicester: History of Education Society, 1979).

Lowell, A.L., *The Government of England, II* (New York: Macmillan, 1920; reprint from 1908 edn).

Martin, J., 'Entering the Public Arena: The Female Members of the London School Board, 1970–1904', *History of Education*, 22, 3 (1993).

Mathias, P. (ed.), *Science and Society 1600–1900* (Cambridge: Cambridge University Press, 1972).

Mathieson, M. and Bernbaum, G., 'The British Disease: A British Tradition?', *Journal of Educational Studies*, 36, 2 (1988).

Mingay, G.E., *The Victorian Countryside* (London: Routledge & Kegan Paul, 1981).

Morris, A.J.A., *Edwardian Radicalism 1900–1914* (London: Routledge & Kegan Paul, 1974).

Morrish, I., *Education since 1800* (London: Allen & Unwin, 1970).

Musgrave, P.W., 'Constant Factors in the Demand for Technical Education: 1860–1960', *British Journal of Educational Studies*, 14, 2 (1966)

Musgrove, P., *School and the Social Order* (Chichester: Wiley, 1979)

Nelson, P., 'Leicester Suburban School Boards', *History of Education*, 6, 1 (1977).

Newsome, D., *Godliness and Good Learning (Four Studies on a Victorian Ideal)* (London: John Murray, 1961).

Peters, A.J., 'The Changing Idea of Technical Education', *British Journal of Educational Studies*, 11, 2 (1963).

Pollard, S., *The Wasting of the British Economy* (London: Croom Helm, 1982).

Price, M., 'The Reform of English Mathematical Education in the Late Nineteenth and Early Twentieth Century' (University of Leicester PhD thesis, 1981).

Purvis, J. (ed.), *The Education of Girls and Women* (Leicester: History of Education Society, 1985).

Reeder, D.A. (ed.), *Urban Education in the Nineteenth Century* (London: Taylor and Francis, 1977).

Reeder, D.A. (ed.), *Educating our Masters* (Leicester: Leicester University Press, 1980).

Reid, T.W., *Memoirs and Correspondence of Lyon Playfair* (London: Cassell, 1899).

Reisner, E.H., *Nationalism and Education since 1789* (New York: Macmillan, 1939).

Rimmington, G.T., *Education, Politics and Society in Leicester 1833–1903* (Hansport: Lancelot Press, 1978).

Roderick, G.W. and Stephens, M.D., *Scientific and Technical Education in Nineteenth-Century England* (Newton Abbot: David & Charles, 1972).

Roderick, G.W. and Stephens, M.D. (eds), *Where Did We Go Wrong?* (Lewes: Falmer Press, 1981).

Sanderson, M., *The Universities and British Industry 1850–1970* (London: Routledge & Kegan Paul, 1972).

Sanderson, M., *The Missing Stratum: Technical School Education in England 1900–1990s* (London: Athlone Press, 1994).

Shute, C., *Edmond Holmes and 'The Tragedy of Education'* (Nottingham: Educational Heretics Press, 1998).

Silver, H., *Education as History* (London: Methuen, 1983).

Simon, B. (ed.), *Education in Leicestershire 1540–1940* (Leicester: Leicester University Press, 1968).

Simon, B., *The Two Nations and the Educational Structure 1780–1870* (London: Lawrence & Wishart, 1974).

Simon, B. and Bradley I. (eds), *The Victorian Public School* (Dublin: Gill & Macmillan, 1975).

Simpson, L., 'Imperialism, National Efficiency and Education, 1900–1905', *Journal of Educational Administration and History*, 16, 1 (1984).

Taylor, A.F., 'History of Birmingham School Board 1870–1903' (University of

Birmingham MA thesis, 1955).

Temple, W., *Life of Bishop Percival* (London: Macmillan, 1921).

Timmons, G.T., 'Secondary Education in Coventry in the Late 19th Century', *Journal of Educational Administration and History*, 13, 2 (1981).

Turner, G.L. (ed.), *The Patronage of Science in the Nineteenth Century* (Leiden: Noordhoff International Publishing, 1976).

Weinberg, I., *The English Public Schools: The Sociology of Elite Education* (New York: Atherton Press, 1967).

Wellens, J., 'The Anti-Intellectual Tradition in the West', *British Journal of Educational Studies*, 8, 1 (1959).

Whitbread, N., 'The Early Twentieth-Century Secondary Curriculum Debate in England', *History of Education*, 13, 3 (1984).

Wintle, J. (ed.), *Makers of Nineteenth Century Culture 1800–1914* (London: Routledge & Kegan Paul, 1982).

Woodhead, D., *A Century of Schooling: The History of a School in Ardwick, Manchester* (Manchester: Manchester Education Committee, 1980).

Worsley, T.C., *Flannelled Fool: A Slice of Life in the Thirties* (London: Ross, 1967).

Wrigley, E.A., *Nineteenth-Century Society* (London: Cambridge University Press, 1972).

INDEX